CAPTURING THE LANDSCAPE OF NEW SPAIN

The Southwest Center Series

Joseph C. Wilder, Editor

Capturing the Landscape of New Spain

BALTASAR OBREGÓN
AND THE 1564
IBARRA EXPEDITION

REBECCA A. CARTE

THE UNIVERSITY OF
ARIZONA PRESS

TUCSON

The University of Arizona Press
www.uapress.arizona.edu

Printed in the United States of America
20 19 18 17 16 15   6 5 4 3 2 1

ISBN-13: 978-0-8165-3142-4 (cloth)

Jacket designed by Leigh McDonald

Publication of this book is made possible in part by a grant from the Southwest Center of
the University of Arizona.

Library of Congress Cataloging-in-Publication Data
Carte, Rebecca A., author.
    Capturing the landscape of New Spain : Baltasar Obregón and the 1564 Ibarra
Expedition / Rebecca A. Carte.
        pages cm — (The Southwest Center series)
    Includes bibliographical references and index.
    ISBN 978-0-8165-3142-4 (cloth : alk. paper)
    1. Obregón, Baltasar de, 1544– Historia de los descubrimientos antiguos y modernos
de la Nueva España. 2. Landscapes in literature. 3. Mexico—Description and travel.
4. New Spain—Discovery and exploration. I. Title. II. Series: Southwest Center series.
    F1211.C38 2015
    972'.02—dc23
                            2015001527

∞ This paper meets the requirements of ANSI/NISO Z39.48-1992 (Permanence of Paper).

Dedicated with greatest appreciation to Maureen Ahern
(1936–2012)

Contents

Illustrations

Acknowledgments

As any study of its ilk, the present work rests on the shoulders of innovative scholars to whom we owe our knowledge of the past, and with whom we dialogue even if we have not met in person. Their names grace the bibliographies of countless studies, including this one. It is also the result of mentors and professionals who have been generous with their time and knowledge. I am profoundly grateful to so many people and institutions without whom the present study simply could not have been realized. Above all, I owe a debt of gratitude to the hard work and tireless dedication of the late Maureen Ahern, who inspired and supported countless scholars in her lifetime. I am forever changed for having been one of them. Daniel T. Reff likewise has lent his time, advice, and support over the years, encouraging me and helping me every step of the way. The scholarship of Johnathan Walker has broadened my scope of vision in thinking about landscape, and his graciousness in accommodating my questions and requests is much appreciated. Ricardo Padrón provided me with essential feedback to my initial draft. No less important have been countless members of the Rocky Mountain Council on Latin American Studies who have inspired and challenged me at conferences over the past several years as I presented my preliminary work. I would be remiss if I did not also express my debt of gratitude to The Leopold Schepp Foundation, whose scholarship support allowed me to continue my education. Finally, I am ever guided by the example set for me by my mother, Judith Carte, whose love of learning and appreciation for people from all different backgrounds and belief systems has left an indelible impression on me. She never ceases to inspire and motivate me.

Time Line

1521   Fall of the Aztec city of Tenochtitlán.

1525   Las Ordenanzas, which would have been followed by Francisco de Ibarra, set guidelines for expeditions.

1531   Núño de Guzmán reaches southern and central Durango. Founds San Miguel de Culiacán.

1533   Fall of the Incan city of Cuzco. José de Angulo reaches Topia district.

1536   Cabeza de Vaca reaches Culiacán after a ten-year odyssey.

1539   Fray Marcos de Niza scouting party sent out from Culiacán. (See Niza [1539] 1987, 1995, 1999). Francisco de Ibarra born. Printing press comes to New Spain.

1541   Mixtón War begins with uprisings in Nueva Galicia.

1542   Coronado Expedition returns after two years, and is viewed as a failure. Las Leyes Nuevas attempt to reign in abuses of the *encomienda* system.

1544   Baltasar Obregón born in Mexico City.

1545   Spanish begin mining Potosí.

1546   Spanish mining extends to Zacatecas.

1551   La Junta de Valladolid ends after one year of debate.

1552   Ginés Vázquez de Mercado reaches Aviño and Guadiana Valley.

1554   Viceroy Luis de Velasco gets royal authorization to explore the north. Francisco de Ibarra leads 2–3 month *entrada* from Zacatecas reaching Río Nazas. Silver mining begins in the region.

1556   Temporary mission in Guadiana established by Franciscan friar.

1558   By this time, mining takes place in Sombrerete, San Martín, and Aviño.

1561   Rustic mission established in the area that would become Nombre de Dios.

1562   July 24, Ibarra commissioned to explore lands north of San Martín.

1563   January 24, Ibarra sets out from San Martín (after a stay of more than forty days) to secure mining settlements and explore the northern borderlands.

1567   Mining communities established in Indé and Santa Barbara.

1569   Indigenous rebellion in San Juan de Sinaloa, a settlement founded by Ibarra.

1570   Settlement founded in the Valle de San Bartolomé.

1572   Mission established in San Juan del Río.

1573   Las Ordenanzas set new guidelines for expeditions.

1574   Jesuit missionaries reach Durango.

1575   August 17, Francisco de Ibarra dies in Chiametla. Villa de Santiago de Saltillo founded.

1581   Chamuscado-Rodríguez Expedition (See account by Hernán Gallegos).

1583   Antonio de Espejo Expedition (See accounts by Espejo [1586] 1966, 1975 and Pérez de Luxán [1582] 1966).

1584   Baltasar Obregón sends his *Historia* to the Consejo de Indias in Spain.

CAPTURING THE LANDSCAPE OF NEW SPAIN

Introduction

What is landscape? A word, an abstraction, a sign, a concept, a mean-
ing, what the eye embraces? It is a "given" which has yet to be proven,
and about which we know little, despite numerous publications. A
formal answer to this question would be as ambiguous as the term itself.
Therefore, it is good that the landscape provokes debate and discussion.
—S. QUONIAM, 1988

Landscapes are links to personal and collective pasts.
—ANNE SPIRN, 1998

In the mid-1980s, a cavernous, 140-mile trail in Mexico stretching from
the pueblo of Tepehuanes across the Sierra Madre Occidental to Culiacán
captured the imaginations of two graduate students at Syracuse University, Johnathan Walker and Jonathan Leib. Walker recalled learning of
the famous trail known as Topia Road from a geography professor he had
studied under, James Parsons. In 1940, Parsons, along with his colleague
Robert West, traversed the rugged terrain of Topia Road, a *camino real*
that in colonial times had served as the main trans-Sierran route linking
the mountain mining pueblos of the interior of New Spain (present-day
Mexico) with the Pacific Coast (see figure 1).[1] The pair crossed formidable
canyons two to three thousand feet deep on horseback and on foot over
a period of ten days, ultimately determining Topia Road to be "the most
outstanding of the trans-Sierran trails" for both its antiquity and the volume
of traffic it had carried during the expansion of the Spanish Empire (West
and Parsons 1941, 408, quoted in Walker and Leib 2002, 556). Inspired
to retrace the same route as their predecessors, Walker and Leib ventured
to Topia Road in the mid-nineties to compare Parsons's photographs and
field notes with the region's contemporary conditions, with the objective
of evaluating landscape alteration. How would the Topia Road of 1940,

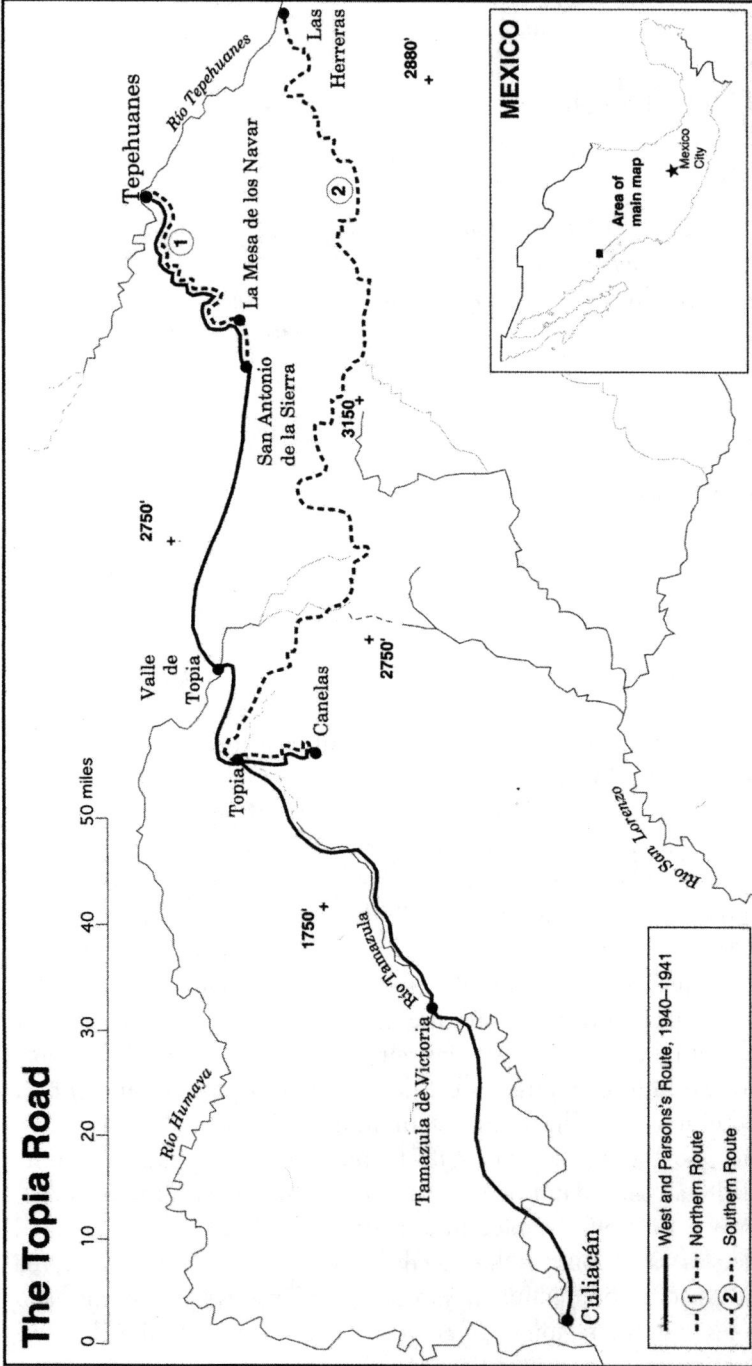

Figure 1. The Topia Road: Tepehuanes, Durango, to Culiacán, Sinaloa (in Walker and Leib, 2002)

home to what Parsons described as some of the most isolated settlements in Mexico, compare to the Topia Road navigated by Walker and Leib fifty-five years later?

To answer this question, Walker used repeat photography, finding the locations where Parsons had taken photographs for use in the 1940 study and taking pictures of the same scenes. These comparative photos (examined in concert with field observations, interviews with locals, and Parsons' field notes) reveal that radical changes had indeed occurred to the *cultural landscape* along Topia Road over the period of more than five decades largely because of the human influences of mining, migration, and drug trafficking.[2] One set of photographs in particular demonstrates how the road, having been abandoned by locals for a newer, more practical route, had begun to erode considerably (see figure 2). Yet, while Walker's purpose in comparing these photos was to demonstrate significant landscape alteration, if we widen the scope to consider the five centuries that have passed since the road's inception—and I would like to propose that we do—one could take the view that the gouges and ruts of Topia Road have rather stubbornly endured. While not as well-traveled as in colonial times, the route nonetheless remains quite visible; the vestige of a foundation that can be traced back to the 1563 expedition of Francisco de Ibarra, first governor of Nueva Vizcaya and explorer of the northern borderlands of New Spain.[3] Given its long history, it is rather remarkable that Topia Road, whose life in years is more than three times its distance in miles, still seems to announce itself in the photographs, as if refusing to go away. The photos taken in 1940 and 1995 show us a mere glimpse of only a few of Topia Road's countless moments in history, freezing it long enough for us to view and to imagine.[4]

So what can we know of Topia Road's long life prior to the 1940s? Obviously, the explorers of the sixteenth century who inaugurated the road lacked the photo technology enjoyed by twentieth-century geographers; however, a few of those explorers that were pushing the frontiers of New Spain ever northward did similarly attempt to "capture" the landscape—to hold it still on paper so that readers back in Spain, and fellow explorers of the *tierras incógnitas* of the north, could likewise "view" it and imagine it in the mind's eye. These narrators attempted to "textualize" the landscape so that it could ultimately be read by those whose eyes had never seen it. In this way, texts, like photographs and maps, serve as a tool to render an image of the landscape.

The present study is inspired in part by a deep appreciation for textual and visual renderings and all they offer and in part by a fascination with their futility. Obviously, while these renderings offer the reader or viewer

Figure 2. The photograph comparison of Topia Road (Walker and Leib, 2002)

a means by which to see landscapes that his or her eyes never experience in real time and space, the oft-observed irony remains: any simulacrum of a landscape is going out of date even while it is being constructed. Just as Peter Turchi (2001) points out that "every map goes out of date, every map asserts a truth that it can never attain" (172), landscape depictions go out of date too, as Leib and Walker's photos elucidate. Furthermore, as many scholars of landscape theory (see Mitchell 2002a, 2002b, 2002c; Olwig 2002; Spirn 1998; Quoniam 1988) have demonstrated over the past few decades, this same futility bespeaks the paradox of the term's usage in the parlance of our times in which *landscape* has come to denote the static stuff of paintings or photographs of "pure" nature, as if nature were somehow untouched by man. These same scholars have pointed out that the word's etymology belies this static conception and denial of human influence, and they argue that across disciplines the usage of the term *landscape* needs to be questioned and (re)considered as an analytical and cultural concept. Heeding this call, the objective of the present study is to explore one particular attempt to textualize the landscape that so fascinated West and Parsons and later Leib and Walker: Baltasar Obregón's *Historia de los descubrimientos de Nueva España* (1584), the account of the same expedition led by Francisco de Ibarra that marked the Spanish inauguration of Topia Road.

Baltasar Obregón

The son of an *encomendero*, Baltasar Obregón was twenty years old when he joined the expedition led by Francisco de Ibarra, the purpose of which was to establish mining settlements in the borderlands of New Spain and to suppress indigenous rebellions in the region. These rebellions were a part of the fifty-year war commonly referred to as La Guerra Chichimeca, which occurred when Spanish settlement inched northward and soldiers began raiding native settlements to capture slaves for the newly established mines of San Martín, Chalchihuites, Aviño, Sombrerete, Fresnillo, Mazapil, and Nieves.[5] Obregón was the descendant of some of the first Spanish settlers and important families of the Americas; he had already participated in an expedition to California at the age of nineteen in the hopes of increasing his family's fortune. Thus, although Obregón's role in the Ibarra Expedition was that of soldier-explorer, and despite his lack of advanced education, he would go on to compose *Historia de los descubrimientos de Nueva España* twenty years after his participation in the expedition, reinforcing his own observations with other reports and expanding the scope of events to include the years before and after his first-hand experiences with Ibarra.[6] Obregón attempted to provide a comprehensive interpretive history of northward Spanish expansion, including two later expeditions (of which Obregón was not a part) that began to push the frontier even farther north into present-day New Mexico: the Chamuscado-Rodríguez party (1581–82) and the expedition led by Antonio de Espejo in 1583. Obregón sent his text to the Consejo de Indias in 1584, probably in an attempt to garner favor with the Crown in the hopes of receiving permission to be a part of, or perhaps even lead, another excursion to the region. Ultimately, this privilege would fall not to Obregón, but rather to another criollo, Juan de Oñate, who would win the commission in 1598.[7]

In the prologue to *Historia*, the soldier-explorer proclaims that the "historia y relación [history and account]" that he has composed will provide "verdaderos hechos de las tierras que han visto y descubierto, haciendo relación de las que son buenas o malas [true information about the lands that have been seen and discovered, making an account of those that are good or bad]" for the officials that henceforth set out to conquer and populate the little-explored lands of the northern frontier of New Spain (43).[8] Arguing that experience is the best teacher, Obregón will provide true information to make a case for which lands are "good" and which are "bad." As part and parcel of this objective, the text abounds with extensive descriptions of the landscape as Obregón interjects itinerary-driven information about the location of mines, population centers, routes passable by horse, and supplies. Landscape textualization, then, performs a primary role in Obregón's retelling, with the landscape emerging at times as protagonist and others as antagonist, but always in vivid, life-like, and dramatic ways. While scholars to this point have focused primarily on what the text tells us about the route the Ibarra Expedition may have taken (Bancroft 1934–75; Hopkins Durazo 1988; Mecham 1927) and historical data regarding the founding of Spanish settlements (Mecham 1927; Jones 1988), no one, to my knowledge, has provided readers with a particularly extensive or thorough critical analysis of the narration of this text.[9] Furthermore, the Ibarra Expedition itself has been comparatively understudied, overshadowed at either end of the time continuum by the popular commemorations of the expedition led by Francisco Coronado (1540–42) and the infamously violent establishment of a Spanish settlement led by Juan de Oñate in 1598, both of which are well known in the southwestern United States and Northern Mexico.[10] This lack of attention and analysis represents a substantial gap of roughly fifty years during a fascinating period of radical transformation in the lands that were home to the Pima, Yaqui, Mayo, Opata, Suma, Concho, Acaxee, and Xixime, among others, as vassals of the Spanish Empire attempted to re-create and negotiate some semblance of an occidental social space as it extended itself northward. As such, not only does Obregón's textualization of the land and its people offer one of the first renderings of the region through the occidental cultural lens, it also offers insight into Spanish cultural perceptions of landscape during a period of important shifts in the occidental worldview. By examining how landscape is put to paper by Obregón, my aim is to rethink the notion of landscape itself to consider the human implications of its textualization during the nascent stages of Spain's centuries-long imperial endeavors. What does this particular narrative act reveal about the worldview of the narrator and his own aims? What fissures exist in his construction that may reveal alternate possibilities? How does Obregón's landscape rendering serve as a means of (re)production of Europeanized social space in and on the northern frontier of sixteenth-century New Spain? I postulate that what at first seems to be mere landscape description is actually the creation of a landscape in which myriad issues relating to space and place, such as discursive mapping, history, and the textual projection of European institutions and indigenous America, all converge to create a *textualscape*.[11] The textualscape is the textualization of the dynamic site perceived: the renderings of a land and its people that posit the reader into the landscape through thick description replete with value judgments that make it a creative narrative act. Just as Parsons and West and later Leib and Walker utilized photographs of Topia Road to examine its cultural record, this study is dedicated to utilizing the text to a similar end.

Pagus

Within and among the extensive discursive records penned by Spanish explorers, missionaries, and government officials for export back to Spain throughout the colonial period, landscape descriptions are perennial as the grass, and the term *landscape* appears no less frequently in studies of these texts from the fields of literary studies, geography, history, and historical ethnography and anthropology. Yet, for as much as scholars across disciplines employ the term, landscape as a cultural concept remains underanalyzed, banalized to a certain degree, or simply taken for granted.[12] While critical theories of space and place have wielded significant influence over the past several decades in Latin American colonial studies, the cultural concept of landscape has largely remained a backdrop: ignored, loosely defined, and even used interchangeably with the more thoroughly and analytically defined terms of "space" and "place."[13] How can scholars from other fields such as geography, anthropology, and even architectural design, help us to rethink what landscape means as well as what it does in colonial texts?

In *Landscape, Nature and the Body Politic* (2002), geographer Kenneth R. Olwig traces the Germanic lexicological heritage of the term, offering insight into how the contemporary notion of landscape as natural scenery has been divorced from its original meaning, a meaning that inherently included the human element. *Landscape*, he explains, originated from the Germanic family of languages wherein the term designated a region, as it also did in older forms of English. To the Dutch *landschap*, the Danes *landskab*, the Swedes *landskap*, and the Germans *Landschaft*, the term carried essentially the same connotations of community and people as *country* and *land*. In *The Language of Landscape* (1998), architect Anne Spirn explains that the word is made up of two roots: "land," meaning both a place and its people, and various forms of the word "shape." However, this original meaning, which conveyed at once the concepts of place, people, and the verb "to shape," has morphed in the English tradition. "Still strong in Scandinavian and German languages, these original meanings have all but disappeared from English" (17). Similarly, the equivalent Italian terms *paese* and *paesaggio*, the French *pays*, and the Spanish *paisaje* have carried the same meaning: country, land, or province. All of these share a common Latin heritage in which the term *pagus* conveyed the idea of territory, field, district, or town (Méndez García 2005). In this way, pagus denoted a socially defined area of land (Cosgrove 1998, 66). This etymology reveals two important aspects of landscape that I consider in Obregón's retelling of the landscape traversed during his time with the Ibarra Expedition: (1) in its original meaning, landscape had included a human element, and (2) the term intended to include an active, dynamic element.

By the beginning of the eighteenth century, the term *landscape* had become "closely associated with its metaphoric qualities and its metonymic use in language" and painted country sides (Quoniam 1988, 6).[14] To this day, *landscape* typically conjures associations with paintings and moreover, within the world of art, the notion of untouched nature, a pristine view devoid of man. Art historian Mark Roskill notes in the introduction to his study, *The Languages of Landscape* (1997, 1), that "landscape represents traditionally the domain of nature as opposed to culture," fomenting the commonly maintained association with pure nature. However, Olwig (2002) argues that from the emergence of the sixteenth century, "the primary subject matter of landscape paintings was not predominantly 'natural scenery.' These paintings usually depicted life in countries filled with culture. Rather than nature, they were concerned with the regional habitation" (xxv).[15] By moving beyond the term's associations with painting and pure, "untouched" nature, we can recognize landscape's essentially human and dynamic elements and thereby begin to consider its function as a cultural concept. This study understands landscape as *process* rather than static backdrop or mere context: the perceived site of the dynamic relationship of land and people with the implication that the landscapes we perceive—that we are conditioned to perceive—vary between cultures and as such may be "translated." As W. J. T. Mitchell (2002b, 2) contends, "landscape" must be changed from a noun to a verb, allowing us to grapple with "the way landscape *circulates* as a medium of exchange, a site of visual appropriation, a focus for the formation of identity." In the chapters that follow, I will examine how landscape emerges as praxis, how it functions as a cultural concept, and how it circulates in a criollo's comprehensive history of northward expansion in sixteenth-century New Spain.

The following chapters are organized thematically, with chapters 1 and 2 examining the two purposes that Obregón purports to address, respectively: (1) to provide a comprehensive historical account and (2) to provide itinerary and mapping information. Chapters 3 and 4 broaden the scope from the narrow lens of Obregón's landscaping processes to a wider view in which the effects of the Spanish presence on the landscape in both natural and human terms may be considered within the sociohistoric context of the expansion of the Spanish Empire, and ultimately the role of landscape as praxis in human endeavors. Chapter 1, "Taking Place," examines the importance of establishing an occidental history on the northern frontier to the cause of imperial expansion.[16] By flashing back to the arrival of Hernán Cortés to Tenochtitlán and Francisco Coronado's famed 1540 expedition, and then flashing forward to the expeditions taking place in the first half of the 1580s, Obregón elects not to limit himself to his own eyewitness testimony, opting rather to provide a wider scope within which to posit his own experience. I examine his motivations for writing a comprehensive history, his status as a criollo, and the implications of historicizing a region that was not formally a part of New Spain. In addition to providing a historical framework, Obregón also refers to the past and to his own eyewitness experiences to provide geographical knowledge and itinerary information for the Consejo de Indias and future explorers. Chapter 2, "'Lo que hay en esta tierra'" (That which is in this land), is dedicated to examining Obregón's discursive mapping project and its value-laden landscape descriptions. Specifically, I analyze how cultural views of landscape, space, and place, as well as the attitudes and values of the narrator, inform his definitions of "good" and "bad" landscapes.

Chapter 3, "Multiple Landscapes, Multiple Frontiers," considers the perspectival nature of landscape and how the indigenous populations of the region may have viewed the lands differently. By attending to issues of human identity, and how Obregón delineates physical and cultural frontiers between Europeans and indigenous peoples and between indigenous groups, we gain insight into his notions of civilization and barbarianism, center and periphery, and stability and instability, all of which allow for the establishment of a human hierarchy. I also consider the effects of previous Spanish encroachment and how the presence of a new, "alien" group would have altered the landscape. Of course, the Spanish presence and the desire to establish permanent, stable settlements in the north were driven at least in part by economics, with important human consequences. Chapter 4, "(Re)producing Social Space and Textualscapes," considers how the dual albeit contradictory missions of the mining enterprise and evangelization in New Spain inform the project of Spanish imperial expansion in the New World and how both institutions' dependence on forced labor significantly changed landscape perception. How is Obregón's perception of the landscape filtered through the lens of the mining enterprise and evangelization, and what does this mean in terms of the imagining of an indigenous Other?

By taking into account the confluence of the material, the spiritual, and the historical complexities of Obregón's *locus of annunciation*, I postulate that his text is demonstrative of an important shift in Spanish perception of the landscape to the north. While certainly some Spanish soldiers participating in the Ibarra Expedition (and perhaps even Ibarra himself) were clearly still out to find wealthy cities like Tenochtitlán and Cuzco, a more guarded view of the north as a troublesome region that would have to be settled or *pacificado* to be mined clearly predominates Obregón's textualscape. The result is a "history" that reads more like a composite of past, present, and future projections onto the landscape of New Spain; a textualscape that not only reflects Obregón's cultural views of landscape, space, and place, but also may play a role in the actual (re)production of this social space.

While names like Coronado and Oñate have enjoyed currency in the study of this region, Baltasar Obregón and the Ibarra Expedition often have been relegated to footnote status. In my research I have found that, although Obregón's text is cited in numerous studies, and it is widely accepted as the most trustworthy account of Ibarra's expedition (Mecham [1927] cites our dependence on it for information regarding the early history of Nueva Vizcaya), the role that it has played in informing our understanding of history and cultural studies has not been examined extensively. To be clear, my purpose is not to provide a historical study of the Ibarra Expedition or the region of Nueva Vizcaya, nor is it to provide an ethnography of the indigenous peoples that inhabit it, although I do draw from those fields. Rather, my aim is to narrow the reader's focus on the *discourse* of one text that has informed scholars from a variety of fields for generations to explore what its language reveals about the perception, creation, and textualization of landscape, and consequently the image of the region and its peoples that has been painted and repainted. It is an attempt to bring attention to the importance of language and landscape in identity creation and in informing perceptions of peoples and their place in history. For this reason, this study is organized thematically, not chronologically (although I have tried to maintain some order for the reader with the aid of endnotes and a timeline); nor is it organized spatially (the exact route taken by Ibarra is debatable). It is my aim to generate a discussion that is, in my view, overdue regarding a complicated but important account composed during a time of cultural, ecological, economic, and political upheaval.

Some notes on translation: The only published English edition of Obregón's text (Hammond and Rey 1928) is unfortunately not based on the original held in the Archivo General de Indias (AGI) in Seville, Spain, rather from a Spanish transcription of the original. Completed by Father Mariano Cuevas in only ten days, the transcription suffers from omissions and errors, so I have elected not to use the Hammond and Rey English translation of it; instead, I have provided my own translations of the paleographic study by María Bravo and reconciled them with Hammond and Rey's. My goal while translating has been to stay as true as possible to what I hear in Obregón's voice and to honor that voice, which is florid and verbose, while making it accessible to as many readers as possible. As a result, the translations are not word for word. For example, I have modified syntax and prepositions, or eliminated one of a triple adjective or verbal sequence in some cases so as to make the English as readable as possible, and not necessarily literal. I have relied on the *Diccionario de Autoridades* (1726–39) and the etymological dictionaries of Joan Corominas (1954, 1987) as sources in an attempt to get the closest approximation to meaning from Obregón's time while still allowing for language that is easily understood. A collaborative English translation of Obregón's *Historia* that draws from expertise in discourse, linguistics, and historical ethnography is greatly needed.

CHAPTER ONE

Taking Place

We need the past, in any case, to cope with present landscapes. We selectively perceive what we are accustomed to seeing; features and patterns in the landscape make sense to us because we share a history with them. Every object, every grouping, every view is intelligible partly because we are already familiar with it, through our own past and through tales heard, books read, pictures viewed. We see things simultaneously as they are and as we viewed them before; previous experience suffuses all present perception.
—DAVID LOWENTHAL, 1975

In the mid-sixteenth century, the landscape that lay beyond the ever-shifting northern frontier of New Spain was still largely an imagined space to European settlers. A constantly contested terrain that was mostly a source of legend, lore, gossip, and stories of failed conquest and bellicose savages, the *banda del norte* (edge of the north) was widely viewed as the mysterious and even terrifying periphery for Baltasar Obregón and his contemporaries, yet one that still beckoned.[1] The dreams of golden cities that had once fueled desire to explore and conquer the lands to the north had waned for a time after the Mixtón War of 1541 (an indigenous uprising that began in Nueva Galicia and spread quickly to Culiacán, Compostela, and La Purificación) and the uninspiring return of the Coronado Expedition to New Spain in 1542.[2] This marked the beginning of a new phase of Spanish expansion that was more cautious and gradual. Moreover, at the time of Obregón's writing, Las Ordenanzas de descubrimiento, nueva población y pacificación de las Indias (1573), which aimed to outline the Spanish Crown's policies of settlement in all of the Americas in both philosophical and economic terms, had prohibited the use of Crown funds in settlement expeditions

14

and forbade the entry of unlicensed parties into new lands under pain of death and loss of all property.[3] Even before 1573, expeditions were privately financed at great economic risk to their sponsors, and participants were paid only in booty and rewards procured in their participation.[4] With no guarantee of recompense, coupled with the fear of juridical proceedings and punishment as a result of accusations of violating the Ordenanzas, Spanish explorers were often loath to be saddled with expedition costs or diminished status. Exploring the unknown north with its unwelcoming lands and indomitable "savages" was largely viewed as a risky endeavor. Aside from documents produced by members of a few expeditions, the landscape to the north remained largely unknown and left to be imagined rather than controlled by Spanish settlers.

In painting a landscape through discourse that takes shape by providing extensive, even chapter-long descriptions of the lands stretching from Nueva Vizcaya (which included the area north of Zacatecas and large areas of the modern-day Mexican states of Durango, Chihuahua, and Sinaloa) further northward to present-day Sonora, New Mexico, and Arizona, Obregón's *Historia de los descubrimientos de Nueva España* (1584) offers its readers a glimpse into how this alien world was perceived by Spaniards trying to overtake and Europeanize it. In the prologue, Obregón explicitly puts forth his two primary purposes for writing the *Historia*. The first is to provide concrete information about the pragmatics of northward expansion that will serve utilitarian reconnaissance purposes and which, as I elaborate in chapter 2, results in an exhaustive description of the landscapes traversed. That all of this information comes wrapped inside a comprehensive history of northward expansion indicates Obregón's second purpose:

> Los reyes y príncipes especialmente constituidos por el altísimo Dios . . . por estar de ordinario muy ocupados en el grave peso e inmensa carga de la administración de tantas regiones y gentes, no suelen poder leer historias ni otras obras que en su progreso sean de relaciones largas, por el poco tiempo que les resta para ver y pasar escrituras prolijas; para cuyo conveniente remedio, deseando servir a V.M. y después a estos sus reinos de las Indias . . . hice y ordené esta general y universal crónica y relaciones de las partes y valles contenidas, reducido a honesta brevedad y compendio sus historias escritas difusamente y otras no bien entendidas y otras casi incógnitas.

> [Kings and princes, specially ordained by God the Almighty . . . , being as they are daily most occupied with the heavy weight and immense charge

of the administration of so many regions and peoples, and due to what little time is left them to view and go over wordy writings, are not usually able to read histories nor other (written) works that are in their composition long accounts; for whose convenient remedy, desiring to serve Your Majesty, and secondly His regions of the Indies . . . I have made and organized this general and universal chronicle and account of the parts and valleys contained (in the Indies), (from) written histories (many of which are) diffuse, others not well understood and (still) others almost unknown . . . , condensed in a compendium of brevity and honesty.] (43)

A sort of executive summary for the powers of Castile, Obregón's text purports to summarize a period of roughly sixty-five years for busy government officials an ocean away. While at first this task may seem to have less to do with landscape and more to do with important figures, politics, and major events, one soon recognizes that Obregón's stories do not happen in a nebulous limbo, but rather in a painstakingly depicted landscape. As de Certeau contends, "Stories . . . carry out a labor that constantly transforms places into spaces and spaces into places" (1984, 118). Obregón's stories carry out a labor of transforming the northern borderlands into a vivid stage on which the Spanish protagonist emerges as the active agent in a larger narrative by historicizing a space that had been "historiless" (from a Spanish or criollo perspective), infusing the unwieldy landscape with a particularly Spanish presence.

In relating stories generated from his own participation in the expedition led by Francisco de Ibarra into the northern borderlands of New Spain, along with expeditions previous and subsequent to it to the same region, Obregón provides a textual retelling of the landscape's role in the history of New Spain and that of the larger Spanish Empire in which the Spanish protagonist is successful, at least potentially, in his campaign to "poblar, pacificar y conquistar [settle, pacify and conquer]" lands. In a sense, he appropriates lands that had remained beyond the firm grasp of explorers and officials alike.[5] In this chapter I first examine Obregón's own expressed purposes in composing a history of the troublesome yet beckoning northern borderlands. Second, I delve into the discursive devices that Obregón employs, "opening up a theatre for practical actions" (de Certeau 1984, 123) in and on the borderlands of New Spain, specifically, how Obregón utilizes the privilege of his own eyewitness accounts and testimony from others, as well as two different but overlapping narrative tropes: that of the epic heroes and the more subtle inclusion of seemingly benign local lore. In doing so, he infuses his "comprehensive history" of the northern borderlands with a sense of thickness and stability that previous histories of New Spain may have been lacking for his readers in Spain. María Portuondo (2009) tells us that in Renaissance cosmography, "in order for a place to exist, it required a historical narrative, whether mythical or factual, that located the place within the human context" (35). By employing a discourse that literally "takes place" in the northern regions of present-day Mexico, Obregón's *Historia* textually transforms and appropriates the mysterious north, a source of consternation and misery for the Spanish imagination, at once bringing it into existence for his readers and implying that it be molded by criollo hands.

The First "Mexican" Historian

Little is known about Obregón's biography aside from his birth in 1544 to an encomendero in Tezontepec in the present-day state of Hidalgo, Mexico. His father and both grandfathers had played important roles in the Spanish settlement of central Mexico, and Baltasar himself participated in an expedition to California when he was nineteen in the hopes of increasing his family's fortune. He would later join the largest expedition led by Francisco de Ibarra, a *peninsular* who had come to Mexico as a young man and had already realized preliminary explorations to the north from Zacatecas between 1554 and 1562 (see figure 3). Obregón joined Ibarra's 1563 expedition in Sinaloa and penned *Historia de los descubrimientos de Nueva España* twenty years after the fact, along with an *información de méritos* to accompany it, ostensibly because of the "poverty of his *encomienda* in the Mizteca Baja, to petition the king for relief" (Mecham 1927, 110–11). As the title would indicate, in addition to relating "verdadero testimonio de lo que vi, anduve y experimenté [true testimony of what I saw, traversed, and experienced]," Obregón also attempted to provide a comprehensive interpretive history of northward Spanish expansion that encompassed the historical events leading up to the Ibarra Expedition, including the odyssey of Álvar Núñez Cabeza de Vaca (1527–37) and the officially sanctioned expeditions led by Fray Marcos de Niza (1539) and Captain Francisco Vázquez de Coronado (1540–42). In doing so, Obregón would earn himself the distinction of being considered by some as the very first Mexican historian (Bravo 1997; Hopkins-Durazo 1988).

The first recorded description of European contact with the indigenous peoples of northern Mexico occurred when Cabeza de Vaca, along with three other companions who had survived the shipwrecked Pánfilo de Narváez Expedition, trekked westward from Florida across the American

Figure 3. Portrait of Francisco de Ibarra, first governor of Nueva Vizcaya

continent between 1527 and 1537 with the goal of reaching New Spain (see figure 4).[6] One of the survivors that accompanied him, an African slave called Estebanico by his captors, returned to the area in 1539 as a guide accompanying the Franciscan friar Marcos de Niza. This group had been sent as an advanced party by Viceroy Don Antonio de Mendoza in the hopes of discovering riches based on tales of wealthy cities to the north. These tales had been generated from the oral and written reports of the four survivors of the Cabeza de Vaca party that had reached Culiacán in 1537. Fray Marcos de Niza and his group were to report back to Mendoza on the territory to the north and its purported riches (see figure 5). The de Niza scouting expedition generated much enthusiasm regarding the

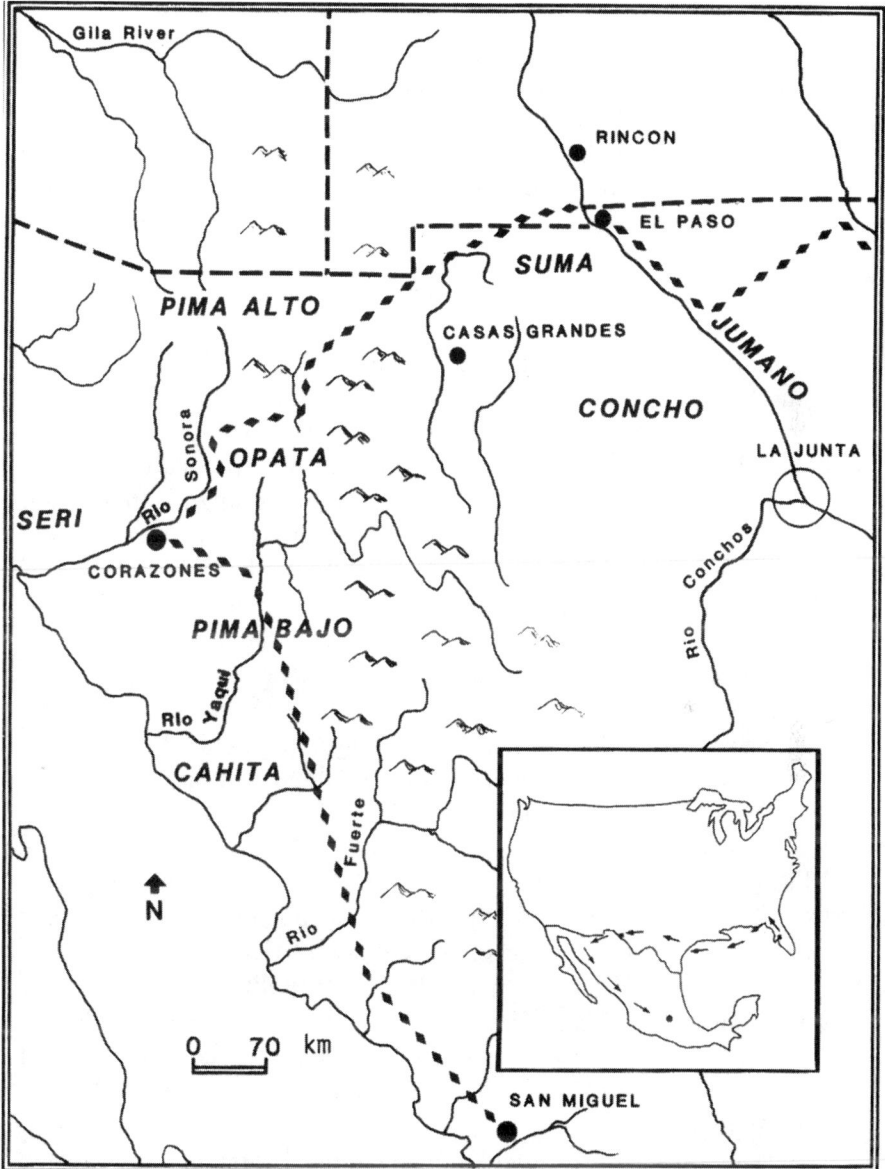

Figure 4. Cabeza de Vaca's route (In *Disease, Depopulation and Culture Change,* Reff 1991)

supposed existence of seven wealthy, "civilized" cities to the north. De Niza reports in his 1539 "Relación," "Solamente ví, desde la boca de la abra, siete poblaciones razonables, algo lexos un valle abaxo muy fresco . . . tuve razon que hay en ella mucho oro y que lo trataron los naturales della en vasijas y joyas [I only saw, from the mouth of the gorge, seven (fairly) large settlements, (and) a bit farther below a very green valley . . . I was told that there is much gold there and that the natives trade in vessels and jewels]" (1995, xix, my translation). The visual observation, combined with what de Niza heard from the indigenous inhabitants, would have called to mind for explorers and soldiers of the time two important legends, one European and one Nahua, inspiring more exploration.

Scholars have long cited the legend of the Seven Cities of Antilia as motivation for Spanish explorers who believed these mythical cities were located somewhere in the New World. The legend, that seven Portuguese bishops had fled the Moorish invasion of the Iberian Peninsula and founded seven cities somewhere in the western Atlantic, was strongly entrenched in the European imagination of de Niza's time.[7] Coming from one who knew Mexico and Peru firsthand, de Niza's report that he had seen seven cities, albeit from a distance, would have echoed the equally influential, yet lesser recognized, foundation narrative of the Nahua tradition. As Rojo's recent study *Return to Aztlan* (2014) argues, the Nahua origin story recounts the "Aztec pilgrimage," the primordial migration of Mexica ancestors from the seven caves of the underworld at Aztlán to a promised land, which the Spanish of course recognized as the wealthy civilization of Tenochtitlán.[8] De Niza's report of the Seven Cities of Cíbola to the north would have fueled rumors of the possibility of "Otro México" that might still be "discovered." The belief that the great Mexica civilization had originated to the north, likely bolstered by the strong tradition of the Seven Cities of Antilia, spurred the huge expedition sent out by Mendoza in 1540.[9] This expedition, led by Coronado, penetrated as far north as Kansas and as far west as the Grand Canyon. However, the Coronado Expedition was largely viewed as a failure on its return to New Spain in 1542 because no fabled cites were found nor any wealth comparable to that of Peru or Mexico (see figure 5).

In addition to the lackluster return of Coronado from the far north, the track record of other Spanish entradas closer to home had not resulted in overwhelming success. The mining frontier of New Spain and its enterprises slowly spread northeast from central Mexico, and slave raids to nearby indigenous communities, repression of indigenous rebellions, and military and evangelization efforts consumed the attention of the Spanish. Most

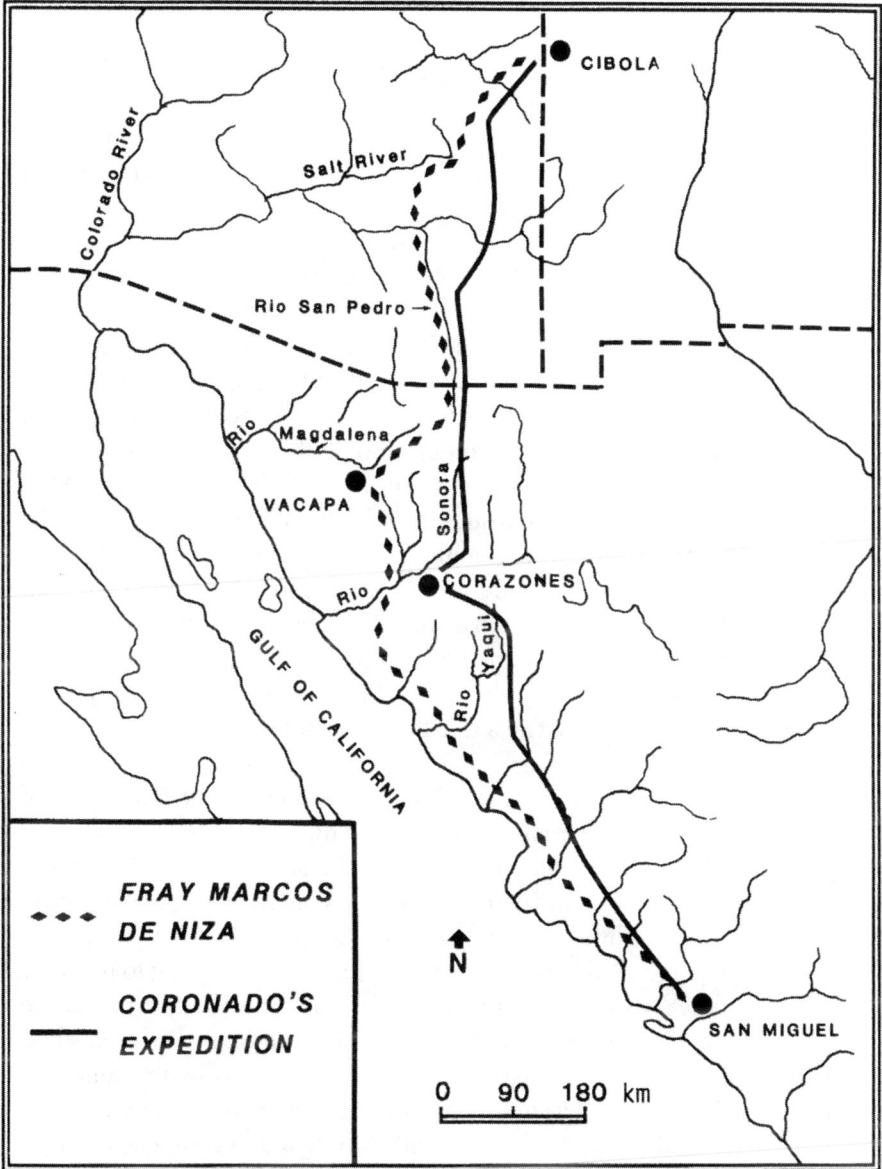

Figure 5. The route of Fray Marcos de Niza and the partial route of Coronado
(*Disease, Depopulation and Culture Change*, Reff 1991)

notable were the infamous forays of the founder of San Miguel de Culiacán, Nuño de Guzmán, who left Mexico City in December 1529 to seek
his fortune and ideally, the famed Seven Cities or Islas Amazonas. For five
years (1530–35) he ransacked the region, raiding indigenous settlements
for slaves and mercilessly squashing indigenous rebellion. His brutality, as
well as his flagrant disregard for the prior rights of discovery of his fellow
countrymen, eventually caught up with him, and Guzmán was arrested and
jailed in 1536. Obregón refers to Guzmán throughout *Historia*, mostly in
terms of the aftermath left in the wake of his brutal tactics.

As Obregón's account attests, the Ibarra expedition of 1563 initially
retraced some of the territory already covered by Nuño de Guzmán and
José de Angulo in the 1530s and Ginés Vázquez de Mercado in 1552.
Mercado had explored the region as far north as Durango under a directive
from the *oidores* (magistrates) of the Audiencia de Nueva Galicia, impelled
ever northward by a tale of a mountain of solid silver (which in fact, turned
out to be a mountain of iron that today is aptly called El Cerro de Mercado).[10] Four years after Mercado, in 1556, the oidor of Nueva Galicia,
Pedro Morones, received royal authorization to undertake an entrada to
Chiametla but lacked the funding and never carried out an expedition.
After Morones's death in 1564, Ibarra would receive a royal *cédula* (a decree
from the king of Spain) "ordering him to continue his work and conquest
and settlement even though he entered lands which had already been
discovered—providing that he found them without churches and religious"
(Mecham 1927, 142).[11]

Composed two decades after Obregón's own experiences as a part of
the Ibarra expedition, *Historia* emerges from the tumultuous milieu of the
second half of the sixteenth century when the far reaches of New Spain,
despite having suffered myriad setbacks in its attempts to expand, slowly
inched its way northward. Although the landscape to the north had been a
source of consternation and failure for explorers who, longing to replicate
the wild successes of Hernán Cortés and Francisco Pizarro, had come
back time and time again empty handed, silver mining settlements had
been established in Zacatecas. Gradually, and perhaps more cautiously,
friars, soldiers, and settlers from these precariously held mining areas were
turning their attention northward again with dual and contradictory aspirations of saving souls and prospecting for mines. Could this landscape,
one of constant resistance from indigenous inhabitants that had thwarted
Spanish efforts and had been a source of constant failure for so many,
still hold promise? Had Pedro de Nájera y Castañeda's 1563 account of
the Coronado Expedition reignited rumors of a possible "Otro México"?

Could a "failed" landscape be turned into a "successful" one? Obregón would argue that it could, and in relating the history of Spanish attempts at settlement in the area, he relies on his own eyewitness testimony and that of fellow explorers to make his case.

Telling His Stories

Obregón emphasizes the privileged perspective of his eyewitness testimony of the Ibarra Expedition (which he joined in Chiametla) to recount the events and descriptions in his text.[12] This makes sense: by the time of his writing, the sense of sight had gradually (over a period of roughly two hundred years) surpassed hearing as the privileged mode of perception and source for knowing in occidental culture knowledge. "The tradition of the high Middle Ages tended to prefer the testimony of the ear to that of the eye: a cultural trait linked to the practices of dominant orality. Hearsay naturally took on the value of authority. Sight, at best, could confirm" (Zumthor and Peebles 1994, 817). His intended readership, the Consejo de Indias and its cosmographers, would have privileged eyewitness reports.

> At the end of the fifteenth [century], this modernity is taken up by those most sure of themselves: that which one knew hitherto by hearsay, one now knew by having universally verified it. This is a topos that we see appear toward 1450 in the Portuguese Zurara, in 1470 in Adorno, and in Columbus with his letter to Santangel. It is true that, having seen, these authors desire to make themselves understood and to lay claim to complete credibility by their word. (817)

At the same time, Obregón also readily employs the oral and written testimonies of other soldiers and prospectors to reinforce his own experiences and to recount those that occurred prior to him joining the expedition, as well as those that occurred during later entradas, particularly those of Chamuscado-Rodríguez (1581–82) and Antonio de Espejo (1583), both of which had begun to push the frontier even farther north into present-day New Mexico. Of course, it is not surprising that Obregón would relate his own deeds; it was common practice for expedition participants in the sixteenth century to compose *relaciones*, both out of an obligation to inform, and to garner favor with, the Crown. However, Obregón's case is peculiar in that he wrote long after his participation in the Ibarra Expedition and was under no obligation do to do so. Moreover, the criollo soldier uses the terms *historia* and *general y universal crónica* to describe his text, the implications of which must be considered.

Obregón employs the terms *crónica, historia, comentario*, and *relación* interchangeably to refer to his document (see figure 6); it is more than likely that he saw them as synonyms to indicate that his work would relate events that had actually happened. However, in 1569, not long before Obregón wrote *Historia*, Las Ordenanzas were revised to outline the historiographical procedures recommended by the Crown for the relaciones written in the New World (Bravo 1997, 14). From that time, the historia began to be distinguished from other discursive modes in their point-of-view of narration and scope. These texts, unlike *cartas* and relaciones, were not written solely out of an obligation to the Crown; rather, they were characterized by their philosophical nature and their wider, potentially public, audience (Mignolo 1982, 77).[13] While there is no evidence that Obregón ever intended for his text to be published, Bravo points out that it nonetheless shares many of the characteristics of the chronicles produced in the Indies in his day and reflects a medieval conception of history. It is reasonable to speculate that this is indicative of his desire to emulate his contemporaries. Moreover, although Obregón did not give his text a title, he does repeatedly refer to it in the prologue as "historia," and the signed description (Legajo 1–1–3/21) in the Archivo General de Indias (AGI) reads, "Historia de los descubrimientos antiguos y modernos de Nueva España y Nuevo Mexico" (Bravo 1997, 26).

Clearly, *historia* was a term that carried particular connotations for Obregón. In fact, he expresses his ideas regarding the function of history and sets out his objectives in writing this one. First, he will provide valuable itinerary information for future expeditions that will help to grow Spanish interests in the region, insisting repeatedly that "la experiencia es maestro de todas las cosas [experience is (the) teacher of all things]" (167).

Para que en esta relación sea vuestra real majestad servida con acrecentamiento de muchas provincias, villas, quintos, tributos y vasallos; y para que los generales, gobernadores y capitanes de su real servicio fueren a descubrir, conquistar y poblar, vayan advertidos e informados de muchos casos y cosas necesarias a la utilidad y provecho de lo que en semejantes jornadas y sucesos conviene, y vayan desengañados de los daños que solían suceder a los primeros, a quien faltó avisos.

[So that by this account your Royal Majesty be served with an increase of many provinces, villages, royal fifths, tributes and vassals; and so that

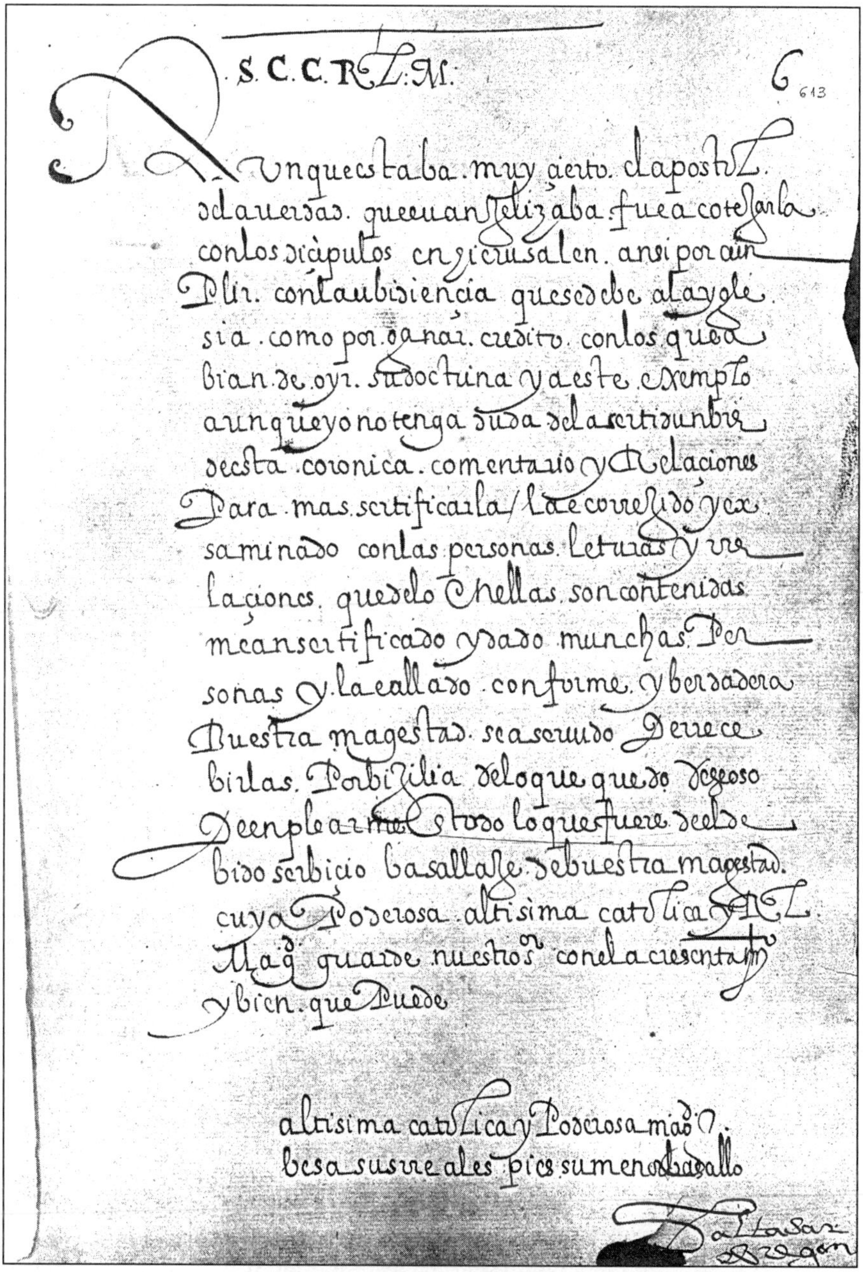

S. C. C. R. L. M. 6 613

Aunquestaba muy cierto del apostol
de a uersas que cuan felizaba fue a cotexarla
con los discipulos en iherusalen. ansi por aun-
plir con tanbisiencia que se debe a la ygle-
sia. como por ganar credito con los que de-
bian de oyr su doctrina y a este exemplo
aunque yo no tenga duda de la certidunbre
desta coronica. comentario y Relaciones
Para mas certificarla la e corregido y ex-
saminado con las personas letras y relaciones que de lo en ellas son contenidas
me an certificado y dado munchas Personas y la e allado conforme y verdadera
vuestra magestad se a seruido de rece-
birlas. Por bigilia de lo que quedo deseoso
de emplear me en todo lo que fuere de su de-
bido serbicio basallaje de vuestra magestad.
cuya Poderosa altisima catolica R. L.
Mag. guarde nuestro señor con el acresentamiento
y bien que Puede

altisima catolica y Poderosa mag.
besa sus reales pies su menor basallo

Baltasar Obregon

Figure 6. Final paragraph of the prologue to *Historia de los descubrimientos de Nueva España* (1584), signed by Baltasar Obregón (AGI. Patronato. 22. R7. fo. 613) the generals, governors and captains of your royal service who go on to discover, conquer and settle, may (do so) advised and informed, for their utility and benefit, of the many necessary cases and things, and that they go advised of the harm that so often befell those first (explorers), who had no warnings.] (43)[14]

Second, he will elucidate the truth amid the rumors and mixed claims regarding territory (and the multiple toponyms) based on his own experience and memory and the testimony of reliable witnesses, thereby ensuring that the truth be told and that "no se sepulten en el olvido y poca memoria de los hombres los buenos ejemplos y casos y sucesos [the good examples, cases, and events not be entombed in the obscurity of man's short memory]" (42). History in Obregón serves three functions: it tells the truth, provides valuable lessons and information, and ensures that credit is given where due.[15]

Obregón is at once author, compiler, and witness as he refers to his *Historia* as a source for his own, personal testimony and for comparing the veracity of information gleaned from various accounts.[16] In terms of point-of-view, Obregón is at times the authorial witness of events that he relates, but at other moments he is an *historiador*, narrating events related to him either discursively or orally by others, such as soldiers, priests, *indígenas*, and settlers. Indeed, Obregón often indulges in *imitatio*, emulating, adapting, and at times even copying verbatim from other sources (a practice the author openly cites in the prologue), likening his role as historian to that of the natural station of the bee, collecting essences from various flowers to create honey. He should not, he reasons, be faulted for having taken examples and arguments from other histories that support his task.[17] Of course, while the practice of borrowing or copying directly from other sources was common in Obregón's time, compilers and authors did not necessarily deem it necessary to cite sources when they did so. Why does Obregón, then, draw attention to his cobbling together of multiple accounts? Bravo (1997, 24) postulates that this may indicate an earnestness on Obregón's part to demonstrate veracity or sincerity, or simply a desire to back up his own testimony. It may also be that, as a relatively undereducated man, Obregón relied on other sources to lend authority to his own work—it was the testimonies of others that assured the confirmation of services as related by the chronicler.[18] The importance of this lies in the recognition that for his intended readership, outside testimony would have lent authority to his self-proclamations (Adorno 1995, 21). Obregón seems determined to at once demonstrate his knowledge and verify that knowledge with other sources and testimonies. While modern-day readers may dismiss his outside testimony as less reliable because Obregón did not witness events first-hand, it must be kept in mind that his potential readers would probably not have viewed it this way because they recognized testimony and other texts as valid sources.

The complexity of the role of the narrator is compounded further given that Obregón is also writing to relate his participation and deeds to garner royal favor, as these sorts of texts informed imperial perception and policy and had important implications for their authors, most of whom were seeking future commissions to explore and settle lands. At once author and witness, Obregón was ultimately seeking recompense from the Crown for his participation in the expansion of the empire. Obregón's desire to earn a commission, or at least the opportunity to participate in one, is evidenced in his openly volunteering to serve as *maese de campo* (first lieutenant, second only to the general captain of an expedition) or *capitán* in his first letter, and reminding his reader of his offer to explore the lands beyond San Felipe on the Sea of Cortés in book two. "Y aunque el menor vasallo de V.M. yo me ofrezco ponerlo por obra y servir a V.M. en ver, saber y descubrir quinientas leguas de tierras desde la provincia de San Felipe en adelante y si no fuere aceptado en este servicio, hay en estas partes capitanes muy suficientes para el dicho efecto [And although the lowest vassal of Your Majesty, I offer myself to put to the work of serving Your Majesty in seeing, knowing and discovering five hundred leagues of lands from the province of San Felipe onward, and, if this (my) service not be accepted, there are in these parts captains sufficient to that end]" (255–56).

It is telling that Obregón points to his peers "in these parts," which may hint at an emerging concern about *peninsulares* (or *gachupines* as the criollos in New Spain had begun to call them) as they began to pose a threat to the sons of the first wave of conquistadors and encomenderos. Certainly, to earn the coveted opportunity to explore and settle the north, Obregón would have to precisely demonstrate his capabilities and his interests in serving the Crown. At the same time, given his status as a criollo, Obregón must have been aware that he may be perceived by his readers as lower in social status than his peninsular-born counterparts, and perhaps even with suspicion. While the term *criollo* was already being used to refer to those of Spanish blood born in the Americas by the author's time (the term's usage emerges c. 1560), Obregón does not employ the term himself, more than likely because it would have been used pejoratively (Vitulli and Solodkow 2009, 24). In their study of the "arqueology" of the term and the cultural concept of the criollo, Vitulli and Solodkow demarcate the period 1560–1600 as the *serie de estereotipo* when peninsulares living in the Americas had already begun to use various monikers to refer to the sons of the first conquistadors and encomenderos, such as "hijos del reino [sons of the kingdom]," "hijos de la tierra [sons of the earth]," "hijos y nietos de los conquistadores [sons and grandsons of the conquistadors]," "hijos de los encomenderos [sons of the encomenderos]," or "beneméritos [the meritorious]," and "criollo."[19] This distinction became increasingly important as issues of "quality" began to surface once those sons who had never seen the shores of Spain began to increase in number in the New World.[20] Le Riverend and Venegas Delgado (2005) demonstrate how various writers in the sixteenth century charged that the criollo had mutated somehow largely, according to the hypothesis of the day, because of the region's climate. For example, Juan López de Velasco argued in 1571 that criollos, as opposed to those born on the Iberian Peninsula, were known to turn out physically different in color and shape, with detrimental consequences to the spirit following. Juan de Cárdenas contended in 1591 that criollos usually died younger, turned gray earlier, and suffered from gastric and venereal illness more frequently than Spaniards (Le Riverend and Venegas Delgado 2005, 20, 25). Similarly, in 1568, Bernardino de Sahagún blamed the climate of the region for criollos who "en el aspecto parecen españoles, y en las condiciones no lo son [in appearance are like Spaniards, but in rank are not]" (Le Riverend and Venegas Delgado 2005, 24). Factors such as place of birth, the "harsh" climate of the Indies, encomenderos' proximity to and inferred interaction with indigenous groups, allusions to "uncertain" lineage, and even having been nursed by indigenous or mixed-race wet nurses all contributed to theories that the criollo person was degenerate (Solodkow 2009; Le Riverend and Venegas 2005).

Whereas the term's origins (Corominas cites a Portuguese origin while Woll sustains that the term originated in the Americas) and temporal and colloquial nuances (racial, social, legal, economic, cultural, biological) may be debated, what is certain is that the first generation of those who would be labeled (by those outside of their ilk) as criollos were coming into a sociocultural hierarchy that would inform social station and standing for generations to come. As a criollo, Obregón would more than likely have been aware that his readers may have viewed him as lower in social status than his peninsular-born counterparts. Even had that not been the case, as an explorer and son of an encomendero, his social standing was always at the mercy of the vicissitudes of fortune. Yet, while he may have written his *Historia* knowing that it would be difficult for him to win a commission to explore and settle to the north, he nonetheless seems to consider himself every bit a part of the larger Spanish empire.

In the first letter addressing the Crown, Obregón directly refers to his familial connection to Castile and his own feelings of obligation to the Crown. Quite literally from the first word, Obregón makes clear that he has inherited the noble obligations of his Spanish family and has continued their service to the Crown:

Obligación es de caballeros, hidalgos y personas nobles servir a V.A. y su real Corona en la defensa de nuestra santa Fe católica y sus reinos, vasallos y señoríos, en cuya obligación y servicios siempre se han ocupado mis ante-cesores, abuelos y padres, así en esos reinos de Castilla come en ésta de las Indias. Y considerando suceder en esta obligación y vasallaje, empecé a servir a V.A. en las conquistas de Nueva Vizcaya y en otras partes, a mi costa, trabajo y riesgo de la vida, y en el viaje de la California, desde edad de diez y nueve años, todo lo cual consta de las probanzas que envío a V.A.

[It is the duty of knights, hidalgos and noblemen to serve Your High-ness and His Royal Crown in defense of our holy Catholic Faith and his kingdoms, vassals, and states, in whose duty and services my ancestors, grandfathers and fathers have always been occupied, in (both) those king-doms of Castile as well as these of the Indies. And mindful to enter into this duty and vassalage, I began to serve Your Highness in the conquests of Nueva Vizcaya and in other parts, at my (own) cost, hardship, and risk of life, and (additionally) in journey to California, since the age of nineteen years, all of which attests to the affidavit that I send to Your Highness.] (37)

In addition to his loyal vassalage (the Crown was concerned with con-quistador and criollo separatists as early as 1521) Obregón also establishes his lineage at a time when, as Solodkow argues, being the "unmixed" son of a conquistador meant having a reliable social stance from which to petition for land and titles (Solodkow 2009, 132). Establishing such legal and social standing would have been useful because Obregón's economic prospects, like many of his peers, may have been waning. Solodkow explains that by the end of the sixteenth century a period of crisis and instability in New Spain had resulted in an economically dispossessed generation. While this first gen-eration of criollos had grown up under the protection and privilege of their fathers' *encomiendas*, they themselves were "practically reduced to misery" and possessed an attitude of "vindication and demands" (106–7). Constant disputes of power between the sons of the conquistadors and the burgeoning metropolitan bureaucratic machine of New Spain left many first-generation criollos worried about their loss of privileges, and it is probable that Obregón found himself navigating a society in which his socioeconomic station was not fixed. Fernando Benítez describes the milieu as one in which the criollos had lost a historic battle as the encomienda was dismantled bit by bit and the knight-errantry their forefathers had emulated during their conquest was in decline. According to Benítez, replacing their world was one in which the Inquisition, newcomers from the Iberian Peninsula, and bureaucrats wielded power, not the sons of encomenderos (Benítez 1962, 237).[21]

These extratextual factors lend insight into Obregón's *situación enunciativa* and may inform Obregón's insistence that growing the empire is both paramount and, more importantly, possible. He insists that, in his experience, the majority of the lands to the north are indeed inhabitable and can be pacified by men such as him. Frequently repeating the mantra, "Experiencia es la maestra [Experience is the teacher]," Obregón utilizes stories from past expeditions' failures to secure the landscape so they may serve as lessons moving forward. He openly criticizes what he views as misdeeds or mistakes from previous expeditions, and even disputes the prominence and importance of their chroniclers (Bravo 1997, 21). He is particularly critical of the maltreatment of the indigenous peoples during the course of the Coronado Expedition, contending that such abuses only result in the creation of enemies. For example, the story of one of Coronado's captains, Diego de Alcaraz, and his abusive treatment of the indigenous people at Sahuaripa ends, from the narrator's perspective, in his violent but justified death. Obregón contends that the indigenous rob and destroy the Spanish settlement in retaliation for the heinous offenses the Coronado party had committed against them, including "taking advantage" of their women and daughters and charging them with "too many tributes and personal services," even taking supplies without paying for them. Worst of all, "those who were present when the [indigenous] enemies entered to destroy the village have certified to me that the captain [Diego de Alcaraz] was laying with two Indias" (155–56). Obregón reasons that God punished Alcaraz for the bad example he set for idolatrous Indians who otherwise would have been converted to the Catholic faith.[22]

Stories that relate failure also serve as a contrast against which Obregón emphasizes the successes of the Ibarra expedition, demonstrating that with morally guided and sound practices, the Spanish can turn the failed landscape around. For example, Nuño de Guzmán's failure to hold Chiametla after founding a small settlement there on his return from Jalisco is contrasted against the success of Ibarra in pacifying the region and making allies of its inhabitants. Obregón contends that the people of Chiametla have, in fact, been at peace for many years, trading with European merchants and promising governor Ibarra that they would be obedient "vassals" to the King, even assisting in pacifying the less compliant native inhabitants occupying the mountains.[23]

Of course, relating stories of failures and successes of past expeditions also provides a kind of didactic function, allowing Obregón to offer advice for future expeditions to the north while emphasizing his service to the king and the Consejo de Indias in the form of useful knowledge. In this sense, while his text explicitly provides itinerary information, it is precisely because it is a *history* that it is permitted to serve as a means to incorporate the exposition of his own deeds and those of other explorers throughout his account.[24] The resultant episodic narration that breaks up extensive landscape description may result in the text seeming uneven, and certainly the mixing of present and past tenses can cause some confusion. For example, historian J. Lloyd Mecham (1927) notes a variety of errors in recording dates on the part of Obregón, and cultural geographer Carl Sauer complains about the text's difficulties, calling the chronicle "confused" and "muddled" and accusing Obregón of having a bad memory:

> He has the very bad failing for a chronicler of letting one event suggest another which happened in another place or another time, without indicating clearly to the reader that he is about to go off on a large tangent. The author is obsequious and verbose, anxious to impress his superiors, and thus wrote an uncommonly lurid tale, in contrast to the matter-of-fact simplicity of most of his contemporaries. Indian ethnography and language meant almost nothing to him. (1932, 91–92)

Sauer does applaud Obregón's visual memory and landscape descriptions, but he concludes that Obregón is at once "dim-witted" and "garrulous" in terms of relating events.[25] However, this scathing critique may exhibit an anachronistic criticism on the part of Sauer; in fact, Bravo (1997) argues that Obregón's text actually reflects the characteristics of the *crónicas indianas* of his day, referring to his messianic conception of history and theological references, the text's function as paradigm of practical information, and his use of personal testimony to reinforce truth (16–18). More interestingly, Bravo recognizes Obregón's attention to quality description and points out that his work breaks the classic mold of history with an exceptional "ethnographical curiosity" for his day, that is, the exact opposite of Sauer's accusation that indigenous ethnology meant nothing to him (28).

While it may be tempting to dismiss these differences as the disparate perceptions of a cultural geographer and a linguist, it may be more useful to acknowledge both interpretations as valid. Obregón admittedly attempts to be universal in his history while simultaneously providing extensive description for future expeditions. Much like travel narratives from the time of Marco Polo to Columbus, Obregón's accounting of history reflects what Zumthor and Peebles (1994, 814) call a "double orality" made up of his own recollections as well as the information he had gathered from outside sources. The result, while confusing to today's readership, is that the text merely reflects the lingering influences of the Medieval travel narrative as are cited by Zumthor and Peebles: repetitions, uneven tone, unexpected breaks in description so as to narrate events, a horizontal projection of experience that ignores temporality, and a view of people only in terms of European political and economic utility (814). That the resultant text is uneven and confusing to the modern reader is not particularly relevant, but what is relevant is that this "universality" provides a platform to relate the grand deeds and laudable acts of courage and sacrifice of his Spanish peers while obsequiously mentioning his own service for Crown and King. One implication of this is that it allows for certain literary elements to emerge as he highlights various protagonists and tells their "heroic" stories, even emulating the great deeds of the Spanish medieval literary tradition.[26] It is precisely this function of demonstrating service to the larger project that allows novelesque stories to interrupt, and indeed to flourish, in the extensive scene setting of the harrowing and often hostile banda del norte.

Metaphorai

It would be difficult to ignore that traditional literary elements abound in Obregón's *Historia*, particularly in relating stories of laudatory deeds of Spanish experience. These deeds are reminiscent of the ballads, romances, and novels of chivalry that were popularly read in Obregón's day. As Weckmann ([1984] 1992) has demonstrated, more than mere entertainment, these tales embodied a true sense of honor and ideals that was established in the Middle Ages and fixed in the fourteenth century by Raymond Lull's *Book of the Order of Chivalry*. This code of conduct lingered in the Hispanic world and was emulated in the *libros de caballería* (novels of chivalry) that were widely read in New Spain by conquistadors, even more so with the arrival of the printing press in 1539. It is not surprising that the juridical textual production of the day would emulate novels of chivalry—the soldiers and explorers who were often their authors were eager to make comparisons with knightly heroes. But what function might the relating of expedition lore and legend serve in a text overtly dedicated to providing itinerary information? I have already cited the desire to win a commission and Obregón's insistence that he tell of such deeds so that they may be remembered. Additionally, they are the hallmark of a first-generation criollo glorifying the recent past and the importance of the first conquistadors, worthy of land and titles. Finally, I propose that such stories also serve a larger, less immediate, or even less obvious function: they allow for the construction of a historical framework in an otherwise "historiless" landscape (from the Spanish perspective of course, not indigenous), one where the occidental has not yet left its mark in a permanently successful way. This is not a limited *relación* or list of population centers, nor is it a simple testimony. As the episodes that follow evince, this text links New Spain to its northern frontier and beyond, and back to its Old World readers in Spain.

The first chapter of book 1 opens with Hernán Cortés in Tenochtitlán (more than twenty years before the author's birth) wherein Obregón establishes the Spanish presence in the very palace of the rich and powerful Moctezuma, king of the great Mexica kingdom:

> En la casa real, palacio y salas del poderoso y riquísimo rey Moctezuma, señor de la insigne y gran ciudad de México Tenochtitlán y reinos del imperio mexicano, halló el marqués don Hernando Cortés muchas curiosas y agradables pinturas, letras y caracteres al modo de su antiguo escribir. . . . Estas antiguas crónicas, historias y relaciones fueron fundamento, principio, causa que el marqués don Hernando Cortés y el virrey don Antonio de Mendoza codiciasen saber y descubrir el origen, venida, raíz y tronco de los antiguos culguas mexicanos, teniendo sospecha sería de gran número de indios, poblazones y riquezas, para sujetarlos al gremio de nuestra san[ta] Fe católica.

> [In the royal home, palace and halls of the very powerful and rich king, Moctezuma, ruler of the notable and great city of Mexico, Tenochtitlán, and kingdoms of the Mexican empire, the marquis Don Hernando Cortés found many curious and exciting paintings, letters and characters in the manner of their ancient writing. . . . These ancient chronicles, histories and accounts caused the marquis Don Hernando Cortés and the Viceroy Don Antonio de Mendoza to desire to know and discover the origin, arrival, root and trunk of the ancient Mexican *culguas*, believing that there would be a great number of Indians, large settlements, and riches, so as to hold them in the bosom of our holy Catholic faith.] (45–46)

Although the *Historia* begins thusly with references to the indigenous historical accounts that impelled explorers to find "Otro México," these accounts have been appropriated and filtered, first by Cortés, the "hero" who conquered a powerful and rich king, and second by the *autor-historiador* who assures the former's role as agent of action in the retelling. From the very first paragraph, it is the Spanish protagonist who occupies the scene of the center of power. In this way, even though the action occurs in a space unfamiliar to the reader in Spain, that space is Europeanized through this narrative act, a narrative act that establishes a familiar spatial connection by populating the previously unfamiliar space with the Spanish hero. No less important, Obregón refers to the possible existence of another large civilization and immediately connects it to an extended European presence with the conversion to Christianity.

Lest it be viewed as tenuous, Obregón cites a direct connection between the Old and New Worlds through Cortés's presence in the latter and the larger framework of European history by pointing out the oft-cited (albeit erroneously) coincidence of his birth and that of the "abominable and poisonous" Martin Luther.[27] To Obregón's mind, Cortés was born expressly for the conversion and salvation of the "idolatrous Indians" as a way to balance the harm caused by the enemy of the Catholic faith. Reflective of the dream of a universal Christian Empire that prevailed at the time, Obregón appropriates the local space and memory (events occurring in the borderlands of New Spain) and incorporates them into what, in his view, is "universal" memory (occidental and Catholic history).

The supposed coincidence of the birth of Martin Luther and the birth of Hernán Cortés in Europe, explained as Providence that allowed for the conversion of the "idolatrous Indian" in New Spain, historically connects the unfamiliar, foreign New World to the familiar Old World, broadening the scope of the Counter-Reformation and presupposing the appropriation of indigenous space as a part of the European imagination and linking these two seemingly disparate worlds. For while Phillip II was putting down rebellions against the Catholic church in Europe, Obregón points out, Cortés was converting the idolatrous Indian, spreading the faith: "el invictísimo César de gloriosa memoria que estaba en el imperio de Alemania, castigando a los rebeldes y enemigos de nuestra santa Fe católica y a la inobediencia de su real Imperio y Corona. [the invictus Caesar of glorious memory that was in the Alemannic Empire, punishing the rebels and the enemies of our Holy Catholic Faith and the disobedience to His Royal Empire and Crown]" (47). Likening the cause in New Spain to that of Phillip II's in Europe, the stories serve as *metaphorai*, linking places and serving as a means of mass transportation (de Certeau 1984, 115). As metaphorai, the Cortés tales traverse the Atlantic and link the Counter-Reformation in Europe with indigenous conversion in New Spain. The hero, the Spanish protagonist, now belongs to both places, and both places are each a part of the other.

Obregón draws similar comparisons between protagonists of the Conquest and European heroes, demonstrating parallels with both recent and distant times. For example, as a prelude to the extensive relation of the battle in the valley pueblo of Sahuaripa (Zaguaripa) in which Obregón fought during the Ibarra expedition, the author humbly likens the victory to that of "el famosísimo y católico rey don Alfonso de Castile [the very famous and Catholic King Alfonso of Castile]" against Alboacén de Marruecos (Abul-Hasan 'Ali) in 1340 in which, despite being gravely outnumbered, a mere 8,000 horsemen and 12,000 foot soldiers vanquished 660,000 Moors (166). Similarly outnumbered, Obregón goes on, Tamorlán (Timur Lang) defeated the largest army ever known (more than one million), and imprisoned its leader, King Bayaceto, in a cage of gold (166).[28] Citing more recent history, Obregón points to Francisco Pizarro's triumph in Peru (c. 1532–33) in which "con pocos cristianos venció a gran suma de indios, poderosos señores de gran Tesoro [with but a few Christians vanquished a great number of Indians, powerful lords of great wealth]" and Don Juan de Austria's naval victory at the Battle of Lepanto in 1571 "adonde venció, mató y rindió gran suma de poderosas galeras mediante su católico esfuerzo, osadía y valor [wherein he vanquished, killed, and subjugated a great number of powerful vessels by his Catholic spirit, temerity and valor]" (166). The battle waged to "pacificar" the people of Sahuaripa (possibly the Jovas, who occupied the area along with the Opata) is paralleled thusly:

Y aunque parezca demasía y agravios a guerras y victorias tan famosas traer a la memoria en este comentario una pequeña batalla que tuvo el general Francisco de Ibarra en las sierras y partes remotas del valle de Señora quise, aunque desigual, honrarla con el final de cosas tan dignas de estimación, loa y memoria con que son, se le dé a ella más de su igual merecimiento y a mí perdón de la culpa que en semejante caso hubiere errado, aunque no me parece más quilate que el que V.M. le diere y los cristianos lectores quisieren aplicar, no quitando de cada caso lo que a su loa y estimación mereciere; pues sin preceder interés de calor de encomiendas, oro, plata, esclavos ni otros despojos de provecho más de querer sujetar a los indios a la ley de nuestra santa Fe católica, vencieron, mataron y rindieron buenos soldados y su general a seiscientos bárbaros

gallardos, esfrozados [*sic*] y señores de flechas enarboladas de ponzoñosa
yerba . . . en parte[s] lejos y remotas de alcanzar socorro de cristianos ni
poderse retirar por ser en tierras fragosas.

[And even if it may seem excessive and (an) affront to such famous wars
and victories to call to mind in this commentary a small battle that General Francisco de Ibarra waged in the sierras and remote parts of the
Valley of Sonora, albeit unequal, I desire to honor (that battle) among
things so worthy of esteem, praise, and memory with the purpose that it
be given proper consideration; and pardon me in the event that I have
erred, although it does deserve the value that Your Majesty might grant it
and the Christian readers might give to it, (and) does not take from any
event the praise and esteem deserved; thus, without acting in any interest
or enthusiasm for encomiendas, gold, silver, slaves nor any other spoils
of profit other than wanting to bring the Indians to the law of our Holy
Catholic faith, the good soldiers and their general vanquished, killed and
defeated six hundred brave barbarians, zealous men brandishing arrows
with the poisonous herb . . . in remote lands, far from any help of Christians and unable to retreat for being in (densely) overgrown lands.] (167)

It has been well argued and convincingly demonstrated in other studies
that drawing such comparisons in a rather "literary" fashion is a prevalent
trope in juridical documents (Adorno 1995; Weckmann [1984] 1992).
What I would like to draw attention to specifically is the role of such stories
in an otherwise (at least from a Spanish or criollo perspective) frustrating landscape and how they provide a place within what Obregón calls
"católica memoria," allowing for the deeds of caballeros to flourish. Even
more importantly, they allow for the unruly, unconquered, uncontrolled
space to take shape in the larger framework of occidentalized landscape
(place) and history (time). As historian, Obregón dedicates the first five
chapters of book 1 to relating what one may consider the "major" events
lived by the Spanish conquistador protagonists that led up to the departure
of Ibarra from San Martín, Nueva Vizcaya, in 1563.[29] Incidents that already
held a place in history are reviewed, such as the travails of Cabeza de Vaca;
the "deceitful ways" of fray Marcos de Niza that had inhabitants of New
Spain clamoring to explore and discover the legendary Seven Cities of
Gold; stories from Coronado's expedition, including the death of the maestre de campo, Lope de Samaniego; Nuño de Guzmán's violent conquest
and settlement of Culiacán; the founding of a villa near Cíbola; and the
exploration of pueblos along the river Tibuex. With each telling of events

featuring Spanish protagonists, one can see the banda del norte beginning to take shape as a historical space throughout which stories of a Spanish protagonist are acted out.

Perhaps even more striking than Obregón's retelling is how these meta-phorai are not limited to the literary or the "major" European fueled narrative acts; rather, they emerge likewise in local lore and even gossip. These anecdotal accounts serve at once to fill in the gaps of history for those who have not personally experienced the landscape and create a space for alternative possibilities. Consider the following account of Coronado's fall from his horse:

> Volvió el general [Coronado] de Quivira marchando con su campo por sus ordinarias jornadas hasta juntarse con su campo, *que estaba en el río de Tibuex, adonde por su desgracia cayó de un caballo,* de la cual caída afirman los antiguos que fueron en su compañía y estuvieron presentes que descaeció y fue a menos su buen entendimiento y gobierno, ocasión de su determinación a la vuelta de la tierra que había descubierto y podía poblar; *otros afirman que la causa fue haber dejado mujer hermosa e hijos y hacienda en la ciudad de México.*

> [The general (Coronado) returned from Quivira marching with his men by way of his daily journey until rejoining with his camp, *which was on the Tibuex River, where to his disgrace he fell from his horse,* a fall from which, the old ones who were in his company and were present affirm, diminished and lessened his good understanding and government, occasioning his determination to return from the lands he had discovered and (could have) settled; *others contend that the cause (of his determination to leave) was having left his beautiful wife and children and hacienda (behind) in Mexico City.*] (59–60, my emphasis)

In the course of the daily journey back to his camp from Quivira, in present-day New Mexico, Coronado was thrown from his horse.[30] First, while it does mark a turning point in the Coronado Expedition in that ultimately the injury incurred from the fall would hasten Coronado's return, Obregón does not limit himself to reporting this consequence; rather, he adds a bit of extra speculation. It is noteworthy that this episode, devoid of the heroic acts expressed in other tales, takes on an almost gossipy tone, suggesting an alternative story. Witnesses have speculated about what could have caused Coronado to fall from his horse, suggesting multiple versions and various possibilities of what happened on the way back from

Quivira to the main camp, near present-day Albuquerque, along the river Tibuex. Why is this tidbit included in a comprehensive history of northward expansion? How does it connect to the other grandiose narratives that report exceptional valor? Is this exemplary of why Carl Sauer (1932, 92) would accuse Obregón of having composed an "uncommonly lurid tale"? Or perhaps these story "fragments," those suggestions that insinuate more stories about the story, allow the reader to experience the landscape in a more profound, even personal way. Borrowing from de Certeau, the "verbal relics" that make up the story then connect it to "lost" stories, to stories not found on the page, to the point where their relations are not thought, "produc[ing] anti-texts, effects of dissimulation and escape, possibilities of moving into other landscapes" (de Certeau 1984, 107). Since the river Tibuex is the location where this unfortunate event/story/ bit of gossip takes place, it moves itself into the broader historical landscape, filling gaps with multiple possibilities.

Another episode that exemplifies the landscape-as-story occurs when Obregón relates the tale of a scouting party that ends tragically in death. When Ibarra sends the maestre de campo, Martín de Gamón, along with twenty soldiers and some indigenous guides on a scouting mission to Topia, the soldiers grow suspicious of the guides when the journey takes longer than they had estimated:[31]

> Habiendo marchado [Gamón] con su campo algunos días más de los que prometieron las guías por tierras de gran soledad, aspereza y frío, unas veces por una senda por donde iban ellos a Topía, otras por montañas de espantable oscuridad y espesura montuosa . . . el maestre de campo y soldados *entendieron que las guías los llevaban con mala intención* a entregar a sus enemigos para que los matasen. . . . Apretó [Gamón] a las guías con grandes amenazas y prisión, de la cual se soltaron con determinación de defender sus vidas y matar a los cristianos. . . . *A los cuales ahorcó el maese de campo Martín de Gamón contra justicia, razón y cristiandad de un hermoso, florido y fértil árbol*, el cual manifestó el delito de la injusta muerte de las guías haciendo señal por divina y milagrosa permisión de manera que después de ahorcados *se secó la madera verde y floridas hojas de él, caso milagroso y digno de memoria y admiración.*

> [Having marched with his men some days more than the guides had promised through desolate, rough and cold lands, sometimes by the path by which they used to go to Topia, other times by way of mountains of a frightening darkness and dense vegetation . . . the maese de campo and

soldiers *thought that the guides were leading them with the evil intention* of turning them over to their enemies for them to kill. . . . Gamón pressured the guides with great threats and prison, which incited them with the determination to defend their lives and kill the Christians. . . . *For which the maese de campo, Martín de Gamón, against justice, reason and Christianity, hanged them (the guides) from a beautiful, flowering, and fruitful tree*, which manifest the transgression of the unjust death of the guides by making a sign, by divine and miraculous permission, that after having been hanged, *the green wood and flowery leaves (of the tree) dried up, a miraculous case worthy of memory and admiration.*] (77, my emphasis)

Gamón hangs the guides from the beautiful, flowering tree and it miraculously withers, leaving a lasting mark on the landscape that denotes the injustice and malice that led to their deaths. Later, the tree "retells" the story when the Ibarra expedition heads for Topia "hasta llegar al valle de los ahorcados que justició Martín de Gamón, adonde vieron el árbol que, sin muestra de ser lisiado de rayo ni fuego, *está seco*, por lo cual se coligió ser por divina permisión [until arriving at the valley of the guides that Martín Gamón had accused and hanged, where they saw the tree that, without any sign of having been damaged by lightning bolt nor fire, *is dry*, which came to be by divine permission]" (82, my emphasis). The use of the present tense connotes the permanency of this indelible mark on the landscape of the northern frontier, a marker that holds a history and tells a story of greater significance for all who pass by it. To borrow a phrase from anthropologist Keith Basso's work on local theories of dwelling, this "fuses setting and situation" (1996, 8). As Spirn (1998, 27) points out, "In landscape, representation and reality fuse when a tree, path or gate is invested with larger significance." The tree now represents a particular Spanish reality. It is invested with a larger significance, representing the repercussions of mistreating "potential vassals." It is history as a lesson, and one told by the landscape itself.

Both stories referenced above—part gossip, part legend—allow Obregón to specify places within the landscape in terms of a Spanish experience as if to say, "That is the tree where those guides died" or "That is the spot where Coronado fell off of his horse." This may speak to the emerging criollo discursive style "plagados de anécdotas y chismes locales configurados de una 'naturaleza oral' [plagued with anecdotes and local gossip configured from an oral nature]" (Kathleen Ross, quoted in Solodkow 2009, 139) wherein adventures are related with the excess and mythology that social rumor has added to them, passed down from conquistadors to their sons

(Solodkow 2009, 140). I warrant that they also allow Obregón to resignify the landscape through storytelling within the context of a larger historical framework. *Landscape*, in this sense, performs a cultural function; it is praxis. Hirsch and O'Hanlon draw a comparison between mapping and what Paul Carter has called "imperial history," "the form of history which 'reduces space to a stage' upon which actors enact significant historical events such as those leading to . . . 'discovery' and 'settlement'" (Carter, quoted in Hirsch 1995, 3). The theatre-protagonist relationship of episodes of knight-errantry and major European figures are "filled-in" and enriched by the seamless relationship between the landscape and its stories of local lore that bespeak something close to the ground; a landscape that is lived and experienced off the page. Obregón's project of discursive mapping coupled with storytelling seems to be reflective of a more embodied and robust experience of landscape, one that provides a thickness and stability to the theretofore historically "empty" northern borderlands.

Ahern has demonstrated that, prior to the Coronado Expedition, the northern frontier had been conceived in the European mind as either the "mythical places of the Seven Cities inherited from medieval lore . . . or as lands known to those born in Mexico as the territory of the Chichimecas" or as *tierra de guerra* (2002, 33–34). Pedro de Castañeda de Nájera's account of the Coronado Expedition (written in 1563, twenty years after the return of Coronado) however, "transformed the geography of North America from the medieval island imagery of Columbus to that of a new continent about to appear on maps, where the toponyms of Cibola, Acoma, Tiguex, Cicuyue, and Quivira configured new political and cultural spaces" (2002, 27). Specifically, in what scholars have described as an "unpolished style" (Montané Martí 2002), and as Ahern demonstrates, Castañeda's account relates the Coronado Expedition in the form of an itinerary by measuring in number of leagues the distance between pueblos and naming places along a north-south axis. What is more, because there was still no precise map that located Cíbola or Quivira in 1563, his account rescued the expedition, its route, and its events, from its "forgotten and tainted status" (Ahern 2003, 280).[32] By the 1580s, it seems that rescue mission had had an effect, and as Rojos points out, the toponym "Nuevo México," previously applied to various places mistaken for the Aztec homeland so desperately sought, was by then fixed to the city of Cíbola.

Written more than twenty years after the Castañeda account, Obregón's *Historia* exemplifies that by the 1580s these recognizable toponyms now hold a history, and as such, represent a landscape in and on which the stories of expeditions now literally have "taken place." That important historical events (related in the language of heroic deeds) have happened in these places is presupposed, serving as what de Certeau has called "foundation narrations." "The story's first function is to authorize, or more exactly, to *found*" (de Certeau 1984, 123). The landscape as perceived through Obregón's cultural filter holds a history that is culturally recognizable and shared with European history, giving it a thickness and stability that arguably may have been lacking in the imaginations of its readers previously. In such an historical discourse, the projection of a particularly Spanish story onto the landscape of the northern frontier has transformed it textually to reflect that cultural identity. Just as Castañeda's account of the Coronado Expedition "realizes the cultural and spatial configuration of a 'new' norte and a 'new' frontier—forming an intersection where the text must confront the terrain" (Ahern 2002, 28), Obregón's text must confront the landscape. However, in the latter's text, the landscape confronted represents a now historicized, and even politicized, spatial configuration. As Obregón describes the landscape and projects future settlements onto it, he simultaneously compiles and relates Spanish stories of expansion and "conquest" (with mixed results) to date, historicizing it in ways that had theretofore been lacking in the Spanish narrative.

Conclusions

History for Obregón is rooted in truth and experience. The explorer-turned-historian's text reveals his view of himself as a part of the larger empire as he filters the banda del norte for his readers through the lens of the Spanish history it holds and the Spanish future he projects onto it. Like the *bricoleur*, or "abeja" to use his own terminology, Obregón draws stories from the landscape and compiles a patchwork history that appears to perform a larger cultural function beyond his own motivations in compiling it. That is, by (re)telling stories about Spanish and criollo protagonists in the region, including himself, Obregón projects a sense of Spanish history onto the terrain of the northern borderlands of New Spain, allowing the frontier landscape to form a part of European imagined experience, fusing setting and situation, presenting a construction of what was, is, and should be—and presenting it as truth.

Obregón was never awarded the commission that he sought; that honor went to Juan de Oñate, also a criollo who had been born in Zacatecas. Do we then read Obregón's discourse as a "failed" text because it did not succeed in advancing its author's own interests? Or do we dismiss the text as badly written and confused? Would the Consejo de Indias have been as unimpressed in 1584 as Sauer was in 1932 with Obregón's chronicling abilities and medieval rhetoric? Probably not, as the profusion of genres was common in the second half of the sixteenth century and the criterion of exactitude and readability had yet to be "imposed on the observation of spaces" (Zumthor and Peebles 1994, 816). Additionally, the cosmography he was informing would have served important legal and administrative issues in the Consejo de Indias, and current information was highly valued (Portuondo 2009). In this way, far from confused, Obregón would have viewed his text as his readers' very remedy for confusion. As the following chapter demonstrates, Obregón is insistent that an integral aspect of providing a comprehensive history includes clearing up the confusion caused by conflicting reports generated from multiple expeditions. Moreover, in addition to providing a comprehensive history of northward expansion, his second aim in writing *Historia* is to provide those who explore the region in the future with pragmatic wayfinding information.

CHAPTER TWO

"Lo que hay en esta tierra"

*In Greek, narration is called "digesis": it establishes an itinerary
(it "guides") and it passes through (it "transgresses").*
—MICHEL DE CERTEAU, 1984

For New Spain to be mapped, it needed to be imagined.
—BARBARA MUNDY, 1996

In addition to serving as a comprehensive history that synthesizes past experience and events in the northern borderlands, Obregón's text is equal
part narrative report that attempts to provide an account of what is there
and how the landscape can best be exploited to serve the Spanish Empire.
While Obregón addresses his text in his first letter to the oidores of the
Consejo de Indias and in the second letter to King Phillip II, the itinerary
function of the text would have serviceable purposes for the viceroy in
Mexico City as well as those soldiers and prospectors living in New Spain
who aspired to explore the north. Notwithstanding the consideration taken
to show readers in Spain what the narrator believes that audience may
want to see, the relación also attempts to relate what is actually seen and
perceived by the narrator to replicate a landscape alien to them. Ultimately,
some type of "on the ground," itinerary-driven information needed to be
compiled if unknown lands were to be settled. As Ahern has argued, the
relaciones became paradigms for the itineraries or guides to be followed by
future expeditions. "On the northern frontier in New Spain, the relación or
written report preceded the map, assuming a normative role in establishing
a spatial order for resolving the articulation of the territory traveled, its

alterity, and above all, its future place in universal cosmography" (Ahern 2002, 37). As Obregón penned his depictions of the landscape after his exploration with Francisco Ibarra, he no doubt had his potential readership, the Consejo de Indias, in mind. A primary purpose of his text emerges: describing the landscape to help his readers to know, locate, and better utilize the "failed" landscape that had thwarted Coronado's exploration.

On the other side of the Atlantic, cosmographers in Spain depended on the copious flow of accounts from the New World for the information they provided about indigenous peoples, resources, important events, and topography. A practice dating back to Rome's Pliny the Elder (AD 23–79), the organization of knowledge under imperial authority had been a means for cataloging and assimilating the unfamiliar "so as to allow the reader's eye to sweep over the *orbis terrarium* as a thing to be possessed" (Murphy 2004, 131).[1] In this way, descriptive mapping was paramount in the production of spatial knowledge on both sides of the Atlantic. So, while it is true that by the 1580s the mathematized geographical map was a large part of the scientific discourse, Obregón's potential readership would have valued and indeed expected such landscape description that he was providing. Exactly what regions held potential for settlement and which inhabitants were hostile to "pacification" was of course included, but also workaday information like where water could be found, where food was readily available or scarce, and where horses could and could not pass. Eyewitness "mapping out" was one of the principal functions of the relación, and every entrada since 1519 had provided this type of information. Inevitably, conflicting accounts emerged in terms of the location of things, but also more subjective debates of landscape "quality" and potential surfaced. The result in Obregón's *Historia* is an intertextuality that allows us to consider occidental ideas of mapping and landscape perception at a time when the very methods of cataloguing such spatial knowledge were experiencing a shifting paradigm.

A Changing Cosmography

Portuondo (2009) demonstrates how, by the end of the sixteenth century, major changes had occurred in the science of cosmography in Spain because of two factors: (1) an imperial mandate that necessitated utilitarianism over curiosity and natural philosophy and (2) a constant flow of new discoveries that exposed the deficiencies of the discipline of cosmography. A century prior, she explains, cosmographers whose worldview was rooted in Aristotelian philosophy had attempted to explain the knowable universe by locating it within a mathematical grid in the tradition of Euclid and Ptolemy while also placing it within a temporal context that accounted for important events and description in the tradition of Pliny the Elder. Cosmographical knowledge was presented both descriptively and mathematically and included texts as well as maps. However, with the discovery of the New World, and under the burgeoning bureaucracy of Phillip II's imperial mandates, it became increasingly difficult to create cosmographies akin to those from the High Middle Ages, when the representation of the knowable universe was not meant to be realistic, but rather intended to "confirm" worldview, to borrow a term from Zumthor (1986). With the dawning of a new world in the sixteenth century, interpretive cartography began to give way as maps "broke with medieval *mappemondes* existing prior to the great voyages of discovery" and geography now "wanted to instantaneously capture a fantasized space that was to be transformed into a place" (Westphal 2013, 146). The Consejo de Indias, charged with collecting and vetting the countless texts generated from the Americas to figure out how to best establish and administer domain there, had very specific informational needs.[2] The project of confirmation was being abandoned for a project of knowledge creation not only by covering, exploring, and measuring alien space to "fill it" but also by knowing it and subsuming it in its own image. How would Obregón's text have compared to other projects of knowledge creation and filling in the "empty" space?

Explicitly charged with compiling a general history of the Indies (both moral and natural) and comparing previously recorded histories, the first cosmographer of the Consejo de Indias, Juan López de Velasco, served the newly created post for more than twenty years (1570–91). During his tenure, he "set in motion the most ambitious and successful program ever attempted during the early modern era for collecting geographical, ethnographical, and historical information about the New World" (Portuondo 2009, 19). Of course, a large portion of this information would come in the form of a relación or history such as that provided by Obregón, but some was generated from the answers to a survey, the *Relación Geográfica*, sent to officials in New Spain to gather longitudinal information (Portuondo 2009; Mundy 1996). (See figure 7.) Mundy (1996) argues that there would have been a disconnect between officials in New Spain and cosmographers in Europe regarding mapping by citing the example of the *Relación Geográfica*, a survey consisting of fifty questions that would have reached New Spain in the 1570s and again in the 1580s, about the time that Obregón was writing his *Historia* and coincidentally when the expansion of the

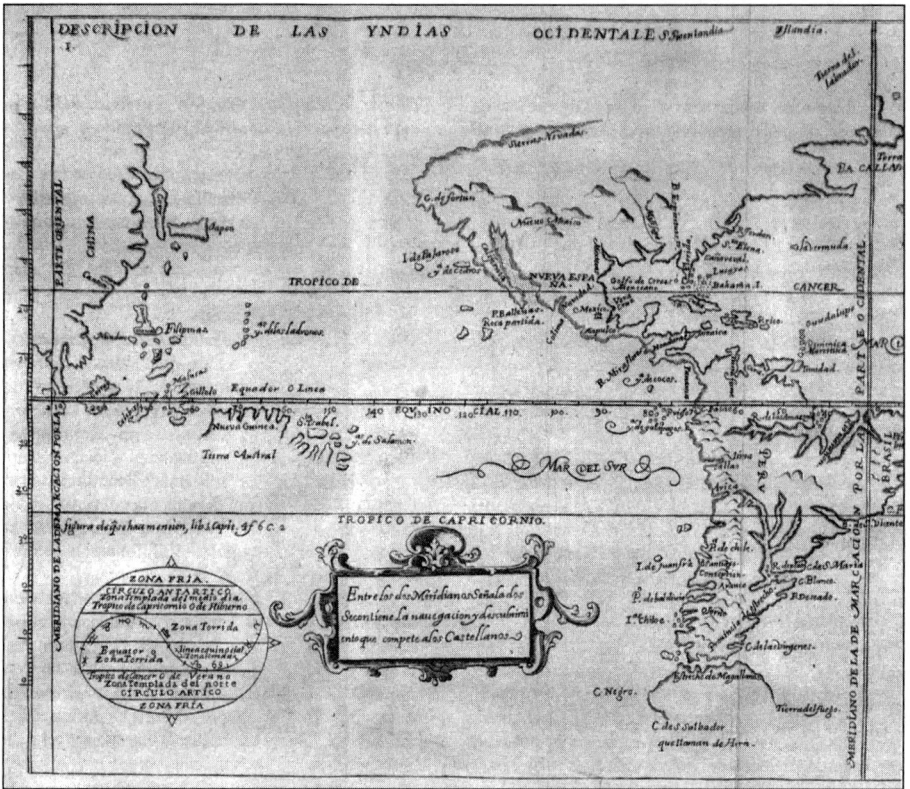

Figure 7. López de Velasco's 1570 map of the Indies: Originally published in Antonio de Herrera y Tordesillas' *Descripción de las Indias Occidentales* (1601)

northern frontier was a point of imperial focus. The *Relación Geográfica* requested both textual information, in the form of answers to the questionnaire, and spatial information, in the form of maps from officials in New Spain. Mundy contends that López de Velasco's survey failed to produce the desired results, specifically gathering information that would aid in measuring longitude to better "view" the New World. Portuondo argues against this interpretation because there is no textual evidence of what the royal cosmographer thought about the responses, nor of his disappointment in the Amerindian maps, hence such interpretations regarding usefulness or failure are speculative (2009, 203–4). However debatable the reception of the survey responses may be, what is germane to the present study is what Mundy's analysis demonstrates about pervading attitudes and ideas toward mapping in New Spain and how they are echoed in Obregón's discourse.

Obregón speculates about the greater issues of cosmography in *Historia*, in particular the possibility of a land connection to *La gran China* and the existence of El Estrecho de los Bacalaos (a much hoped-for entrance to the ocean to the West) just beyond Quivira connecting New Spain to Europe.[3] In chapter 36 of book 1, Obregón contends with the misinformation perpetuated by chroniclers who lacked first-hand experience. How could historians and ancient chroniclers write about longitude and leagues, let alone know the extent of these *tierras firmes*? In the first place, he notes, they have been proven wrong regarding the extent of contiguous lands in the New World, and in the second place, the lands from Quivira onward and New Mexico and beyond have yet to be traversed. Additionally, they have included the New World as part of the uninhabitable *zona tórrida* (the torrid zone, a term used since the time of Aristotle to refer to lands closest to the equator). In fact, he argues, most of the lands are inhabitable and produce many of the same crops grown in Castile. Moreover, he reasons, these lands may reach as far as China and be filled with new discoveries of wealth, peoples, and civilizations. These contemplations may reflect Obregón's desire to emphasize the value of experience and to promote the possibilities for future discovery, but they also demonstrate his awareness of the larger imperial mapping project. His recognition of cosmographic mapping more than likely reflects the level of knowledge of the typical explorer of his time, who would have been familiar with and even tried to imitate the cosmographies of the day. At the same time, his text reflects a navigation of the landscape that is arguably closer to the ground and emulates itinerary and travel narrative as much as cosmography.

A mode of discourse dating from late antiquity, the narration of the itinerary brings the reader down to the ground to travel alongside the narrator in a manner akin to, as Ahern (2003) and Turchi (2004) have proposed, the American Automobile Association's "Triptik" maps of today. "The itinerary addresses a reader who is embodied, earthbound, and dynamic" (Padrón 2004, 61).[4] Much like today's GPS devices mounted on windshields and streaming through smart phones, the itinerary guides the reader from "here" to "there," traveling through space and time with the reader, pointing moment to moment and announcing how many miles are left to travel. Explorers writing from the New World would have often likewise been covering space to arrive to a (perceived) place wherein "space" is a distance to cover—a void to be filled—that "can only be made to exist by peppering it with sites" (Zumthor 1986, 51). Put another way, "Medieval space takes us simultaneously to a 'hole-y' vision of space and temporality, to a 'space-time.' There is a tight association between the philological itinerary and the process of 'reading' of 'space'" (Westphal 2013, 39). In this way, the narrative report serves to plot out the itinerary taken by participants to relate the length of time and number of leagues traveled between pueblos, stops along the way, orientation, and wayfinding, all of which are observations grounded in experience. In the mid-sixteenth century, these reports read like travel narratives "striving toward a rhetoric fit to account for displacements of the body and the particular emotions those displacements arouse" sharing in common the characteristics as cited by Zumthor and Peebles (1994, 812): a focus on the privilege of eyewitness, the description of the departure, the duration of travel from place to place, the encounters in unknown country, and the binary of welcome or rejection by native inhabitants.

While Obregón specifically addresses his text to the royal authorities in Spain who read from a different vantage point (physically, but not necessarily philosophically), he nonetheless emphatically proposes to provide on-the-ground itinerary information, privileging what Olwig (2002, 26) has called the "bottom-up nature of the itinerary" as opposed to the "top-down nature of the map." It is by way of this conception of the itinerary that Obregón directs his reader through the landscape to bring his own mapping project to fruition, a mapping project that he expressly describes as relating and verifying information from multiple sources about lands and provinces and the distance between settlements, and, in his words, the "where, how and what" for this readers (Obregón 60). In doing so, Obregón depicts the landscape in terms of distance and population centers, thereby creating a textualscape that attempts to embody that particular way of thinking it. At the same time he refers to other textualscapes that rely on the same type of distance reckoning and landscape description to support his own claims and reconcile conflicting reports. He will set the record straight to give a clear picture of what "is" in dialogue with texts that spoke the same language of the itinerary.

Conflicting Reports

As is common in relaciones from this period, Obregón's distance measurements are almost invariably communicated in terms of leagues, days of travel, or a harquebus shot. Means of orienting direction in the text are grounded in experience: by the position of the sun or relationships to prominent landscape features or characteristics (Mundy 1996, 57–58). Phrases that exemplify orientation grounded in experience abound in the

Historia, such as "a la banda del nacimiento del sol [at the edge of the sunrise]" (187), "hacia el poniente [toward the sunset]," "hacia Irlanda [toward Ireland]" (192), and "doscientas leguas a la mano izquierda [two hundred leagues to the left hand]" (196). This intimates an attitude toward space wherein stories of on-the-ground-experience, passability, and wayfinding in the vein of dead reckoning hold a privileged place. Of course, explorers would have been keen to find their way so as to gain wealth, the principle means of which was the exploitation of native labor for work on encomiendas. Consequently, directional narratives to large indigenous settlements became so important in the sixteenth century that "territorial records were often little more than lists of population centers" (Mundy 1996, 57). The primacy of distribution of land and native labor are reflected in Obregón's descriptions of population centers and the routes taken to reach them. It is by utilizing mathematical and population mapping in concert with Spanish toponyms that Obregón attempts to clear up the emerging confusion stemming from conflicting reports.

By the time Obregón sent his *Historia* to the Consejo de Indias in 1584, various expeditions had already begun pushing the frontier of New Spain northward, at times retracing the steps of their predecessors; prior to Ibarra's expedition, the southern part of the modern state of Sonora had already been traversed by Diego de Guzmán, Álvarez Núñez Cabeza de Vaca, Fray Marcos de Niza, and Coronado (3). (See figure 8.) Multiple expeditions to the tierras incógnitas north of New Spain produced manifold itinerary information, impelling Obregón to undergo the daunting task of clarifying the confusion stemming from conflicting reports containing itinerary information such as multiple toponyms, the distance and length of time between pueblos, and the presence and size of pueblos found in other accounts. For Obregón to report on the landscape he would have to contend with the clarification of contradictions and conflicting accounts found in various narrative reports. These passages draw from multiple sources (some copied verbatim) but principally rely on Cabeza de Vaca's *Relación* ([1542, 1555] 1999), documents and interviews with members of the Coronado Expedition, Obregón's own experience with Ibarra, and documents from the expeditions of Chamuscado and Espejo. Armed with these documents and testimonies, Obregón grappled discursively with textual and oral verification of finding one's way through the northern landscape.

Perhaps the greatest confusion for today's reader of Obregón's text (and ironically what he hoped to remedy for Spanish officials trying to map the north) stems from the multiple toponyms that refer to the same locations. Seed (1993) explains that the cultural practice of renaming conquered

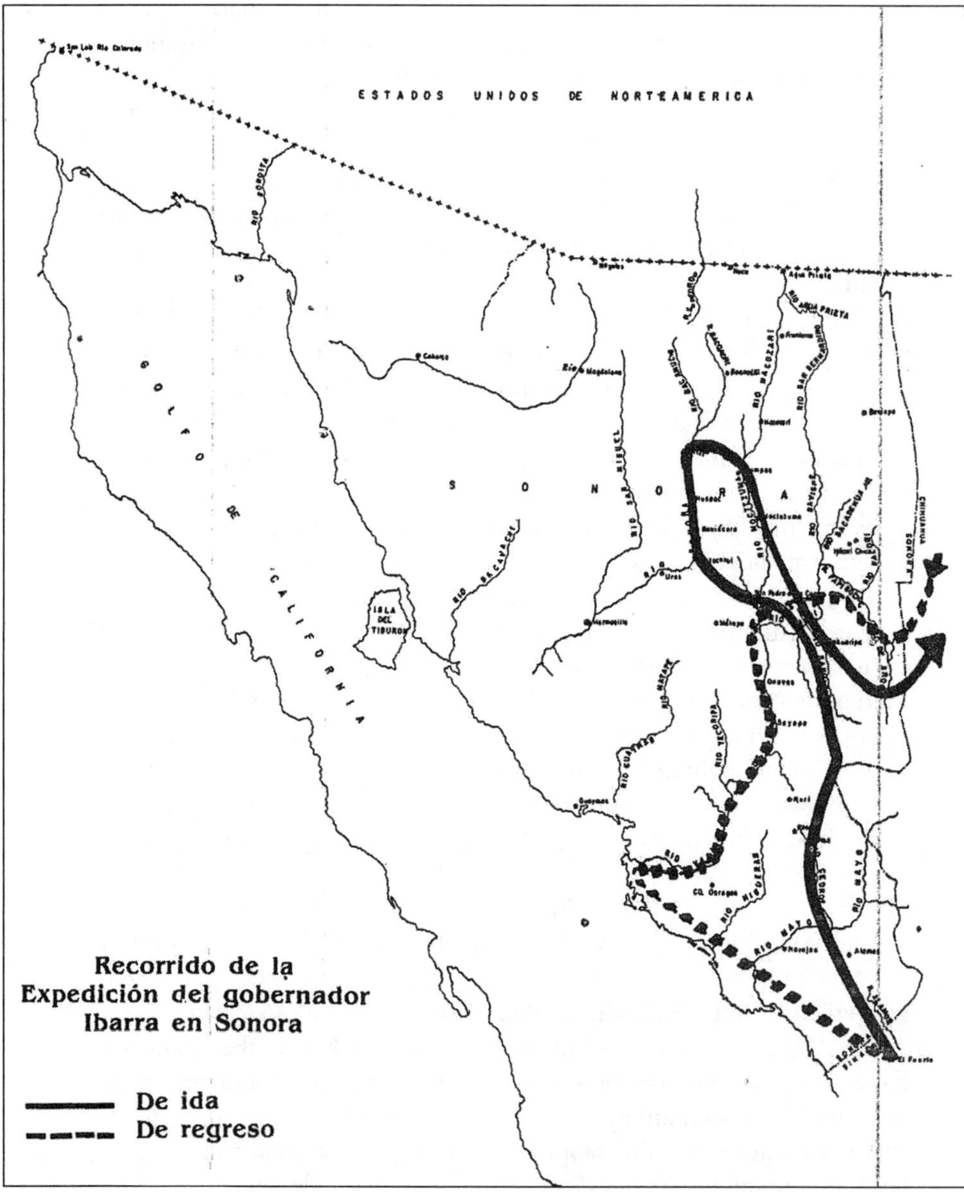

Figure 8. Ibarra's route according to Armando Hopkins Durazo (1988)

territories, inherited from the Roman tradition, was transported to America intact beginning with Columbus and continuing throughout the period of European expansion. Of course, this Europeanized the landscape for occidental minds but disregarded the indigenous landscape. Spurr (1993, 32) points out that "by naming things, we take possession of them," and naming was a privileged rite of sorts enjoyed by Spanish explorers as they pushed the frontier northward, naming and renaming pueblos, rivers, mountains, valleys, and deserts as they went. The "magical powers proper names enjoy," as de Certeau calls it, and their ceremonial cachet is evinced in the Las Ordenanzas of 1573, in which imperial authority makes clear the importance of naming in the act of taking possession, stating that once explorers and officials arrive in "new" lands they must name the region and all of its features, including prominent population centers (such as pueblos and cities) and topography (such as mountains and rivers).[5] "Naming is at the heart of mapping," Mundy (1996, 138) observes, and expedition participants bequeathed places with the names of their choosing, often unwittingly renaming a place that had already entered the Spanish record or memory by another name from a previous expedition.

In addition to naming's violent function of seizing landscape for one's own, the practice also would have provided a means of transporting a familiarity both in terms of culture and orientation. Places were often named for a saint because it was founded on that saint's feast day, as Ibarra does in the case of San Sebastián in Chiametla, to cite one of many examples (129). This practice, based on the concept that settlements needed a saint to defend and protect them, also "Christianized" the landscape. "The use of ritual speech to name territory is analogous to the process of baptism practiced upon the peoples of the New World" (Seed 1993, 122). In other cases, a geographical feature of the area inspired the toponym, as in the case from the Chamuscado party described by Obregón in which the men find a large quantity of ram horns: "Hallaron cantidad de cuernos que al parecer eran de carneros grandes y de diferente modo y naturaleza que los de cristianos . . . por esta causa nombraron los descubridores a este valle el de los Carneros [They found a (large) quantity of horns that appeared to be from large rams of a different manner and nature than those (familiar to) Christians . . . and because of this the discoverers named this valley 'Valley of the Rams'" (235). Similar to the function of stories as foundation narrations related in chapter 1, (re)naming pueblos and regions, in addition to establishing possession, would have provided Spanish explorers and the readers of *Historia* with a sense of orientation and thickness, giving direction and meaning to the vast and unfamiliar lands lying to the north of Nueva Vizcaya. After all, these lands had been depicted as "empty," perceived by Europeans on both sides of the Atlantic as unfamiliar, unknown space, as Agnese Battista's World Map (c. 1544) evinces (see figure 9). As geographer David Lowenthal (1975, 9) explains, naming over the landscape with portable symbols from the past serves a fundamentally human need for some semblance of continuity rooted in history: "Those who gave classical eponyms and architecture to New World locations sought identification with antiquity as much as continuity." This is the case even more so when confronted with terrain that seems "empty" and alien to the narrator or where topographical difference was not recognized by Spanish explorers, as in the case of the *Llanos de las Vacas*:

> Y así prosiguió [Coronado] su viaje seis jornadas, al cabo de las cuales toparon los llanos de las Vacas, que afirman son de más de cuatrocientas leguas, de tan extraña suerte y manera que no se ven ni divisan sierras, lomas ni cerro de ninguna manera, ni señales para atinar, conocer la tierra, ni de donde se apartan ni salen de una jornada a otra, ni de un lugar a otro; *y es en estos llanos muy necesario la aguja del marear como si fuese por la mar*. Y el riesgo que hay de andar sin guía y solos se ha experimentado con riesgo de que aconteció salir a cazar algunos soldados y no acertaron a volver, ni tuvieron señales por dónde ni cómo poder atinar a su salida al campo de donde salieron a tierras pobladas, de manera que nunca más se supo de ellos ni adónde salieron ni y si los mataron.

> [And thusly (Coronado) continued his journey for six days, at the end of which they came upon the *Plains of Cattle*, which they affirm are more than four hundred leagues (and) of such a strange nature that no mountains, elevations nor hills may be seen or devised in any way, nor signs for finding or recognizing the land, nor from where to exit or leave from one day's march to the next, nor from one place to another; *and in these plains a compass is as necessary as if one were at sea*. And the risk of traveling alone without a guide has been proven, as it happened that some soldiers who left to hunt could not ascertain how to return, and they did not have landmarks for where or how to find egress to the lands from whence they had left. They never learned of them, where they went, or if they were killed.] (55–56, my emphasis)

While still a source of confusion and fear, the extensive plains named by the Spaniards for the "cows of small stature" that inhabited them at least are identifiable—they are knowable. That is, where there is the absence

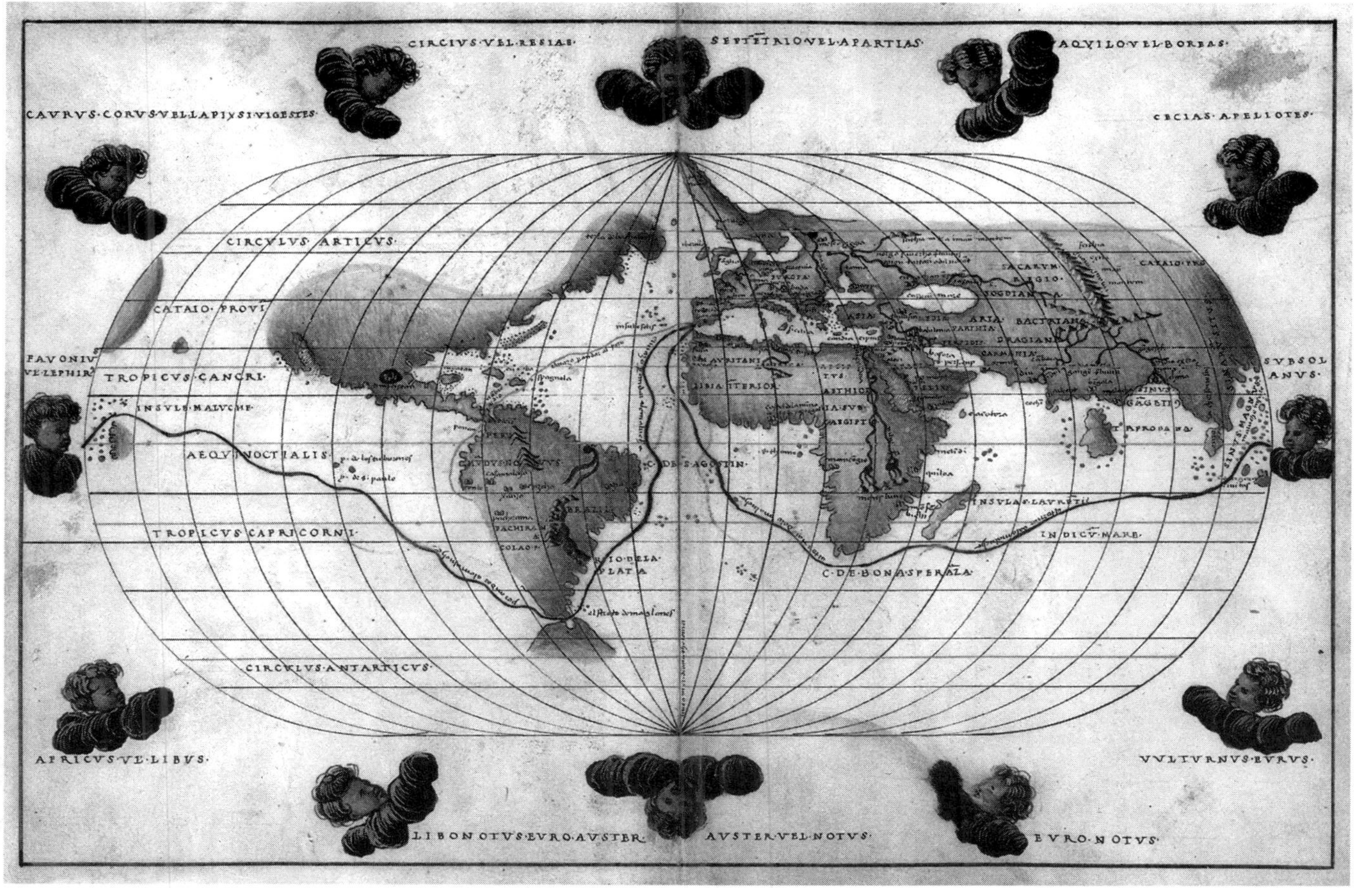

Figure 9. World Map c. 1544 by Agnese Battista In *Portolan atlas of nine charts and a world map.* Library of Congress Geography and Map Division

(in the narrator's viewpoint and orientation) of a positional "here," such as mountains, a hill, or a river, one is imposed, "hypothesized, rhetorically asserted by way of names . . . [that] signified differences that made a difference" (Hirsch 1995, 3). An imperative function of Obregón's discursive project is to make sense of and give meaning to these plains that seem as vast as the sea. One means of accomplishing this is to establish fixed proper names that serve as orienting signposts, allowing for directional viewpoint, movement, and passage.

Naming, at once a means of taking possession, Christianizing the landscape, and making sense of a seemingly vast and unfathomable territory, served explorers on the ground like Ibarra and Obregón by giving them some sense of direction and stability in a world not their own. Rojo (2014) rightly points out that even "Nuevo México," a toponym completely devoid of European projection, is based on something "known" to the explorers, something "civilized," and even something desirable.[6] Yet this enthusiasm for naming over the course of multiple expeditions also produced multiple toponyms, a phenomenon that only caused problems for both explorers and officials in terms of geographical clarity and land rights. Obregón's remedy is to sort out multiple toponyms to explain the locations of pueblos in relation to one another, their number, the distances between them, and even their populations, allowing him to construct direct itineraries and travel paths for future expeditions. To set the record straight, Obregón refers to the toponyms imposed by various parties as he relates particular events, thereby signaling double nomenclatures. For example, as he retells Coronado's route from Tibuex to Quivira by way of Cíbola, he explains that the party discovered the river and town of Tucyan, which Antonio de Espejo named Mohoce (58). By comparing accounts, he reasons that these places are one in the same, thereby generating geographic knowledge of the areas while simultaneously establishing the order of events of "discovery" for future claims. This is significant because the clarification of who had discovered what lands first would have been vital in securing a commission from the Crown to settle a territory or to be named *gobernador* with the legal permission to distribute lands and indigenous laborers or conduct an expedition for settlement or exploration. Las Ordenanzas are clear on this point: "Ningun descubridor ni poblador pueda entrar a descubrir ni poblar en los términos que a otros estuvieren encargados o ouieren descubierto [No discoverer nor settler may enter to discover nor settle lands that have been charged to others or have been (previously) discovered]" (*Transcripción de las Ordenanzas* 1973, 30). The significance of first discovery in terms of booty and rewards cannot be overstated as explorers like Ibarra were trying to earn land, titles, and wealth at their own expense without Crown funding. Who had traversed the lands prior mattered a great deal, and establishing the order of "discovery" meant stating claims, witness accounts, and appeals to authority. This is probably why Obregón includes a clarification regarding Acuco (Acoma), a pueblo that was visited by Spanish-led excursions on more than one occasion. Obregón explains that the pueblo was first "seen and discovered" by Coronado, then Francisco Sánchez Chamuscado, and finally Antonio de Espejo:

[Acuco] ha sido visto y hallado por Francisco Vázquez de Coronado primeramente y los segundos que le visitaron fueron los de Francisco Sánchez Chamuscado y los terceros fueron los de Antonio de Espejo . . . y según lo que he experimentado, sabido y examinado a los descubridores, parece que la poblazón que nombran los descubridores de Francisco Sánchez Chamuscado son éstas del río de Tibuex, por razón de que los de Coronado afirman que Acuco, pueblo fuerte, está quince leguas del río de Tibuex, que los de Francisco Sánchez Chamuscado nombraron Guadalquivir y provincia de San Felipe. Los compañeros de Antonio de Espejo afirman está este río de Tibuex quince leguas de Acuco, y Cíbola cincuenta leguas, de manera que es averiguado ser las poblazones que descubrieron antiguamente Francisco Vázquez de Coronado.

[(Acuco) was seen and discovered by Francisco Vázquez de Coronado first and the second ones who saw it were (those led by) Francisco Sánchez Chamuscado and the third ones were (those led by) Antonio de Espejo. . . . According to what I have experienced, learned and examined from the discoverers, it appears that the (large) settlement that the Chamuscado group are naming, are those of the Tibuex River by reason that the Coronado party affirm that Acuco, a fort town, is fifteen leagues from the Tibuex River, which those from the Francisco Sánchez Chamuscado party named Guadalquivir and province of San Felipe. The companions of Antonio de Espejo affirm that this Tibuex River is fifteen leagues from Acuco, and fifty leagues from Cíbola, by which manner it is figured to be the settlements that Francisco Vázquez de Coronado discovered previously.] (54–55)[7]

Acknowledging that Chamuscado's party called this river Guadalquivir (after the great river that flows past Sevilla), Obregón employs the testimony of participants from the Coronado and Espejo expeditions to demonstrate that the toponyms of Guadalquivir and the Río Tibuex (the Rio Grande) refer to the same body of water. He concludes that, as the river of Guadalquivir is reported to be fifteen leagues from Acuco (Acoma) and fifty leagues from Cíbola, it stands to reason that the rivers are one and the same, and thus the *poblazones* (large settlements) to which Chamuscado refers must be those that Coronado had already discovered. This again serves the double function of creating geographical knowledge (that there is one, not multiple, pueblos, and its distance from the river and from Cíbola) and establishing who arrived first. In short, Obregón makes it clear to the reader, albeit erroneously, that Chamuscado had discovered nothing new.[8]

In a similar instance, Obregón employs the testimony related to him by a descendent of Bernardino de Luna, a participant from the Espejo expedition, as well as testimony from surviving Coronado expedition members and accounts from the Chamuscado party, to resolve the seemingly conflicting reports emerging from these expeditions (268).[9] By comparing the names of the pueblos (toponyms) that Coronado discovered and counting leagues (mathematical mapping) in combination with counting people and pueblos (population mapping), Obregón deduces that both Espejo and Chamuscado were retracing old discoveries, thereby clarifying the number of pueblos that exist in the same area and the size of their populations. In this way, although the Ibarra Expedition never traveled as far north as Cíbola and Obregón has no personal experience there, he identifies its location textually, supporting his finding with declarations and testimony of participants from various expeditions.

Likewise, population information buttresses mathematical mapping and toponyms to dispel or confirm rumors of purported areas of "significance" in terms of settlement and resources, such as the rumor of "El Turco." A guide from the Coronado Expedition who had claimed that pueblos of clothed people who cultivated maize existed about ten days' travel from Quivira to the west, "The Turk" was presumed to be lying in order to send Coronado on a wild-goose chase, and his claims had been dismissed. Yet after studying and examining information about later expeditions that report similar circumstances, Obregón concludes that the existence of such pueblos is quite possible:

> Asimismo tuvo el general Francisco Vázquez de Coronado algunas noticias de Quivira que fue la última tierra que anduvo en su viaje, aunque no se conformaron las guías que fueron el Hisopete y el Turco y en las noticias estuvieron varios y diferentes; y en particular *el Turco, por haber mentido en las noticias*, mandó darle garrote el general Francisco Vásquez Coronado. Dieron noticia que diez jornadas de Quivira hacia el poniente

había un gran río poblado de muchas gentes vestidas y que cogen mucho maíz y andan y se sirven de muchas canoas; *túvose por mentira, por la experiencia que se hizo del Turco y así esto está dudoso aunque se tiene por cosa cierta*, porque después acá han dado esta noticia a los descubridores que han estado en estas tierras y en particular Antonio de Espejo.

[Francisco Vázquez de Coronado also received some accounts from Quivira, which was the last land he visited on his journey, although the guides, Hisopete and the Turk, did not correspond and the accounts were varied and different; and in particular the general Francisco Vázquez de Coronado ordered that *the Turk be garroted for having lied.* They (the guides) gave accounts that ten days' march from Quivira toward the sunset there was a great river settled by many clothed people who cultivate much maize and (who) travel by canoes; *this was taken for a lie, due to the (prior) experience (Coronado) had with the Turk . . .* , however it (may be) taken to be true, because later discoverers that have been in those lands gave the (same) accounts, in particular Antonio de Espejo.] (189, my emphasis)

All of these examples demonstrate how multiple expeditions to the north had attempted to provide itinerary information in the form of proper names and directional location of "discoveries" by plotting them onto a discursive map, fulfilling a very similar function of the map. As Mignolo (1992, 60) suggests, in the context of "discovery," *la carta* (in the sense of written information that *describes* the position of these new lands) and *la carta* (in the sense of the map, graphic information that *designs* the position of them) forges a relationship between two sign systems that articulate the same conceptual modification. At the same time, as evidenced in the communication of rights of discovery, the discursive itinerary serves other practical purposes as well, most notably conveying valuable information regarding the landscape's passability or impassability, food and water sources, number of inhabitants and their customs, and of course, potential wealth for future exploitation.

Topophilia and Topophobia

Obregón is effusive in his contention that experience is the best teacher, arguing that future explorers will only avoid the mistakes of the past if they embark "advertidos e informados . . . de los daños que solían suceder a los primeros [advised and informed . . . of the harm that often befell the first (explorers)" (43). As Obregón states in the preface, the purpose of his textual rendering is to provide information about the lands that have been seen and discovered, accounting those that are "good" and "bad" for the officials that henceforth set out to conquer and populate tierras incógnitas. Obregón interjects his history with itinerary-driven information about the location of mines, population centers, supplies, and routes passable on horse. He also highlights the difficulties of passage through rough lands, the hardships endured in harsh climates, and the dangers faced in hostile encounters.

As elucidated in chapter 1, Obregón's narrative project attempted to provide a historical framework within which to situate the expedition led by Ibarra and its role in the expansion of the Spanish Empire. The first five sections of book 1 of *Historia* provide a summary of the historical context and events leading up to the departure of the Ibarra Expedition, including some of the more political aspects of attaining commissions to lead explorations. Specifically, Obregón relates how, before departing for a new post in the viceroyalty of Peru, the first viceroy of New Spain, Antonio de Mendoza, had advised his replacement, Luis de Velasco, regarding the importance of discovering the roots of the powerful Aztec empire (70). Of course, it had been during Mendoza's tenure as viceroy that Hernán Cortés, having learned from Mexica codices in Tenochtitlán that the Aztec empire's founders had migrated from the north, petitioned without success to lead an exploration there.[10] Ultimately, that expedition would be sanctioned and led by Coronado, and even after Coronado returned in 1542 without having found the roots of the Mexica or another great empire, the possibilities still beckoned. On the discovery of massive lodes of silver in Zacatecas in 1546, the distant north became a priority for the viceroy, and when Luis de Velasco took over in 1550 his administration implemented a strategy of establishing a system of defensive towns and presidios to provide safe stopping points for caravans, merchants, and travelers going to and from the mines (Powell 1944, 181). Around that time, the newly appointed viceroy's daughter married Diego de Ibarra (one of the impresarios who had become enriched by the silver mines of Zacatecas). Ibarra promptly informed his father-in-law that his haciendas were on the route to the banda del norte and that he was entertaining plans of putting together an expedition to Copala to the north.[11] Velasco, having secured royal authorization for an expedition, urged his son-in-law to send Ibarra's nephew, Francisco de Ibarra, to secure mining areas from rebelling indigenous groups and establish permanent settlements for food and supplies and for further exploration. Although Diego de Ibarra was reluctant to send his nephew, apparently concerned about his youth and lack of experience, he relented, and Francisco de Ibarra set out on January 24, 1563, after a stay of forty days in San Martín to secure the settlements of Nombre de Dios and Durango.[12] Soon after the establishment of these strongholds, Ibarra and his men were intrigued by rumors of silver and gold deposits in Topia, and Obregón's depictions of "lo que hay en esta tierra" begin in earnest when he recounts the scouting expedition Ibarra sends to Topia and the subsequent departure of Ibarra himself.

In *Topophilia: A Study of Environmental Perception, Attitudes and Values* (1974), geographer Yi-Fu Tuan defines topophilia as "human love of place" (92). Coupling sentiment with place, two important implications emerge: (1) human beings respond to their physical setting—or better said, their perception of it—and (2) they place value on it. Tuan writes that "the word 'topophilia' is a neologism, useful in that it can be defined broadly to include all of the human being's affective ties with the material environment. These differ greatly in intensity, subtlety, and mode of expression" (93). Tuan further reasons that the human individual, at once a biological organism, a social being, and a unique individual, experiences topophilia on all three of these levels, and this is reflected in perception, attitude, and value, respectively (245). Moreover, Lawson-Peebles argues that these cognitive landscapes would have been informed, or even formed, before actually experiencing landscape. In this view, there is no such thing as "the unknown" because "those who are about to enter an undiscovered area project upon it a collection of images drawn from their personal experience, from the culture of which they are a part, from their reasons for travelling, and from their hopes and fears regarding their destination. On occasion these projections are so strong that they shape the terrain they encounter" (Lawson-Peebles 1988, 9). Environmental geographer Kurt Abrahamsson similarly argues that the landscape perceived—and we may include projected—is laden with value judgments. He calls this creative process of perception "landscaping": "Landscaping is a process that creates meaning in the landscapes and helps us to fill our cognitive landscapes with details, with areas we like, topophilia, and some that we dislike, topophobia" (Abrahamsson 53). Obregón's own "landscaping" is revealed throughout the text as myriad instances of his own topophilia and topophobia emerge, lending insight into the narrator's worldview (attitude) and his individual information project (value).

Moments of topophilia emerge frequently in Obregón's text; in a sense it is a topophilic cognitive projection that spurs the Ibarra expedition to its first destination. Ibarra and the soldiers hear of a place called Topia from the indigenous inhabitants of Nueva Vizcaya, and more specifically, of purported riches that can be found there: "[Topía] del cual habían traído y manifestaron una rodela de pluma de muchas colores y gala y un plumaje de plata y ropa de algodón tejida de hilo torcido [(Topia) from which had been brought and shown a feathered shield of many colors and regalia, a crest of silver, and cotton clothing woven of twisted thread.]"[13] However, before the reader may "arrive" at the topophilic place of Topia, Obregón first leads him or her through the space that must be traversed to get there:

Haciendo cortas jornadas por no fatigar los soldados y caballos de silla y carga, pasando por sierras de gran altura, de grandes montañas, riscos y hondables barrancas y quebradas, y cargando y descargando los caballos de carga que muy a menudo caían por la mucha aspereza de las sierras. Lo cual hacían con mucho ánimo y contento aunque en tierras solitarias, pobres y desaprovechadas y adonde ni aun aves no habitan ni se divisaban volar en las alturas y regiones, hasta llegar a las sierras de las Cruces, sierra de mucha más aspereza y que parecía dar consejo que no pasasen de allí; la cual está cercada y murada de espantables riscos, peñas y terribles quebradas, de manera que para que pasasen los caballos fue necesario quitar algunas piedras.

[Taking short daily marches so as to not fatigue the soldiers and the pack and saddle horses, passing through ranges of great height, tall mountains, cliffs, and deep ravines and gorges, and loading and unloading the cargo from the horses, who quite often would fall due to the great roughness of the sierras. All of which they (the soldiers) did with great spirit and contentment although in solitary, poor and wasted lands where not even birds lived nor were espied flying in the elevations and environs, until arriving at the Sierra de las Cruces, (a) mountain chain of even more roughness which appeared to advise (them) that they not pass there (and) which is closed and walled off with frightening cliffs, crags and terrible gorges, so much so that in order for the horses to pass, it was necessary to remove a few rocks.] (82)

Here it is topophobia, a descriptor for the areas we do not like, which reveals itself in the extensive description of the rough journey over imposing mountains and deep crags. It is precisely the passage—or better stated, the (im)passability—the arduous task of the moving through, that is the focus of the description. The difficulty for the horses to pass is paramount because, as Obregón argues, "sin caballos no podemos ser señores de nuestros enemigos [without horses we cannot be lords of our enemies]" (215).[14] Not only is this land difficult to traverse by horse, it is simply land wasted, a rough and inhospitable landscape in which not even birds can be spotted. The group is walled in by crags and ravines. The adjectives "huge," "frightening," and "terrible" pepper the textualscape.

Indeed, Obregón's perception of the landscape is so negative that when the reconnaissance group reports having finally spotted houses and a fort, a report that should animate the group, Obregón describes the soldiers as incredulous, "por ser la tierra tan inhabitable y desusada de sendas y caminos [due to the land being so uninhabitable and desolate of paths and roadways]" (82). It is as if they wondered who could live here, and even cursed Ibarra and accused him of leading them to their doom. Adding to the topophobia was a huge storm, lasting two days and nights, and "tan terrible y espantosa peñolería que imposibilitaba al entendimiento poderla pasar [such terrible and frightful cliffs that made perception (so as to) be able to pass it impossible]" (83). Thirty-eight horses froze, among them one of Ibarra's who "amaneció yerto, helado, arrimado a un árbol [awoke rigid, frozen tied to a tree]" (83). Even after finally reaching the pueblo, the soldiers had trouble viewing it as a "place" but rather seemed to view it as a "nonplace" that emerged in the horrible space that they had traversed thus far:

Fue a ganar a Topía por sierras de mucha aspereza y montañas, muy dudosos de la certificación que habían dado los cinco descubridores, aunque personas de crédito. Y como empezaron a ver cuervos, estuvieron más certificados de su esperanza y llegada a Topía; al cual, habiendo pasado la barranca y una subida de una muy alta sierra, le divisaron y señorearon con la vista el valle y comarcas, todas semejantes a las pasadas, como de gente serrana, indómita y fuera de buena orden, vida y costumbres. Y aunque no parecían las casas, fue grande la alegría que recibieron el gobernador y su campo, entendiendo conseguían el efecto de sus esperanzas de riquezas y gente política para descansar de los trabajos que habían padecido en el viaje. (83–84)

[He left to win Topia by way of mountain chains of great, rough mountains, very doubtful of the assurance that the five discoverers had given, although credible individuals. Once they began to see crows, they were more assured in their hope of arriving to Topia. Having passed the ravine and climbing a very steep mountain, they espied the valley and its surroundings, all similar to those (just) traveled (which were) of indomitable mountain-dwelling people, contrary to good order, life, and customs.

And although the houses were not in view, the joy that the governor and his men received was great, understanding that they had realized the fruition of their hopes of riches and civilized people so as to rest from the trials that they had suffered in the journey.] (83–84)[15]

What is striking about this passage is that the transition from the perception of the land to the expectations held for the people who occupy it is seamless: the soldiers' doubt about the people stems from their perception of the land, land that in their view could only be inhabited by "cultureless" people. While the sighting of crows gives them some hope, they are still dubious because this land is as rough and mountainous as that just traveled. How could the fine artifacts they had been shown in Nueva Vizcaya have come from such people in such a nonplace? Moreover, Obregón claims that even the indigenous inhabitants wonder at the arrival of the Spanish through such rough lands: "Preguntaban los naturales si eran los cristianos hechiceros, porque entendían que habían bajado por los aires, imposibilitado la venida por tan espantosa serranía [The natives asked if the Christians were witch doctors, thinking they had come down from the air, (believing) the arrival by way of such frightening mountains to be impossible]" (87).

Reinforcing Lawson-Peebles' notion of landscape as perspectival, Obregón relates how the soldiers' perception is influenced again, and they are heartened because they spy crops of maize, beans, and squash, "lo cual les acrecentó el ánimo [which lifted their spirits]" (85).[16] They are even more encouraged upon seeing six indigenous women dressed in cotton clothes and houses with multiple rooms constructed of walls of stone:

Pasado [el río] fueron por labores de maíz, frijol y calabaza, lo cual les acrecentó el ánimo, contento y mayor ver seis indias vestidas de la cintura debajo de mantas de algodón . . . Fueron divisando las casas y un hermoso fuerte, y otra casa de tres cuartos y muralla de piedra . . . *todo lo cual con la primera vista les pareció poblazón de mucha importancia.* Movidos de la codicia, ansia y deseo de lo que habían significado vieron los autores de Topía, dando a entender habían hallado *otro México.*

[Past the river they (came across) cultivations of maize, beans, and squash which lifted their spirits, contentment, and even more so upon seeing six Indian women dressed from the waist down with cotton cloth . . . they espied the houses and a nice fort, and another house with three rooms and a stone rampart . . . *all of which upon first glance appeared to them to be a large settlement of great importance.* Moved by greed, impulse, and the desire for what the (scouting party) of Topia (had) thought it meant, they were given to understand that they had found *another Mexico.*] (84–85, my emphasis)

The above passage presents a paradigm, which continues throughout the text, in which depictions of population centers and their clothing, housing, and crops dominate the textualscape (a topic considered at length in the following chapter). However, Obregón explains that years before, during his five-year foray into the north (1530–35), Nuño de Guzmán had tried to settle Topia from Culiacán without success. Obregón expounds on the reason for this failure: "Por ser sus habitaciones en tierras tan fragosas y ocasionadas a la huída de los riscos y estar tan apartados de tierras llanas y de provecho, no pudieron ser sujetos [en la santa Fe católica]. [Because their dwellings are in such densely overgrown lands, and conducive to escape from the cliffs, and being so remote and far away from flat, useful lands, they could not be made subjects of the holy Catholic faith]" (87). This can be read as a suggestion that the very land itself actually impedes the evangelization of the indigenous people of Topia (a perspective that of course does not account for indigenous agency in accepting or rejecting Christianity, nor their own landscape perception) and furthermore, establishes a profound connection between land and people.

When the inhabitants of Topia inform the participants of the expedition that the surrounding villages are few and the lands are rough, impossible to pass on horse, Obregón describes the soldiers as "descontentos de no hallar tierras a su gusto [discontent to have not found lands to their liking]" (87). These explorers, imagining the wealth of the conquered city of Tenochtitlán, appear to still hold out hope of finding wildly wealthy cities in the New World. There is not even mention of a more realistic hope of a potential "Zacatecas." In Topia, they have not found "Otro México," and their disillusionment only increases when they move on and find themselves lost, retracing lands that others had already discovered (91). Ibarra even fears desertion: "Temió [Ibarra] la huida de algunos soldados arrepentidos, cansados y atemorizados de pasar otros trabajos semejantes a los que habían pasado [Ibarra feared some soldiers, full of regret, exhausted, and terrified of experiencing trials similar to those they had passed (already), would flee]" (92). For his part, Obregón laments the inability of the indigenous people of Topia and its environs to be Christianized: "por estar como están en tierras tan remotas, ásperas e imposibilitadas de poblarlas cristianos, ¿dónde se harán cristianos si no es poblando algunas minas buenas o poniendo Dios nuestro Señor el remedio necesario? [for being as they are in such remote, rough lands (that are) impossible for Christians to settle; How can they be made Christians if no good mines are settled there or with God our Lord's necessary assistance?]" (90). Christians cannot live here, and why would they live anywhere in which there is no wealth, material or spiritual, as their culture perceives it? In short, this place lacks one crucial element: mines. In Obregón's cultural worldview, the material is a prerequisite for the spiritual, a point that will be elaborated in chapter 4, but here I wish to note that this land is viewed by most of the soldiers as holding little value, and its inhabitants are subsumed in this perception.

A similar narration occurs at Ocoroni and Tegueco along the Cinaro River (present-day Tepantita de Ocoroni, Sinaloa). Obregón describes Tegueco as "el más poblado y mejor pueblo de la provincia de Cinaro [the largest and best settlement in the province of Cinaro]" and the people the "más afamado y temido de los naturales [the most famed and feared of the natives]" (100).[17] Ocoroni is likewise described in relatively positive terms:

> Están poblados y congregados en el río y sus riberas de una y otra parte, en cuyos rededores hay mucha montaña y cerrados arcabucos, de los cuales se aprovechan de fortificarse y defenderse de sus enemigos. Está de la Mar del Sur catorce leguas, todo él poblado de gente desnuda que sólo traen [*sic*] un pañete de algodón ceñido en la cintura. Ellas *visten* de la cintura arriba con unos faldellines de cueros de venados adobados. *Siembran y cogen* maíz, algodón, frijol y calabaza; tienen cerca la serranía de la cual tienen experiencia de *ricos metales* de plata y poblezuelos pequeños de *casas de terrado*.

> [They are settled and grouped together along both sides of the river and its tributaries; in the surroundings there are many mountains and brambly enclosures, of which they (the Indians) take advantage to protect and defend themselves from their enemies. It is fourteen leagues from the South Sea, all (of it) populated by naked people that only wear a piece of cotton tightened about the waist. The women *dress* from the waist with skirts of tanned deer skin. *They plant and harvest* maize, cotton, beans and calabashes; they are near the mountains, where there are *rich metals* of silver and small settlements of *earthen houses*.] (95–96, my emphasis)

Just as in the case of Topia, the population center, clothing, housing, and crops make up the foci of the narrator's attention. Additionally, Obregón depicts the water sources, the natural defense that the mountains provide, and of course, the presence of precious metals for mining. Obregón's reference to naked people that "visten con cueros [dress with skins]" should be noted here, a point regarding cultural perceptions of clothing to which I will return; however, it is the happiness of the soldiers that specifically stems from the presence of people of "orden y concierto [order and accord]" and the provisions and permanent shelter that they supply that captures attention (98). Obregón describes these people in more detail in a section titled "Lo que hay en esta tierra [That which is in this land]":

> Éstos de este río [Cinaro] son dispuestos, diestros y cursados en el uso y ejercicio de la guerra; son buenos labradores, señores de labranzas de maíz, frijol, calabazas y algodón y buenos pescadores. Habitan este río hasta la Mar del Sur, que está de allí catorce leguas, y hasta la sierra que es seis. Es río ahocinado [*sic*], ancho, bravo y florido de arboledas de mucha frescura; tiene cerco de fértiles riberas llanadas para ganados y labores; es el más ancho que hay en aquellas provincias desde el de Centicpas, ciento y cuarenta leguas atrás y mejores llanadas, pastos, temples y calidades que el de Chiametla ni Culiacán. Pueden echar por él abajo pequeños navíos cuando a de avenida y tiene mucho pescado y caimanes. Es poblado de mucha caza de pie y vuelo.

> [These (people) of this river (Cinaro) are orderly, skillful, and studied in the exercises of war; they are good agriculturalists, owners of crops of maize, beans, calabashes, and cotton, and good fishermen. They inhabit this river until the South Sea, which is fourteen leagues away and six (leagues) away from the mountain range. The river is flared, wide, rough, and florid with forests of much coolness; it has fertile, flat tributaries for livestock and crops; it is the widest that there is in these provinces from Centicpas, one hundred and fifty leagues behind and (has) better plains, pasture, climate, and characteristics than those of Chiametla and Culiacan. Small sailing vessels can depart from there when the water is high and it has many fish and caiman. It is populated with abundant game of both land and air.] (101)

The people here are skilled and referred to as *señores*, a term which would have connoted respect and indicated ownership (Corominas 1987, 531). The positive description of the inhabitants is noteworthy, but perhaps even more so is how this positive description seamlessly flows into that of the river and the land surrounding it. Additionally, the area along the river Cinaro is fit for foundation because, above all, it presents a population center that is viewed as suitable, perhaps even ready-made, for a mining enterprise:

Habiendo visitado el gobernador y su maeso [*sic*] de campo los ríos, sierras y comarcas de la provincia, acordó fundar una villa en el río de Cinaro, así por la mucha cantidad de gente que en aquella provincia estaba sin lumbre de fe, como por el servicio que se conseguía al servicio de la real Corona de su majestad, para cuyo efecto vieron y visitaron pueblos y repartimiento que bastaban para la comodidad de los vecinos que pudiesen sustentarla y defenderla de los naturales si se pusiesen en defensa de su fundación. Y asimismo había sierras cómodas y dispuestas para minas de plata que los naturales habían dado noticia de cantidad de metales que para sus embijes sacaban de la serranía; y asimismo había cantidad de valles y tierras para ganados y labores para los aprovechamientos de los dueños.

[The governor and his first lieutenant, having visited the rivers, mountains and environs of the province, agreed to found a settlement on the Cinaro River, as much for the great quantity of people in that province that were without the light of the faith, as for the service that was attained for the royal Crown of your majesty. To that effect, they inspected and visited pueblos and *repartimientos* that would be sufficient for the comfort of the residents so they could sustain and defend it from the natives if they were to impede its foundation. And furthermore there were comfortable mountain ranges suitable for silver mines; the natives had indicated that they retrieved a great quantity of metals from the mountains for their ornaments; and likewise there was a (large) quantity of valleys and lands for livestock and labors for the profit of the owners.] (103)[18]

Again, the textualscape is defined by the quantity of people and the projected ability to sustain a mining settlement.

Despite this potential, Obregón notes that shortly after the founding of Cinaro a state of discontent arises among the soldiers yet again. It must be remembered that the soldiers were not being paid in monies but rather in potential land grants, and while Obregón perceives the landscape through a topophilic lens, this is not the "Otro Perú" or "Otro México" of the soldiers' dreams. The other soldiers do not share Obregón's values nor, it would seem, Ibarra's. Obregón relates a lengthy speech that Ibarra gives in which the latter empathizes with the soldiers but also appeals to their sense of duty.[19] He, too, according to the speech, would like to have discovered and conquered another wealthy Constantinople or prosperous Venicia or, at the very least, another Mexico or Peru. He emphasizes his aim to empower his men by making them *señores* of titles and wealth, but, he insists, only in such a way that God is served. Foremost is consideration to saintly service and holy obedience to spread the Catholic faith in this "barbarous, rustic nation, ignorant of God their creator and savior" and save the indigenous people from the eternal pains of hell (103–4).

Ibarra's speech as related by Obregón (who was probably not present when it was delivered) emphasizes the empathy and understanding of the expedition leader in identifying with the soldiers' desires to find a rich city (perhaps of gold) and gain titles and wealth. It identifies the "thick" European places of Constantinople and Venice, at once elevating Mexico and Peru to their ranks and identifying all of these places as a part of a larger imperial framework, a shared cultural attitude. Still, it tempers this empathy with the reminder of their primary purpose of exploration: the conversion of these ignorant people to save them from eternal damnation.[20] However, Obregón reports that the soldiers are unmoved. Shortly after this grand speech is delivered, the *maestre de campo* tries to organize the men to build a fort, but the soldiers refuse to help, complaining bitterly that they are not receiving payment, that it is doubtful they could ever even finish, and therefore why should they do the work?: "si estaba [el maese de campo] determinado a concluirla [fuerte] fuese rogando a los naturales le ayudasen o fuesen para su efecto compelidos [if the first lieutenant was determined to finish the fort, he could beg the natives to help him or compel them to do it]" (105–6).

This episode demonstrates perception driven by a cultural attitude, i.e., the soldiers expect indigenous workers as part and parcel of land distribution — if not voluntary then "compelled" — but also a plurality of perception resulting from the individual level of value. As the speech intimates and the soldiers' resistance to work indicates, they are disenchanted with the landscape. In fact, Obregón reports that when Ibarra leaves Cinaro, the soldiers are extremely restless for Ibarra to distribute the pueblos and encomiendas; however, Ibarra is reluctant to do so just yet (140).[21] According to Obregón, by failing to dole out land grants, Ibarra created his own desertion problem, a problem with which he would contend for the duration of the expedition.[22] This tension reflects the differences between the members of the expedition in terms of individual values; interests and motivations that may inform their individual perceptions of the landscape. Is land without laborers or land that remains undistributed "good" or "bad"? As noted in the case of the arduous route to Topia, however, some landscapes seem to transcend individual value, and the soldier's Europeanized perspectives of other landscapes are charged with a shared, extremely intense topophobia. Such landscapes are vividly depicted by Obregón despite a twenty-year lapse between experiencing them and recreating them.

Landscapes of Fear

Above all other landscapes that Obregón depicts, the Valle de Señora (Sonora) may represent the paragon of a culturally shared topophobia as well as the intimate connection between the land, people, and perspectival notions of landscape. Obregón dedicates two chapters to what he labels the *árbol ponzoñoso*, or venomous tree, and mention of it emerges throughout the text to the point where it takes on a personage of sorts (see figure 10). Known to the Opata as *magot*, the scientific name of the bush is *Sapium biloculare*, but Hopkins Durazo (1988, 53) notes that it is known in Sonora primarily as the *hierba de flecha* precisely because of the indigenous peoples' use of it as a weapon. Obregón first mentions the tree when he relates his first personal experience with it, an experience full of fear and panic:

> En este alojamiento fui a cortar dos horcones para componer la tienda de mis compañeros y de tomar la madera de un árbol en las manos me dio notable comezón en ellas y llevando los horcones al real conocieron las guías era del árbol ponzoñoso, de lo cual se alteraron haciendo muchos visajes y exageraciones hacia el árbol, diciendo que le dejase que era dañoso y muy ponzoñoso mayormente el jugo y leche de él, con la cual untadas sus flechas al que herían moría, padecían extraño dolor y rabiosa muerte aunque fuesen pequeñas las heridas.

> [In this encampment I went to cut down two posts in order to build a pavilion for my companions and upon taking the wood of the tree in my hands, it gave me notable irritation in them; and carrying the posts to the camp, the guides recognized that they were from the venomous tree, which made them agitated and (they made) many grimaces and exaggerated (gestures) toward the tree, telling me to leave it alone, that it was dangerous and very poisonous, chiefly the milky sap from it, with which (the natives) smear their arrows; those injured by it died and would suffer strange pain and a rabid death even from small wounds.] (152)

Obregón's simple act of touching the wood frenzied the indigenous guides. From this point forward, the *árbol ponzoñoso* becomes a terrifying antagonist in Obregón's textualscape. He calls it "el más terrible y extraño y ponzoñoso árbol de cuantos hay en lo descubierto del mundo, ni se halla escrito en historia ni relación ni igual ni semejante [the most terrible and strange and venomous tree of all there are in the discovered world, (and) nothing equal or similar to it is found in any written history or account]"

Figure 10. El árbol ponzoñoso, *Sapium biloculare*. Phillip James, photographer

because in addition to being of an "infernal nature," it covers more than three leagues of territory. Although beautiful and always green and flowery, the tree is so toxic, claims Obregón, that anyone who sleeps in its shadow swells up and dies if not helped with medicine:

> El jugo y sustancia de él es blanca y cuajada como de leche bien sazonada, la cual es en extremo perjudicial, ponzoñosa y de infernal naturaleza; con la cual untadas sus flechas la herida que dieren con ellas aunque sea pequeña, dan tan terrible y temeroso dolor que mueren los heridos de ella rabiando y si es en pierna o brazos se les cae a pedazos la carne porque la cancera, pudre y hace caer de las partes donde es la herida, aunque no haga más efecto de tocar y comunicar la sangre las heridas un momento. Y es notable caso que si la ponen apartada de la herida o sangre en cualquiera miembro, aguija y embiste a ella con extraña presteza y velocidad como si fuera cosa viva.

[Its sap and essence is white and coagulated like spoiled milk, extremely harmful, venomous, and of a diabolical nature; . . . they smear their arrows with it, (and) the wound from those (arrows), no matter how small, gives terrible and terrifying pain and one dies from the wounds of it raving; if it (wounds) the leg or arm the flesh falls off in pieces because it cancerates and rots the flesh and makes the (body) parts where the wound is fall off, even if the poison only touches or contaminates the blood for one moment. And it is notable that if it is brought near the wound or close to the blood in any limb, (it) spurs and charges toward it with strange quickness and velocity as if it were a living thing.] (158)

Obregón goes on to explain in horror that nothing grows under the shadow of this tree, and the wounds that it causes are incurable, lasting twenty years without ever completely closing. Worse still, this menacing weapon is not the only source of fear, and the landscape depicted is directly, seamlessly, associated with the people who occupy it. The indigenous peoples of the lands of the árbol ponzoñoso have successfully used their knowledge of the tree as a tool against their enemies, even poisoning the drinking water with it. Obregón describes these indígenas as cruel and bestial. The "salvajes" of the Valle de Señora are associated with the poisonous tree and the rough terrain on which it grows:

Y los cristianos que fueren a sus tierras a poblar o pasar de camino por ellas, vayan advertidos y recatados de ellos [los naturales] porque son en extremo codiciosos, traidores, ladrones y belicosos. Y en este valle y lenguaje hay la mayor gruesa de árbol ponzoñoso, de lo cual su daño con más diestros y cursados que los atrás.

[And the Christians that go to their lands to settle or journey through them, go forewarned and cautious of them (the natives) because they are extremely greedy, treacherous, thieving and bellicose. And it is in this valley where the most venomous trees are found, and (the people) are more skilled and knowledgeable in using (the tree) to harm (enemies) than those seen before.] (153)

Likewise, the people of Uparo, enemies of the Yaqui who also occupy the valley, are viewed as savages who do not cultivate fields; they sustain themselves on a diet of amaranth grains, fish, game, and insects, which Obregón seems to find distasteful (153).

The extensive descriptions of the soldiers' intense fear of the Valle de Señora and its inhabitants, beyond a mere topophobia, seem to speak to what Tuan has called a "landscape of fear." Tuan concedes that fear does have its origins in external circumstances that are truly threatening. Yet, he cautions, the notion of landscape is a construct of the mind as well as a physical and measurable entity. The term *landscapes of fear* refers to both psychological states and tangible environments (Tuan, 1979, 6). The landscape of the Valle de Señora, remembered and textualized by Obregón twenty years after his personal experience, materializes as a terrifying and hostile textualscape, one that reflects the force of this perception and memory of fear. "With time lapse concepts may form; a person can stand back and interpret the perceptual cues in different ways as an exercise in rationality. One interpretation is preferred, and strongly adhered to, because it seems true" (Tuan 1974, 61).

One indication that lends itself to such an interpretation is the intensity of the descriptions. For example, while the árbol ponzoñoso does in fact exist and takes its name for its violent purpose, Hopkins Durazo points out that Obregón exaggerates a bit when he describes the height of the tree as "doce estados," or the equivalent of twenty meters, as typically *Sapium biloculare* grows to four or six meters high (53). Yet, rather than dismissing Obregón as a teller of tall tales, it is fair to consider that his hyperbole may be indicative of an intimidating landscape driven by a fear that, while originating from external circumstances that were truly life-threatening, results in a construction of the mind—a psychological perception that Obregón then textualizes. Lowenthal (1975, 28) explains that "the remembered past is also a more emphatic landscape than that experienced today. Just as we forget or elide scenes that failed to strike us, so we exaggerate those that did." To wit, Obregón recalls that Ibarra's group was so terrified of the árbol ponzoñoso and the "tierras de los infieles" that they chartered a new route on the return to Culiacán to avoid it entirely. This indicates a fear that transcends Obregón's individual values and is likely reflective of the expedition's cultural attitudes as a whole. Regardless, the textualscape that Obregón provides his readers is indeed horrifying and would have fed into his readers' notions of the wild, untamed, and desolate lands that no "civilized" person would inhabit.

Conclusions

As the cosmography project for officials in Spain shifted to adapt to a New World, Juan López de Velasco would eventually abandon the cosmographer's practice of interpretation of accounts to make them fit cosmographical knowledge for a more "unmediated" (to borrow from Portuondo) approach that valued the information found in the accounts streaming in from the Americas, whether that information confirmed past cosmography or not. Obregón's text would have aided in producing new knowledge to fill the "empty space" on maps with "places," made all the more familiar with European toponyms for geographical markers such as rivers, mountains, and valleys, and clarification of distances between population centers. Moreover, the type of earth-bound, discursive itinerary mapping reflected in Obregón's *Historia* breaks up the relating of historical events and the account of his own travel narrative with meticulously detailed descriptions. His resultant value judgments regarding the potential for establishing more permanent, stable settlement in the northern borderlands allow us to explore the highly perspectival perceptions, attitudes, and values of the culturally informed notions of topophilia and topophobia. Recalling the travel narrative's attempts at "striving toward a rhetoric fit to account for displacements of the body and the particular emotions those displacements arouse" (Zumthor and Peebles 1994, 812), we can see Obregón's "land-scaping" project unfold, as he constructs his textualscape with topophilic passages about Chiametla that inspire desire as well as topophobic passages about the Valley of Sonora that inspire terror.

Yet fissures exist in Obregón's textualscape. These same moments of topophilia and topophobia reveal cracks through which moments emerge that suggest a wholly different cultural attitude that views "nonplaces" as "places," or even a landscape perception not restricted by such binaries. For the indigenous peoples already living in the landscape that Obregón attempts to transcribe, landscapes of fear are actually landscapes of refuge and defense from an enemy introducing an unprecedented upheaval to the landscape. Where Obregón perceives an "uninhabitable" landscape in which the expedition's very survival is at risk, indigenous inhabitants not only survive but thrive. These differences in perception, attitudes, and values suggest multiple landscapes.

CHAPTER THREE

Multiple Landscapes, Multiple Frontiers

Every river is more than just one river; every rock is more than just one rock.
—GREIDER AND GARKOVICH, 1994

Geography is made . . . largely in terms of the country we perceive, or are conditioned to perceive: the country of the mind.
—JAMES WREFORD WATSON, 1970

In "A Painter, Geographer of Arizona" (1988), French geographer Stephane Quoniam presents his notes from a trip through Arizona, making the case for landscape as something to be read and decoded. Quoniam's notes are purposefully illegible, save for a few trigger words such as "Coronado," "suggest[ing] the possibility of geographical knowledge and the impossibility of communicating personal geographical understanding" (Cosgrove and Domosh 1993, 34). This turns our understanding of the roles of text and image on its head: "In my perceptions of Arizona . . . the painting describes what the text illustrates" (Quoniam 1988, 12).[1] In this (re)presentation, no significant meaning is drawn from the words at all, resulting in a study in which geographical knowledge is stored yet is inaccessible to the reader. Similarly, while the representations of "good" and "bad" landscapes reveal the myriad ways Obregón's perceptions of the lands and its peoples inform one another and his textualscape, at the same time the very creation of that textualscape means an inherent "writing over" a pre- and coexisting indigenous landscape that would have stored copious geographical knowledge, but which Obregón simply does not or cannot access.

Obregón provides chapter after chapter replete with thick description of the landscape that, to the modern reader, may seem benign or even redundant. However, as Padrón reminds us, "description" while seemingly "the most mundane of discursive modes, the most innocent, most purely referential way of utilizing language" holds much more power than we tend to realize: "'Description,' like 'emplotment' entails the encounter between data and expectations, between observations and culturally contingent assumptions about the production of meaning" (2004, 21). While Obregon's textualscape does offer one of the first textual renderings of the region, we must bear in mind that it does so through the occidental cultural lens, not a kaleidoscope. Just as cultural studies of landscape have come to recognize the complexities of authorship and representation, so too must discourse analysis of the textualscape.

> Cultural studies of landscape are no longer regarded as part of a "coherent body of knowledge," slowly assembling, growing and developing like an architectural structure. Rather they seem disassociated fragments, shards of reflecting glass which at once illuminate, reflect and distort—in sum, re-present—the world of individual and intersubjective experience. It may be that those shards imply a potential single sheet of transparent glass through which a single reality might be visible, but the task of reassembling them is fruitless and we are obliged to deceive as we perceive. (Cosgrove and Domosh 1993, 29)

The value of this point of view in attending to Obregon's discourse is that it accounts for the ways landscape that cannot be *read* is simply *rewritten*. The vivid imagery in Obregón's text is filtered through his own perception and appropriation of the landscape, resulting in a textualscape that doubtless has been designed with the Iberian reader in mind. However, this does not mean that it should be dismissed. Much like the rebuilt landscape in the painter's mind expresses a truth, the textualscape likewise expresses its composer's truth (Quoniam 1988, 3). That this textualscape is not objective is not viewed in this study negatively because it is subjectivity that allows for the examination of assumptive attitudes and values.

In addition to providing a window into the culturally informed phenomenon of landscape, by positing the extensive topophilic and topophobic descriptions in Obregón against historical ethnography, his blind spots are revealed, suggesting alternative landscapes. Put another way, the natural resources and cultural capital that Obregón does *not* see reveal as much about the perspectival and human nature of landscape as those that he *does* see. This notion gets to the heart of how the landscape is lived, experienced, valued, and even "read" differently by various cultures, groups, and individuals. It also presents the caveat that any textualscape by its very nature implies the appropriation and writing over of some human element. This chapter explores how landscape may have informed indigenous identity and the ways Obregón "writes over" that identity in his textualscape by projecting frontiers—both spatial and corporal—onto the landscape, one that was shifting even as he wrote.

Language, Landscape, and Identity

Just as the *Sapium biloculare*—which Obregón calls the *árbol ponzoñoso* (venomous tree)—was the salvation of the indigenous and the perdition of the Spanish, the landscapes in which Obregón doubts the very survival of the expedition would have provided, at the most basic level, defense, food, and shelter to their inhabitants. The fact that pre-Hispanic Xiximes and Acaxees were able to organize production and trade to survive with higher population densities than were achieved under Spanish Imperial rule indicates that they lived in a very different landscape (Deeds 2003, 1125). For example, while the rough terrain and the impassability of many areas of the northern landscape confounded the Spanish, they often served the indigenous inhabitants against their enemies, providing an extremely effective weapon against invaders and even a means of escape from them, particularly when their pursuers were on horses. In fact, on more than one occasion Obregón describes how the indigenous inhabitants lead the expedition's soldiers into the highlands specifically to escape them. When Ibarra learns that the residents of Sahuaripa plan on attacking the expedition, he attempts to dissuade them from doing so with a show of arms, a ploy which appears to work at first. However this does not mean that the Opata do not adapt:

Aunque en presencia del gobernador mostraron contento y alegría, estuvieron después tristes y desanimados y con menos esperanza del efecto de su acuerdo de guerra, por cuya causa y crecer en ellos la codicia e industria del demonio tornaron a consultar dos cosas en su consejo de guerra: la una que atento a que iban los cristianos vestidos [para] la batalla no diesen la batalla con arcos y flechas por no ser de provecho ni efecto; la otra, que llevasen con engaño el campo a lo alto y áspero de la serranía fingiendo ser lo mejor y más poblado de la serranía y a parte que no pudiesen aprovecharse de sus caballos por la gran aspereza y peñolería de la serranía y valle de Saguaripa, adonde en llegando a él desampararon el campo las guías y todos escondieron sus bastimentos, mujeres, hijos, atavíos de sus casas y personas, y se escondieron y ausentaron de Saguaripa.

[Although in the presence of the governor (Ibarra) they showed contentment and happiness, later they were sad and disheartened and less hopeful (about) the effect(s) of their war tactics, which caused the greed and work of the devil to grow in them (and) they came to implement two things in their practice of war: one, attentive to (the fact that) Christians would go dressed for battle, not to do battle with bows and arrows because they are not beneficial nor effective; the other, that they deceptively lead the expedition to the high, rough mountains, pretending that it is the best and most populous (area) of the mountain chain, (but in reality is) an area where (the Spanish) could not use their horses due to the great roughness and cliffs of the mountains and valley of Saguaripa, where upon arriving, the guides deserted the expedition and the inhabitants hid their supplies, women, children, utensils, and the people all hid, abandoning Saguaripa.] (154–55)

Evidently, the same landscape that so horrified Obregón was a safe haven for the indigenous inhabitants and a source of defense and power. In fact, the Yaquis that Ibarra encountered would take refuge in the mountains from Spanish and Mexican military forces well into the twentieth century (Radding 2005, 212). Northern New Spain, Guy and Sheridan point out, is a region of "topographical extremes" in which desert valleys are punctuated with mountain ranges that, in addition to isolating the region from the center of power, "also provided regions of refuge and resistance for Indians fleeing Spanish dominion, and impregnable bases of operations for Native Americans raiding Spanish settlements" (1998, 5). Quite often, autochthonous resisters were able to take advantage of the landscape that Obregón dismisses as "malas tierras," ironically aiding them in frustrating the Spanish Imperial project.

Radding demonstrates in her meticulously researched comparative study *Landscapes of Power and Identity* (2005) that in addition to providing defense against Spanish slave raiders and encroachment, indigenous groups such as the Yaqui-Mayo, Pima-Tepehuán, and Opata-Eudeve peoples depended on their desert, piedmont, and mountainous landscapes for their subsistence and survival (see figure 11). Not surprisingly, Obregón's textualscape reflects a perception of the landscape that often undervalues

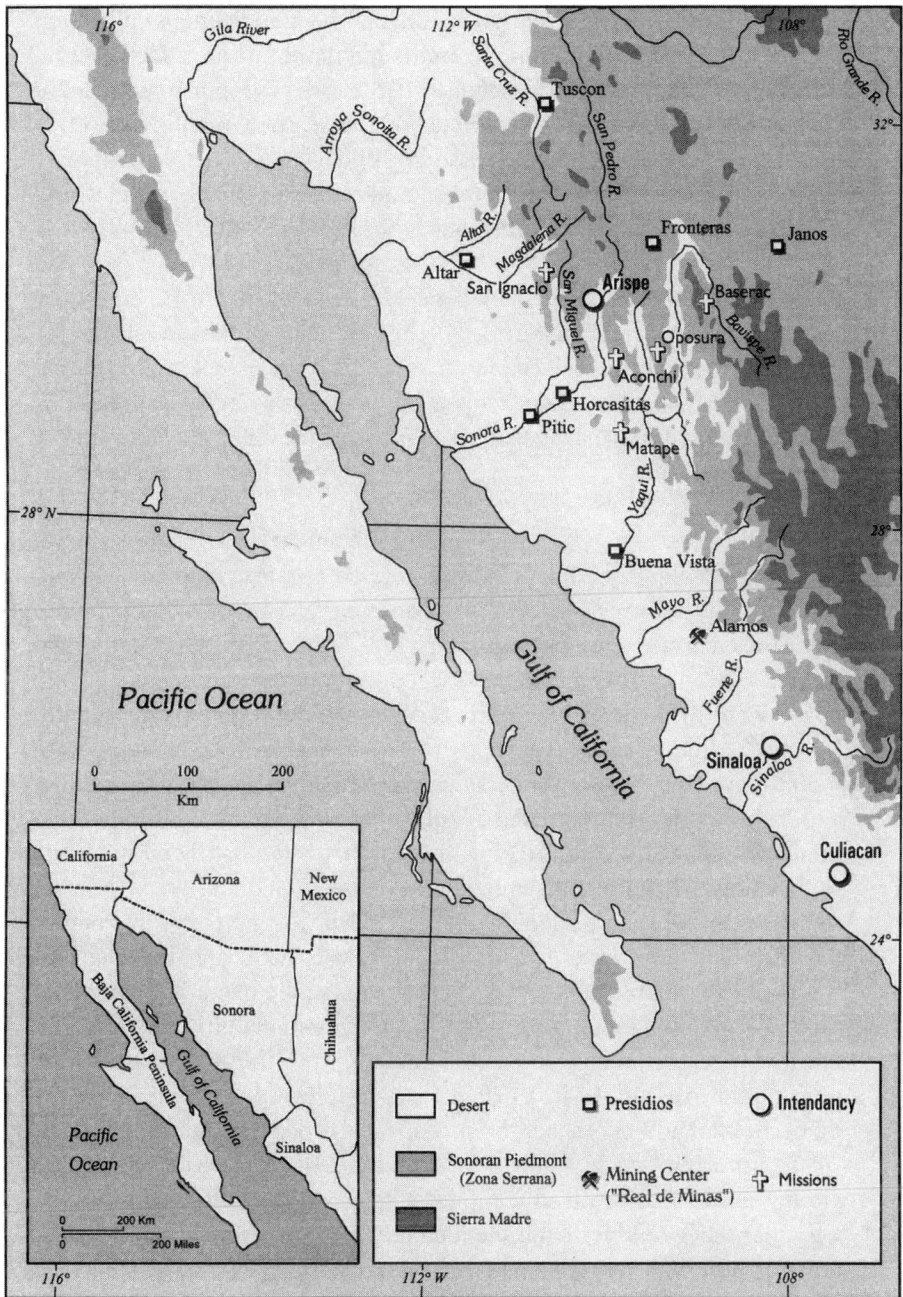

Figure 11. Sonora, place map drawn by Jason Casanova under the direction of Jane Domier (*Landscapes of Power and Identity*, Radding 2005)

or simply does not recognize what would have been indigenous cultivation practices and shelter. For example, in the highlands, where effective cultivation was dependent on seasonal rainfall, the valleys supported permanent villages while temporary shelters were built for seasonal planting as well as hunting and gathering activities (Radding 2005, 24–25). These temporary shelters, dismissed at once by Obregón and his companions, in fact would have supported a rather sophisticated agricultural system.

> Constructed spaces in the cordillera were distinguished by ribbons of narrow irrigated fields in the floodplains with small gardens and shallow wells at their edges; swidden plots in different stages of seeding, harvesting, and fallowing; and stone terraces built in canyons and close to caves and natural springs that provided planting surfaces, water and protection against predators. (27)

Also, in the *zona serrana*, or piedmont, groups such as the Opata, Eudeve, and Pima practiced floodplain farming consisting of irregularly shaped *milpas* that flowed through fence-like rows of trees planted at different angles along the edge of the river and utilizing small dams, or weirs, that controlled water flow (29). Some of the territorial configurations were seasonal while others went through specific periods of construction and abandonment. In other words, what Obregón describes as "rústicas habitaciones" were more than likely smaller shelters that would have been used for hunting and gathering by seminomadic peoples. For their very way of life, it was imperative that "architecture of desert peoples rested lightly on the land" so that houses could be assembled and disassembled and areas revisited from season to season (Radding 2005, 33). Nonsedentary groups such as the Cunca'ac (Seri) and O'odham, in addition to gathering, hunting, and fishing, likewise utilized the cycle of the seasons, the rivers, and rainfall to their full potential to support a sophisticated system of cultivation (31–32). Clearly, where Obregón perceives "nomads" dwelling in the space that must be traversed to get to a place, those peoples would not have shared his occidental notion of space. For nonsedentary peoples, Zumthor tells us, "place unfurls in space" (quoted in Westphal 2013, 162). Moreover, these groups' landscapes involved complex strategies of mobility that informed identities that would have transcended the binary of "nomad" and "sedentary."[2] Where Obregón sees spatiality, then, the indigenous inhabitants see something very different and in some instances, even sacred.

Equally important as defense, shelter, and subsistence, the landscape's spiritual function for the indigenous cultures would have likewise been difficult for Obregón and his contemporaries to recognize. Radding notes that in addition to taking refuge there from Spanish and Mexican military forces for hundreds of years, the same mountains held a profound spiritual power as "the Indian's moral cosmologies of life and death, good and evil, were envisioned in terms of the natural environment in which they lived" (2005, 212). The Yaquis associate the Sierra Bacatete (The Tall Cane-Reed Mountains), a mountain range that marks the eastern boundary of their traditional territory, with the sacred world of *huya aniya*. Griffith (1993, xi) demonstrates that well into the twentieth century the Tohono O'odham and Yaqui "express[ed] their relationships with the land in many ways— through belief, legend, custom, and even art and architecture." The same seminomadic Pima-O'odham referenced by Radding call the Baboquivari Mountain the center of their universe, the dwelling place of I'itoi, the creator god of the Tohono O'odham (Griffith 1993, xiv). To this day, many older rural Mexicans and Mexican Americans share a "supernaturally sanctioned relationship" with the Pimería Alta region in which mythical stories shaped landscape (xviii).[3] The mountains, rivers, flora and fauna, rocks, and trees all would have held (and still hold to this day) untold spiritual and cultural wealth. However, Obregón and the Ibarra Expedition are simply not able to read the sacred landscape that is already there, instead writing over it with Christian toponyms, crosses, and churches.

Various studies have demonstrated that the envirocultural regions that Obregón depicts would have comprised a highly complex landscape rich in natural resources, cultural capital, and spiritual sustenance for its indigenous inhabitants (Deeds 2003; Griffith 1993; Radding 2005; Sheridan-Prieto 2002). Certainly Obregón registers little of it. These omissions are the result, at least in part, of the culturally informed phenomena of topophilia and topophobia, a phenomenon not intrinsic to the landscape but rather residing within individual people (Abrahamsson 1999, 57). Certainly it bespeaks the perspectival nature of landscape. Yet another theory would suggest that Obregón could simply not communicate in writing that which he could not read himself: that landscape is more than mere perception. Architect Ann Spirn argues in *The Language of Landscape* (1998) that landscape is language itself: humans' native language, and not merely in a metaphorical or metaphysical sense. Landscape, read by humans long before their inventions of signs and symbols, is translated into signs and symbols.[4] She contends that landscape has all the same features of language with its own equivalents to words, parts of speech, syntax, formation, and function: "Like the meanings of words, the meanings of landscape elements (water, for example) are only potential until context shapes them. Rules of grammar govern and guide how landscapes are formed, some specific to places and their local dialects, others universal" (15). Through this critical lens we can approach Obregón's textualscape as one of many possible translations, and moreover a translation crafted by a nonnative speaker. Of course, while this may explain in part his inability to recognize that those "uninhabitable" nonplaces are actually rich in human history and culture, more importantly, the language of landscape allows for a closer approximation to the intimate connection between landscape and human identity.

The indigenous landscapes that held so much in terms of sustenance, protection, and spiritual cosmology would have informed, and indeed shaped and reshaped, indigenous identity over the centuries prior to European contact in copious ways. Sheridan-Prieto examines how identity is resignified in specific socioeconomic situations, contending that in sixteenth-century northeastern New Spain, territoriality would have been the very expression of native diversity itself: "territoriality is how identity is formed and transformed in order to resist and adapt socio-economic situations" (2002, 16, my translation). Citing the "inconsistencies" traditionally found in the literature as an obstacle to creating an ethnic map of the region, Sheridan-Prieto argues that these "inconsistencies" instead provide the key to a much deeper explanation of the processes of territorialization of social relations and of specialization of different groups (17).[5] Long before and after the Spanish entradas into the region represented in Obregón's *Historia* took place, diverse groups spanned the landscape and territory was contested between them. These issues of cultural identification with the land often eluded Europeans who simply did not or could not read conflicting claims to resources and territory.

Far from fixed, indigenous population clusters were culturally and ethnically dynamic, argues Deeds (2003), and the Spanish "certainly did not understand their systems of government, subsistence, kinship, and relationships with other groups" (345).[6] Moreover, as Rojo (2014, 1464) points out, the "flexible relation with the territory they occupied, and the loose political structures that bound them together were not based on permanent subservience," which was far more difficult for the Spanish to contend with than the civilization of the Nahua auxiliary soldiers traveling with them. The Mexica are referred to positively throughout the text, and the favorable commonalities drawn between the pueblos in Nuevo México and the Mexica belie a preference for Nahua culture and perhaps explorers' lasting hopes for Nuevo México to fulfill the origin story of the Aztecs. In fact, the inability of the Spanish to recognize difference would have only been exacerbated by the Nahuatl-speaking auxiliary soldiers that accompanied the expedition, who viewed their neighbors as "savages" and privileged their own, more sedentary, way of life. These Nahua auxiliary soldiers referred generically and pejoratively to these peoples as Chichimecas, a moniker the Spanish picked up on and used to refer to any indigenous group that resisted Spanish incursion or attacked Spanish settlements. Adding to all of these factors that eliminated difference, Obregón was ascribing cultural, political, and ethnic identities to groups that had already been rocked by violent slaving expeditions that had brought, war, rape, forced labor, migration, and diseases, all historical processes that would have profound effects on indigenous identity so deeply rooted in territoriality.

A Shifting Landscape

Evidence of prior contact abound in the Obregonian textualscape in the form of material items documented as having been traded to the region's inhabitants or left behind by the explorers, including beads, glassware, iron objects, broken cart pieces, a trunk, and a book (which was extant forty years after Francisco Vázquez de Coronado left it behind in Zuni). In fact, Obregón notes that in the Valle de Señora one of the referents to the Spanish explorers used by the aborigines is "hombres de hierro [men of iron]" (155): "Y de ordinario siguieron el campo mostrando tener codicia de las cosas y atavíos de los cristianos, mayormente de cosas de hierro para cortar o labrar sus tierras [And frequently they followed the expedition showing envy of the things and equipment of the Christians, principally the items of iron for cutting or working their lands]" (153). Furthermore, Obregón reports that Antonio de Espejo's group meets an indigenous chief in possession of tools for removing silver given to him by Bernardino de Luna (267–68). For his part, Ibarra perpetuates this practice, presenting glass items and blankets to various indigenous groups encountered, typical gifts of exchange at the time of first contact.

However, Spanish-led expeditions had left behind much more than glass and blankets. According to Obregón, on arrival at a pueblo in the Valle de Señora, Ibarra learns of two mestizos residing in Sahuaripa, "hijos de indias naturales de allí y de los cristianos que ellos habían muerto [sons of indigenous women and Christians that had died]" (152).[7] The mestizo progeny of a Spanish settlement founded during the time of the Coronado Expedition, and later governed by Diego de Alcaraz, were the children of Spanish soldiers and Opata women (Hopkins Durazo 1988, 37). As previously noted, far more complex than a meeting between Spanish and Indian, these expeditions included indigenous auxiliary soldiers, interpreters, and guides who would have also had more fluid notions of identity.[8] There is evidence that some of these individuals chose to remain behind and not return to New Spain. Riley (1974, 30) points out that in various accounts there is mention of unnamed Mexica soldiers who had accompanied Coronado and remained in the Pueblo region.[9] Obregón refers to "dos indios ladinos de la lengua mexicana" in Tucayan as reported by Espejo who tell the latter that they are from the barrio of San Hispólito in Mexico City (188). In Cíbola, four Nahuatl-speaking "indios cristianos" come out to receive them who had also stayed behind from the Coronado Expedition (263). This is not to say that cultural contact had not taken place before auxiliary soldiers accompanied Spanish expeditions; in fact, there is evidence to suggest that cultural exchange between the northern region and Mesoamerica had been going on long before the arrival of the Spanish.[10] While Deeds (2003) cautions that the degree to which Mesoamerican sociopolitical organization may have penetrated the region is not well understood, what is certain is that during this period any cultural interaction would have been taking place under incredibly different sociohistoric circumstances, not least of which includes the phenomenon of forced displacements.

As the Spanish pushed northward, indigenous people were increasingly displaced or forced to migrate, a phenomenon embodied in the case of Luisa, "una india cristiana" residing in Ocoroni: "Diéronle noticia de una india cristiana que sabia la lengua mexicana y otras tres de aquellas provincias [They told them about a Christian Indian woman that knew the mexica language and three other (languages) of those provinces]" (96). According to Obregón, Luisa had been born in Culiacán and "Christianized" but later escaped to avoid paying tribute. The presence of the multilingual indígena in Ocoroni is a direct result of Spanish expansion and growth in mining enterprises. Luisa's liminal status results from her forced migration: "Esta Luisa fue cautiva en cinco parcialidades, desde donde vino derrotándose de valle en valle, desde donde quedó huida u olvidada de los de Francisco Vázquez Coronado viniendo del viaje de Cibola [This Luisa (had been) captive in five places, from where she roamed from valley to valley; she escaped or was forgotten by the Coronado expedition returning from their journey to Cibola]" (98). Far from an isolated case, Luisa's displacement is part of a larger trend. According to Obregón, the people of Matoen had also fled Culiacán to escape the encomiendas (90).

In addition to fleeing their native homeland to escape encomienda, many aborigines had been taken prisoner in slave raids and relocated hundreds of miles away. Deeds (2003) points out that as the Tepehuanes and

Conchos resisted being forced into encomiendas, the Spanish began to look outside the region for labor, slave raiding into Sonora and relocating their captives. Often, indigenous scouts were sent to *rancherías* to capture and deliver residents to fulfill grants for laborers already issued. Obregón's textualscape reflects the terror that these raids had instilled in the inhabitants. In Urique the people fled on seeing the Ibarra Expedition for fear that they would kill them or take them prisoner (111). Obregón also reports that the Chamuscado and Espejo Expeditions encounter aborigines who are deathly afraid that the Christians will take them prisoner and make them slaves.

Of course this intense fear was not unfounded. Reff has proposed that references to "la mala cosa" in Álvarez Núñez Cabeza de Vaca's relación represents indigenous reactions of fear stemming from slave raids and diseases introduced to the region: "The native peoples he encountered in Texas and northwestern Mexico undoubtedly had learned from trading partners about the destruction taking place to the south. Arguably, this information gave rise to Indian fear of bearded, sword-wielding men, who had a strange and frightening power to kill with disease" (1996, 118–19).[11] It is noteworthy that the effects of disease are wholly absent in Obregón's text despite the fact that inhabitants would have already been exposed to disease before the Ibarra Expedition (see Reff 1996).

The radical changes to the landscape caused by only one of this litany of factors cannot be overstated: the introduction of new flora and fauna (particularly the horse); the erosion and deforestation caused by mining and grazing; constant war; miscegenation in and between groups (autochthonous, African, and European); the rapid spread of strange diseases; migration and displacement; forced labor; the sudden loss of physical cosmography; the introduction of new tools; and disruption of trade (Deeds 2003; Sheridan Prieto 2002). As Sheridan-Prieto (2002) has argued, aboriginal reaction and adaptive strategies would have informed the formation of alliances and group relations with temporary or definitive effects to original identity and the complete reorganization of lived space (26). Recent studies call for the recognition that the Spanish may very well have been seeing and depicting indigenous populations at varying stages of immeasurably disorienting sociopolitical upheaval (Reff 1996; Deeds 2003; Sheridan-Prieto 2002). Deeds argues that the ranchería patterns the Spanish saw may have reflected varying stages of population transformation that resulted from Spanish incursion: "There is considerable evidence to indicate that colonial stresses and new or shifting alliances resulted in the name a people used to identify themselves as a people with a distinct identity" (2003, 1245).[12]

While scholars continue to research and attempt to better understand the complexities and subtleties of indigenous ethnic and cultural identities before and during "first contact," they are confronted with what Deeds (2003) cites as a dearth of archaeological investigation and paleopathological studies, and a "sparse and fragmentary historical record that begins in the later sixteenth century" (1274). Authors like Obregón offer only so much information, as they simply could not read the long and complex envirocultural histories that the landscape held nor their dynamic territoriality identities. However, despite what is lacking in Obregón, he does at least attempt to describe indigenous peoples; in fact, he provides highly detailed descriptions of various groups that scholars continue to cite to this day. Recalling the seamlessness of the land-and-its-peoples descriptions of "buenas" versus "malas" lands referenced in the last chapter, we begin to see how Obregón's textualscape features inhabitants just as much as the lands they occupy. In fact, albeit from a skewed view informed by European notions of civilization, Obregón dedicates significant effort to describing inhabitants. However, he does so in his own native "language of landscape," reading the cultural manifestations most valued by those of his own ilk: clothing, cultivation, and permanent shelter.

Humanscapes and Frontiers

The topophilic passages already reviewed reveal the discursive paradigm that emerges in Obregón's textualscape in which clothing, cultivation, and permanent structures are repeatedly the foci of depiction. These three manifestations mirror what Sauer described as the *cultural landscape*, a critical framework through which to consider the "phenomenology of landscape" and "the reality of the union of [its] physical and cultural elements" (1925, 29). In this view, landscape is dynamic in space and time, with man as its shaping force.[13] Approaching his textualscape, we must bear in mind that Obregón's own identity and language of landscape would have been informed in large part by occidental conceptions of these cultural markers, conceptions different from those of the original (or most recent) inhabitants. For example, to the Spanish, "the architectural entity defined a given human community" and permanent shelter would have been a sign of civilization to Obregón, whereas "rústicas habitaciones" would have meant its absence (Mundy 1996, 91). Clothing, presupposed to mark the beginning of the history of civilization when God expelled Adam and Eve from Paradise, would have also been a barometer for measuring a group of people (Glantz 2005, 67). Antithetically, scantily clad indigenous peoples would have been viewed as vulnerable and at the mercy of the natural elements, an "exposure" associated with irrationality and a lack of civilization (Gerbi 1973; Glantz 2005). Finally, while the focus on crops may be dismissed as mere desire for a ready-made food supply, it should be noted that by the time of the Ibarra Expedition the Spanish had already begun attempts at modifying the flora and fauna to "Europeanize" it. Obregón cites the introduction of animals and plants that would have resulted in significant changes to the landscape, including livestock left behind by Coronado and the settlers of Culiacán as well as new crops of melon and beans.[14] Rooted in the firm belief that "the only possible 'civilized' diet was the European one," Obregón seems to seek out the knowable, readable crops of his culture (Verdesio 2002, 140).

It is precisely the "reading" of these markers of civilization (clothing, crops, and shelter) and the *inability* to read others that at once erase and write over indigenous identity in the textualscape. Ahern (2003) introduces the term *humanscapes* to signal a sort of narrative shift from a gaze that privileges the architectural environment to one that includes more detailed information about the dress, hairstyles, and sexual and marriage practices among the Zuni people in Pedro de Castañeda de Nájera's account of the Coronado expedition, "drawing on it real figures that fleshed out the nebulous mythic landscapes fray Marcos had proclaimed" (2005, 277–78). Akin to chorographic mapping, which deals with the partial and particular views of a whole, these depictions focus on both the built environments of human settlements and the specificities of the human occupants themselves (Mundy 1996, 3). Like Castañeda de Nájera before him, Obregón's textualscape is dominated by his perceptions of people. How they are identified and defined comes to the foreground, with the caveat that their "potentiality" for pacification informs description, aiding Obregón in erecting frontiers between and among groups. Humanscapes in Obregón, while detailed, belie an obsession with "civilization" and the (re)establishment of stably held settlements. Consequently, indigenous cooperation (or lack thereof) with the Spanish expansion project informs human frontiers.

De Certeau (1984) argues that spatiality is organized by the determination of frontiers, and in sixteenth-century New Spain, the northern frontier was continuously organized and reorganized as it expanded and retracted. Spanish settlements in the banda del norte were held only precariously and under constant attack, a situation that spurred the establishment of a system of presidios under Viceroy Velasco.[15] Unlike the notion of the frontier as a great expanse of opportunity that has prevailed in Anglo-American culture in the United States, "in both Latin American historiography and popular culture the frontier was a place to be feared, a spawning ground of barbarism and despotism rather than democracy" (Weber and Rausch, quoted in Guy and Sheridan 1998, 8). Although Obregón lauds the security established by Ibarra in the region, from a privileged historical perspective we know that within only about four years from its founding, indigenous raids on Nombre de Dios were at their peak. Local resistance to European invasion was a part of daily life on the banda del norte both before and during the period commonly referred to as La Guerra Chichimeca (1550–1600). Powell notes that "the new mines at Indé and San Martín continued only precariously active under heavy handicaps imposed by the hostility of the nearby natives" (1944, 188). Indigenous resisters frequently fled from encomenderos, raided settlements, and attacked travelers, all activities that Obregón references.

Constructed from a position of vulnerability, the banda del norte came to represent an open, exterior, distant space that, while still much desired, was unknown; it was full of potential riches, but also different, barbaric, pagan, and bestial (Bolaños 2005, 16). The threat posed by "uncivilized savages" inhabiting the periphery surrounding Spanish settlements permeates every aspect of the Obregonian textualscape, so it is not surprising that cultural information that identifies groups as potential allies or enemies comes to the forefront of his humanscapes. "The natives too are always discussed from the viewpoint of their relationship with the Spaniards: as vassals, enemies, converts or allies" (Gerbi 1985, 98). As a result, the frontier landscape is described as much in human terms as it is in topographical ones wherein uncivilized peoples maraud the periphery of the stable "centers" of settlement. Obregón repeatedly depicts the borderlands as the wild, untamed area that needs to be brought into the fold of what Westphal calls the political omphalos; the fixed center and principle of orientation: the Spanish Empire (2013, 24). But again, such control is far from established, and in many cases has already failed. Obregón depicts, far from a space of domination or even mutual exchange, a frontier between a landscape that is tamed and one that is untamed, or to be more precise, one that has yet to be "pacificado."[16] As part and parcel of this attempted absorption, a primary function of the frontier in the textualscape is to delineate for the purpose of identity construction (Trigo 1997, 80).

Obregón complains that miners and merchants, and their slaves and servants, are all under constant threat of violence from the hostile groups that inhabit the periphery of Nombre de Dios, stressing that Ibarra's two most important accomplishments in founding Nombre de Dios and Durango from the start include the establishment of (1) security ("pacificando y castigando a los rebeldes y enemigos [pacifying and punishing the rebels and enemies]") and (2) supplies ("mantenimientos en abundancia y moderados precios [food supplies in abundance and regulated prices]") so that commerce on the borderlands can be established and maintained (75). To that end, the first order of business is to establish a presidio to curtail raids and to spread among the indigenous populace what Obregón views as "policía, razón y buenas costumbres [civilization, reason, and good customs]" (75).

[En] el valle de San Juan, cincuenta leguas de la villa del Nombre de Dios adonde, por ser parte cómoda y aprejada para conseguir y poner por obra el efecto de su jornada, mandó [Ibarra] hacer y fundó un buen fuerte para que desde él fuesen a traer de paz y castigasen a los caribes salteadores y que asisten en aquellas serranías fronteras haciendo hurtos, daños y matanzas en los mineros, mercaderes y caminantes, y en sus esclavos, criados, haciendas y ganados. Y siendo regalados con amonestación de paz y concordia y ofrecimiento de amistad para reducirlos al servicio de Dios nuestro Señor y de la imperial Corona, no les satisfizo al apetito de su viciosa y bestial vida en que estaban obstinados y viciosos, a cuya respuesta y satisfacción enviaron a hacer muchos fieros y amenazas de muerte si no les desembarazaba el gobernador sus tierras, lo cual ponían por obra con daño de sus haciendas y vidas por fuerza de armas . . . hurtaron, llevaron y mataron doscientos y cincuenta caballos.

[In the Valley of San Juan, fifty leagues from Nombre de Dios where, since it was a comfortable and suitable place to put into effect the purpose of his journey, Ibarra ordered to make and found a good fort so that from it they would bring peace to and punish the *caribes salteadores* that lurk about in those frontier mountains robbing, harming and killing the miners, merchants and travelers and their slaves, servants, property, and livestock. And (yet despite) being entreated with peace and agreement and (an) offering of friendship so as to compel them to the service of God our Lord and the imperial Crown, the appetite of their vicious and bestial life was not sated. . . . They were obstinate and vicious . . . they sent threats of death and threatened to do ferocious things if the governor did not leave their lands, which they put to work by harming their properties and lives by force of arms . . . and they robbed, stole, and killed two hundred fifty horses.] (76)[17]

This depiction is loaded with pejorative language in describing indigenous resistance and associates it with mountain-dwelling peoples, a point to which I will return. At this point, however, I would like to draw attention to Obregón's use of the term *caribes salteadores*. While "salteadores" communicates the offenses of assault and robbery in sparsely settled areas (*Diccionario de Autoridades* 1726–39), i.e., the actions that create instability and chaos for the Spanish settlements; *caribe* is the more culturally charged word.

Among the myriad epithets Obregón employs to distinguish between aboriginal groups, the term *caribe* is particularly perennial. *Caribe*—the first neologism produced from the New World, Jáuregui (2005) point out— was used considerably in New Spain during the period of first encounters throughout the sixteenth century to refer to any person that inhabited the extreme south of present-day Florida and the regions of the Caribbean. Additionally, the term carried the connotation of the practice of anthropophagy but later would be used throughout New Spain for centuries to refer to any "hombre sangriento y cruel, que se enfurece contra otros, sin tener lástima, ni compasión [blood-thirsty and cruel man, who rages against others, without shame or compassion]" (*Diccionario de Autoridades* 1726–39). *Caribe* is a corruption of the word *caníbales*, the word used in Columbus's journal to describe a reportedly hostile indigenous group he hears about from the local Arawak Indians he first encounters. Columbus tells of the Arawak's intense fear of their neighbors, the "caníbales," who are extremely warlike and eat their enemies (Hulme 1986). It is thus from a second-hand account in a language the Spanish could not have possibly understood that the people of that island are connected to the soldiers of *Gran Can* of Marco Polo and Heredotus' man-eating savages (Hulme 1998, 22).[18]

From this initial contact and subsequent usage, *caribe* and *caníbal* (which in the native inhabitants' language likely meant "guerrero bravo" or "comedor de mandioca") eventually came to replace the previously used etymologically Greek term *antropófago* (Boucher, quoted in Jáuregui 2005, 28). The term *caribe* represents the resignification of a trope dating from classic Greek, a trope for which the Spanish were predisposed. These New World cannibals were a merely "modernized" version of the trope wherein the idea of "strange monsters" eventually disappeared, but the cultural practice of eating human flesh (not for survival but out of savagery) remained (Jáuregui 2005, 60). Just as quickly as the labels *caribe* and *caníbal* became synonymous with savagery and difference, they morphed again to signify simply any aboriginal resistance, allowing for the erection of human frontiers between various aboriginal groups in relationship with the "good savage" of lascasian humanists (59). "Civility and cannibalism were born together in the colonial imaginary, insofar as the former made of the latter its absolute moral antithesis" and "encouraged a certain moral violence against the unity of humankind, that is, the hierarchical division of peoples into races, states, and types" (Phillips 1998, 192–93).

While the distinction between Arawaks and Caribs as different ethnic groups has been rejected by historians, anthropologists, and linguists (Hulme points out that "Arawak" was never used by any Caribbean Amerindians to self-identify), this initial demarcation would inform Spanish perception of aborigines as either "easily pacified" or bellicose (*buen salvaje* or caribe) for centuries. Subsequently, the notion of the caníbal or caribe "came to play an important part in the moral justification for imperial rule" (Ashcroft 2000, 31).[19] This justification is written right into Las Ordenanzas: "Deseles a entender (a los indígenas) especialmente que les hemos embiado quien les ensene [*sic*] la doctrina xpiana y fee en que se pueden salbar . . y que no se maten ny coman ni sacrifiquen como en algunas partes se hazia [Especially make the Indians understand that we have sent them those (friars) to teach them the Spanish doctrine and faith by which they can be saved . . . and that they not kill and eat nor sacrifice one another as in some parts it used to be done]" (*Transcripción* 1973, 106). Encomenderos were keen to claim that their labor force was made up of violently savage caribes or slaves rescued from their capture so that their enslavement or forced labor would be legally justified (Jáuregui 2005, 27). In this way, as Jáuregui astutely points out, a trope dating from the Ancient Greeks played a critical role (albeit an anachronistic one) in expanding mercantilism and Modernity (59). Recalling the economic aspirations of Spanish entradas, Obregón's labeling of a group of people as caribe would have been read as marking that group as the epitome of the unhospitable rebel. It is "a work of *realpolitik*, establishing which Amerindians [are] prepared to accept the Spaniards on the latter's terms, and which [are] 'hostile,' that is to say prepared to defend their territory and way of life" (Hulme 1986, 72).[20]

Obregón enlists the term *caribe* frequently, often tacking on the accusation of anthropophagy or sodomy. Of the people of Caguaçan in the environs of Chiametla, he writes, "vivían contra la ley de Dios nuestro señor, siendo glotones de carne humana [they lived outside the law of God our Lord, being gluttons of human flesh]" (119). Also outside of Chiametla in Cacalotlán, in the "sierra alta y fragosa, les habían muerto y comido muchas mujeres e hijos [tall and (densely) overgrown mountains they had killed and eaten many women and children]" (120). At times it seems that Obregón uses a variety of monikers interchangeably, with little or no distinction between *los serranos, fieros bárbaros,* and *los caribes,* all presumed sodomites who eat human flesh. Not coincidentally, these circumstances are more often than not described within what Obregón seems to perceive as the periphery of emerging or potential centers.

The only instances of association between anthropophagi and what Obregón views as a permanent settlement occur in two cases. The first is in Topia, where "cómense unos enemigos a otros; halláronse infinidad de huesos y calaveras de los que mataban y comían [the enemies ate one another; finding there an infinite number of bones and skulls of those they would kill and eat]" (87), and where he ultimately decides that the Acaxee cannot be Christianized or pacified. The second is in Cumupa (home to the Opata): "Son belicosos como gente de frontera y raza de los querechos, los cual mostraron por las insignias que tenían en su pueblo y casas de altos maderos en las calles, y cantillos colgados de cuerpos muertos, cabezas, brazos, piernas, lenguas y orejas, repartidos y divididos en todas las calles, lo cual hacen como gente cruel y carnicera [They are bellicose people, on the frontier with the *querecho* race, which showed by the insignias that they had on the streets of their town and houses of tall wood, where dead bodies, heads, arms, legs, tongues and ears hung about, distributed and divided throughout the streets; they do (this) as cruel and murderous people]" (160). However, when the residents explain to Obregón that the hanging body parts represent a "señal de victoria [sign of victory]" over their enemies, and are not the byproducts of consumption, Obregón accepts this explanation. Thus, only in the case of Topia is the link between anthropophagi and permanent settlement made and maintained by Obregón, while this moniker is overwhelmingly associated with mountain-dwelling peoples.

In addition to identifying a group as hostile, the epithet *caribe* (human) is perennially linked throughout the text to "serranías fronteras" (land). Caribes recurrently tend to be depicted as barbarous people who occupy the untamed and unwieldy "nonplace" of the mountains (which as noted previously had served the indigenous inhabitants quite well), the periphery that has yet to be incorporated into the center. Rooted in the European tradition in which the city-versus-wilderness trope had abounded in theology and philosophy since Aristotle, the "barbarian" was a savage, wild man that lived alone in the wilderness without religion or society (Barrera 2001, 29). The notion of the "barbaric frontier" arrived in the Americas fully intact with explorers who no doubt had difficulty viewing the regions outside of the architectural center of Tenochtitlán as civilized. Interestingly, the spatial binary of center/periphery exemplified in Obregón's textualscape seems to correlate directly to and be inextricable from the human notion of civilized/barbarian, with the latter exacerbated in the constantly contested northern frontier that Obregón presents. For example, the mountain-dwelling people who occupy the "periphery" of the "center" of Culiacán are depicted as wild, marauding rebels:

En este tiempo y sazón, antes y después de haber poblado y conquistado el gobernador Nuño de Guzmán la provincia de San Miguel de Culiacán, han estado los más pueblos e indios de las serranías alzados y rebelados contra los vecinos y moradores de ella y contra sus pueblos, haciendas y esclavos que están y asisten en sus fronteras. De ordinario les han molestado y hecho notables daños, matándoles y comiéndolos a ellos y a sus mujeres e hijos, cautivándolos y quitándoles sus mantenimientos y haciendas, quemábanles sus casas, traíanlos amedrentados, cuidadosos y congojados. Asimismo mataban a los criados y esclavos de los señores de haciendas y estancias y no les dejaban ganado seguro ni casa que no les quemasen. De manera que aconteció que hacer junta general de los rebeldes y entrar de guerra en la villa de noche con gran osadía, coraje, desvergüenza y con gran alboroto y vocería; robaron cuanto podían, hasta los ornamentos que hallaron puestos en la iglesia. . . . Bebían como brutos animales carniceros de su propia naturaleza humana; comíanse unos a otros haciendo extrañas crueldades en los que cautivaban, tomaban y robaban y lo mismo en los caminantes, tratantes.

[During this period, before and after being settled and conquered by the governor Nuño de Guzmán, the province of San Miguel de Culiacán had the most rebellious mountain towns and Indian uprisings against the settlers and inhabitants and against its towns, properties and slaves that are in and about its frontiers. They frequently harassed them and had done notable damage to them, killing and eating them and their women and children, kidnapping them and taking their supplies and properties from them, burning their houses, and making them terrified, worried, and distressed. In addition, they would kill the servants and slaves of the lords of the properties and ranches, and there was no cattle left safe nor house that they did not burn down. And so it happened that the Indians formed a group of rebels to enter into war; they entered the town at night with great temerity, audacity and impudence and with great uproar and shouting; they stole as much as they could, even the ornaments that they

found placed in the church. . . . Like brutal, murderous animals they
ate of their own kind; they would eat one another, committing strange
cruelties to those they captured, stealing and robbing and they did the
same to the travelers (and) merchants.] (92)

Of course, Obregón is describing people who themselves had fled in fear
from the violence and forced labor of the encomienda, seeking refuge in the
mountains where they could find escape and shelter and launch resistance
against the Spanish. However, as Obregón puts it, it is the Spanish who are
at the mercy of the "indios del despoblado [Indians of the wilderness]" that
occupy the "tierras de guerra [lands of war]" surrounding Culiacán (93).

While the twenty-first-century reader may be struck by the contradiction
of using *despoblado* (which would have communicated the notion of unin-
habited wilderness) to describe an area and its inhabitants and "guerra" to
describe indigenous defense, the reader may equally recognize that these
terms help us to better understand Obregón's worldview: lands not populated
by Europeans—or at least by a civilization "readable" to him—were simply
not populated, and lands in which Spanish encroachment was resisted were
by default lands of war. Furthermore, the indigenous people are depicted as
wild and animalistic and are accused of anthropophagy, although Obregón
does not witness this practice himself. Obregón is also quick to point out that
under Ibarra, these barbarous people have been "re-encomendados" and
have promised to "recognize, pay tribute to, and obey their encomendero,
don Pedro de Tovar" (93).[21] This indicates that the "policía, razón y buenas
costumbres [civilization, reason and good customs]" that are the prerequi-
sites for order and civilization can indeed be imparted to the indigenous
peoples near Culiacán, albeit with effort and proper leadership.

The center-versus-periphery trope is repeated when the expedition
begins exploring Chiametla, a region also once raided by the infamous
Nuño de Guzmán and subsequently abandoned after the indigenous population rebelled and took it back. Despite its turbulent history, the soldiers
are intrigued by Chiametla, famous for its riches of gold and silver, clothing, lands, pastures, fish, salt, and fruits, all of which "levantaron a muchos
los ánimos y pensamientos a que deseasen, codiciasen y pretendiesen la
conquista y pacificación de ella después que se le despobló a Nuño de
Guzmán [raised the spirits and thoughts of those who desired, coveted, and
hoped for the conquest and pacification of (Chiametla) after (the Indians)
ran away from Nuño de Guzmán" (115). The narration indicates that Chiametla does not disappoint.

Asomaron trescientos *gandules* en mucho concierto y ordenanza de guerra, lucidos, galanes y compuestos de mucha plumería, conchas, caracoles y dijes de la mar, con arcos, flechas, lanzuelas, macanas y rodelas. Y con esta orden, concierto y recato recibieron al gobernador y los de su campo con mucho respeto, amor y comedimiento y con presente de muchas [*sic*] gallos y gallinas de la tierra, maíz, frijol, calabaza, frutas y caza y lo demás necesario para los caballos y servicio personal. . . . Ofreciéronse a la ayuda y pacificación y conquista de *los caribes serranos, gente salvaje, vil y villana, indómita y glotona de carne humana* y tan *fiera* que por gala trae cola y espejo en la trasera, *aunque belicosa y valiente.* Habitan y asisten ocho leguas del río de Chiametla en las sierras ásperas, quebradas cóncavas y riscos de su altura, la cual [gente] de ordinario había sido contraria y enemiga de los de Chiametla.

[Three hundred *gandules* appeared in great organization and martial order, resplendent, strong, and arrayed with much plumage, sea shells, and ornaments of the sea, with bows, arrows, small lances, clubs and shields. With order, concert and prudence they received the governor and those of his expedition with much respect, love and restraint, and with gifts of many chickens and hens of the earth, maize, beans, squash, fruits and game and other things necessary for the horses and personal service. . . . They offered themselves to assist in the pacification and conquest of the *caribes serranos, savage* people, *vile and despicable, indomitable gluttons of human flesh* and so wild that they wear cues and mirrors on their backs as regalia, *they all be bellicose and strong.* They inhabit eight leagues of the river of Chiametla in the rough sierras, deep gorges and tall cliffs; they regularly had been adversarial and enemies of those of Chiametla.] (118–19, my emphasis)

First, Obregón subtly yet clearly differentiates himself and the Spanish from the aborigines with his use of *gandul*—a term used for a militia of Moors in Africa and Granada and employed by the Spanish in the Americas to refer to any "bellicose Indian."[22] Of course, as a criollo born in Campostela, Obregón would not have had any first-hand experience with Moors in Africa or Granada, but here he aligns himself with a particularly Spanish "we" in opposition to a "they." He then goes on to describe the warriors of Chiametla very positively and largely in terms of their adornment and cultivation. Lastly, he depicts the caribes serranos in terms antithetical to those used to describe the Indians of Chiametla. These are "gente indómita y glotona de carne humana [indomitable gluttons of human flesh]" (although once again there is no direct evidence of anthropophagy cited).

After spending roughly eleven months in the environs of Chiametla, Ibarra departs and leads his expedition on a seven-month journey that reaches as far north as Paquimé (modern-day Casas Grandes, Chihuahua) during which time the group comes in contact with Pima-Tepehuán, Yaqui-Mayo, and Opata-Eudeve peoples referenced previously. On their first encounter with "indios serranos" after leaving Chiametla, the expedition's top priority is to find out from the outlying populace through the interpreter "cuántos pueblos había en aquella sierra y comarca y de qué calidades, cantidad y partes y qué vestían y comían [How many villages there were in that mountain chain and its environs and of what qualities, quantity and areas and what they wore and ate]" (147–48). The serranos tell them about people farther along in Oera.[23]

> Hay gente de mucha más policía que ellos, así de casas como de vestidos y bastimentos; y que los serranos habitan en casas de terrado para ampararse del frío y que las suyas son de cañas de estera para amparo de la [sic] gran calor que hace en sus tierras; y que la gente de adelante viste mantas de algodón y pita de magueyes pequeños y cogen mucho maíz, frijol, calabaza y melones, tunas y pitahayas y muchos géneros de caza y pescado de todos géneros, en todo lo cual trataron verdad porque así lo vimos.

> [(They) are people of much greater civilization in terms of housing, clothing and supplies; and the serranos (of Oera) inhabit earthen houses in order to protect themselves from the cold, while theirs are made of reed mats for protection from the great heat that occurs in their lands; and the advance people dress in cloth of cotton and thread from small maguey plants and they harvest much maize, bean(s), squash and melons, prickly pears and dragon fruit and many types of game and fish of all kinds, all of which is true because we saw it like this.] (148)

Again there is an aspiration to find a potential "center," and a narrative pattern emerges in which the peoples of the periphery that reside outside of a center are quickly dismissed as beneath those residing in the (perceived) center. In the emerging human hierarchy, identities are invented in opposition to one another and then transported from landscape to landscape, typically in terms of cultural markers the Spanish aspire to see and the establishment of a center of power from which to operate. Moreover, there remain those "uninhabitable" regions that are presented as the hostile passage, the space covered and the uncivilized people who (oxymoronically) inhabit the "uninhabitable."

Despidióse de éstos [los serranos] y fue marchando el campo por las más hondas y espantosas sierras y quebradas que pasamos en aquella provincia; eran de extraña oscuridad y peñolería, de manera que gozan poco de la claridad y luz del sol. *Hallamos que en estas espantosas cóncavas y cuevas de esta inhabitable serranía visten* de cueros de venados, pocas mantas de pita, andan los más *desnudos*, traen crecido el cabello hasta el ombligo, cubren sus lugares secretos con cueros de venado, traen caperuzas de mismo cuero puntiagudas. Es su *habitación* en estas hondables quebradas por gozar el vino de maguey y de uvas silvestres. Fueron llamados del fraile, guías e intérpreta [*sic*], los cuales no quisieron aguardar razones, antes se pusieron en huída desamparando sus *rústicas habitaciones*. En esta *inhabitable tierra* anduvo el campo tres jornadas en las cuales pasaron los soldados intolerable trabajo, oscuridad y peligro de sus vidas porque pocos indios nos podían estorbar el paso y salida o matarnos desde lo alto echando a rodas peñascos y flechándonos . . . salimos a lo alto aunque la subida fue por altas sierras, riscos y quebradas pobladas de cantidad de robles, pinos y albarradones, vetas de metales y muchas señales y rastro de metales.

[(Ibarra) took leave of these people (serranos) and continued marching his camp by way of the deepest and most frightening sierras and gorges that we passed in that province; they were strangely dark and mountainous, to where they enjoy little of the clarity of the light of the sun. *We found that in these frightening concavities and caves of this uninhabitable mountain chain* they dress in deer skins, a few blankets of hemp fiber, and most go about nude, they wear their hair grown down to the bellybutton, they cover their secret places with deer skins, wear head coverings of the same sharp material. Their *dwellings* are in these deep gorges so that they (may) enjoy the wine of the maguey and of wild grapes. They were called upon by the friar, guides and interpreter (who did not want to wait for a pretext) before they fled, abandoning their *rustic dwellings*. In this *uninhabitable land* the expedition walked three days march in which the soldiers experienced intolerable trials, darkness, and danger of their lives because a few Indians could block our passage and exit or kill us from above, tossing rocks and shooting arrows at us . . . we exited at the top, although the climb was by way of tall sierras, cliffs and gorges populated by a quantity of oak trees, pines and ramparts, seams of metals and many signs and traces of metals.] (148–49, my emphasis)

As the expedition travels on, the term *querecho* is employed to describe the "uncivilized" people who resist the Spanish encroachment or who are enemies of those who do not. Outside of Guaraspi, according to Obregón, the mountain-dwelling herdsmen deceive the Spanish by leading them into rough lands, spying on the Spanish, and stealing their horses, all offenses which, despite being "the most valiant and strong people of these provinces," leads Obregón to call them "querechos" (159). Just as the Spanish and Nahua auxiliary soldiers glibly employed the term *chichimeca* in reference to any and all indigenous groups north of Mesoamerica, Obregón applies the moniker *querecho* to any indigenous group that is "savage" in his view (Hopkins Durazo 1988, 28). Similarly in Sahuaripa, Obregón describes the town as surrounded by savages: "en la frontera de los indios de los llanos, gente la más diestra, belicosa y cursada en el uso y ejercicio de la guerra de todas las demás naciones y provincias, hasta los vaqueros llamados querechos con los cuales tienen guerra [on the frontier of the plains Indians, the most bellicose, warlike, and skilled in the exercises of war of all the other nations and provinces, as far as the herdsmen called *querechos* with whom they are at war" (163).

Interestingly, at Sahuaripa Obregón holds the people in esteem despite a days-long battle fought there; it emerges as the "center" outside of which reside the bellicose *querechos*. That is, despite their resistance, the people of Sahuaripa are not counted out, perhaps because they reside in a permanent settlement and Obregón recognizes their determination to defend themselves and their women and children (169). Resistance is not the only determinant of frontiers, and human hierarchy, it seems, is negotiable. In Obregón's textualscape perhaps no site better exemplifies this than Paquimé, which he describes in detail in chapter 30 of book 1.

Located in present-day Casas Grandes, Paquimé is an archeological site that dates back to the eighth century; a multistory adobe pueblo that was once one of the largest of the pueblo towns. For three centuries (c. 1060–1340) it was a major trading and spiritual center with extensive irrigation for sedentary agriculture.[24] As it stood in 1563 before Spanish explorers, Paquimé would have represented the built landscape par excellence, and its architecture impresses Obregón, who likens its structures to those of the ancient Romans. The buildings are a marvel to see, Obregón insists, and are six or seven stories high, sturdy whitewashed structures with patios, towers, and stoves for heating during the winter. He raves about the beautiful, fertile river valley that could easily be irrigated at little cost, and the shady, bountiful mountains that surround the valley. A system of canals is already in place and paved roads are found. Finally, the group finds metal slag and copper plates worked from molds "as if made by skilled Spanish artisans" (181–82). Obregón views the numerous advantages that the place holds for settlement: fertile land, access to water, permanent structures, protection from enemies, and, perhaps above all else, precious metals. Despite all of this, he describes the people living in the area surrounding the abandoned structure as "silvestre animales." Epstein has argued that, while never stated overtly, Obregón concludes that the former inhabitants of Paquimé must have worked the metal, and not the indigenous people who present it to him. This seems highly plausible given his description:

> Había cerca de ellas [las casas] gente silvestre, rústica y advenediza que dejaban de habitar en casas de tanta grandeza por asistir y morar en bohíos de paja como silvestres animales al sol, aire y fríos. Son cazadores, comen todo género de caza y sabandijas silvestres y bellotas. Andan desnudos; ellas traen faldellines de cuero de venado adobado y algunos de las vacas.

> [Near the houses there were wild, rustic and wandering people that had quit living in houses of such grandeur so they could reside in straw huts like wild animals in the sun, wind, and cold. They are hunters, they eat all type of game and wild reptiles and acorns. The men go about naked; the women wear skirts of tanned deer skin or cowhide.] (182)

Once again noting shelter, diet, and clothing, the people are represented negatively. Yet concurrently Obregón recognizes the site of Paquimé as one of potential, even reasoning that the people that populate the river of Paquimé can be "sujetas y señoreadas [subjugated and ruled]" (182). However, the soldiers remain disillusioned with Paquimé despite the virtues that Obregón perceives: "La buena esperanza que les había sostenido de descubrir grandes poblazones, según y como tenían noticia, lo cual duró hasta que llegaron a esa ciudad despoblada de Paquimé, adonde del todo perdieron sus buenas esperanzas en no verla poblada de gentes conforme a la medida de sus deseos e imaginativa [The great hope that had sustained them of discovering great towns, according to the account they had heard, which lasted until they arrived to this abandoned city of Paquimé, where all lost their good hopes were lost upon not seeing it populated by people according to the measure of their desires and imagination]" (183).

The plurality of perception is evident. While the architectural structures are impressive, and Obregón sees potential for permanent settlement, the soldiers do not *based solely on their perceptions of the people*. It is my view that Paquimé exemplifies the tensions that exist in landscape perception even among those of ostensibly the same culture and worldview. The soldiers and Obregón do not seem to view the same landscape, and Obregón certainly differentiates himself from the "cobardes soldados" (186). While the soldiers continue to insist on finding a landscape that reflects the landscape of their minds, "Otro México" or "Otro Perú," the criollo views the land strategically as part of a broader imperial society.

Conclusions

Much like an image drawn on a transparency that is laid over another image, Obregón's textualscape lays over an a priori indigenous landscape. While this may eclipse much of that landscape, ethnohistorical studies help to illuminate it, helping us recognize the fissures that exist in *Historia* that reveal multiple landscapes. Moreover, during a period of radical changes, the identities that these multiple landscapes inform would have been constantly up for grabs—negotiated and renegotiated, constructed and reconstructed. The erection of frontiers emerges as part and parcel of this process. Time and time again Obregón depicts the borderlands as areas that need to be brought under imperial control, repeatedly employing the trinity "conquistado, pacificado y poblado [conquered, pacified, and settled]"—all actions imparted by the larger Empire onto the existing, indigenous landscape and always carried out by hastily erected "centers" in the peripheries of the periphery.

Throughout this textualscape the reader is confronted with spatial frontiers imposed by the author—mountains versus plains, desert versus riverbed—but which are just as often delineated in human terms. The culturally constructed system of glib binaries (in Obregón's words, "salvaje"/ "de policía," "serrano"/ "pueblo," "caribe"/ "no comen carne humana," "desnudo"/ "vestido," "silvestre"/ "cultivan la tierra," and "infieles"/ "cristianos") allows for fluidity, portability, and flexibility in depicting indigenous groups. Even when groups are described positively at first, they may quickly be dismissed as savages inhabiting the "uninhabitable," and those described negatively can at least be "subjugated" if residing in desirable lands. Furthermore, "los naturales" (a term that only reinforces their closer association with the wild, untamed realm of nature), regardless of their depiction as "salvajes" or "gente de policía," by virtue of these terms are depicted en masse. The indigenous individual disappears into the imperial landscape. With the exception of Luisa the interpreter, Obregón does not describe with any significant detail any indigenous individual.[25]

The multiple frontiers found in the *Historia*, spatial and corporal, are repeatedly defined and redefined by a hierarchical conception of civilization by humans rooted in the Spanish cultural markers of clothing, permanent shelter, and cultivation. Obregón's descriptions of people would have been informed by an Aristotelian hierarchy that informed the "historias naturales y morales," a new literary genre which had emerged by the mid-sixteenth century that incorporated cosmographical and historical traditions wherein "the natural world sustains human beings' moral actions, that is, actions stemming from God-given free will. . . . man's moral soul and free will placed him in a category apart from other creatures inhabiting the natural world, at the apex of a natural hierarchy and yet distinct from it" (Portuondo 2009, 31–32). Frontiers in Obregón's textualscape are established without regard to cultural identities but rather solely to Obregón's perceptions of civilization and barbarity. The human hierarchy that emerges from this process does not account for territoriality, ethnicity, parochial politics, language, ecology, cosmology, and so much more, revealing as much about his cultural attitudes and personal values for what it omits as it does for what it includes.

Recalling the moment of emergence from the horrifying "tierras de los infieles" when Obregón describes a return to the "buenas tierras" of Guaraspi, he warrants that these lands and people are the best of all that Ibarra traversed in the region, and they are compared positively against their warring neighbors, the querechos (159–60). However, Obregón ultimately concludes that they are "codiciosos, ladrones, cautelosos [greedy, thieving, and sneaky]" (159). Hopkins Durazo (1988) points to this description's contradictions: how strange it is that at first Obregón perceives them as more civilized ("better behaved and more urbane") only to condemn them later (27). In addition, although Obregón concedes that the region is "the best from the Valley of Sonora to Sahuaripa," he rejects Cabeza de Vaca's view of the landscape of Guaraspi as the best and most fertile land of the Indies:

> Porque aunque es abundante de bastimentos, hay muy poco algodón y es tierra muy cerrada y espesa de arcabucos y montañas y áspera de sierras y en extremo cálida y poblada del árbol ponzoñoso. Pedregosa y la gente

de ella ladrona, traidora y desnuda por la mayor parta hasta empezar a entrar en las faldas de la sierra, en tierras templadas, que empiezan casas de terrado.

[Because although abundant in supplies, there is little cotton and the land is very closed (off) and thick with impenetrable vegetation and mountains and rough mountains and extremely dry and inhabited by the poisonous tree. (It is) rocky and the people of it are thieving, traitorous and naked for the most part until beginning to enter the hillsides of the sierra, in temperate lands, where earthen houses begin.] (174)

Obregón's personal hierarchy aside, can these contradicting perceptions of the landscape be explained by cultural difference, such as those noted previously between the European and the indigenous? While Cabeza de Vaca, a peninsular, and Obregón, a criollo, were born on opposite sides of the Atlantic, would they have not shared many of the same cultural attitudes? One may speculate to a certain degree that these differing visions are, at least in part, due to the odyssey that Cabeza de Vaca had experienced, a ten year trek that certainly would have affected his landscape perceptions. Westphal, in fact, embraces Cabeza de Vaca as a great man who defied his cultural background, took the "prison" of space, and not only confronted it, but conformed to its dimensions and conditions. "He agreed to leave it open. Practically, he became naked. He faced what was for him a parallel reality. He defied the suspension of bearings, standards. He accepted the challenge, and this allowed him to probe space and pure humanity with it, through it" (Westphal 2013, 105). [26] The difference in perception may also belie Obregón's criollo identity and desires as elucidated in chapter 1. I propose that an equally compelling factor is that Obregón perceives the landscape through the lens of the mission of evangelization and mining, a lens that filters his perception of various lands and the peoples shaping them.

CHAPTER FOUR

(Re)producing Social Space and Textualscapes

The place of the past in any landscape is as much the product of present interest as of past history.
—DAVID LOWENTHAL, 1975

Haunted places are the only ones people can live in.
—MICHEL DE CERTEAU, 1984

Sensory stimuli are potentially infinite: that which we choose to attend (value or love) is an accident of individual temperament, purpose, and of the cultural forces at work at a particular time.
—YI-FU TUAN, 1974

As Phelan succinctly observes, "No colonial empire in modern times was built upon so extensive a philosophical and theological foundation as that empire which the Spaniards created for themselves in the New World" (1970, 5). Perhaps no document better illuminates the overlapping convergence of this theological foundation with an economic one than Las Ordenanzas of 1573. Composed with the aim of outlining the policies of settlement in all of the Americas in both philosophical and economic terms, the document represents what Vas Mingo calls the "crystallization of a new policy" steeped in ethical and religious thinking that "unites Christian morality and justice with political and commercial interests" (Vas Mingo 1985, 98). In addition to forbidding the entry of unlicensed parties into new lands under the penalty of death and loss of property, as well as condemning the loaded term *conquistar* in favor of the euphemistic *pacificar*, the Las Ordenanzas make explicit that any lands appropriated for Spain must be

101

those "de indios y naturales a quien se pueda predicar el evangelio pues este es el principal fin para que mandamos hazer los nuevos descubrimientos y poblaciones [of Indians and natives who can be evangelized, as this is the principal end for which we order new discoveries and settlements to be made]" (*Transcripción* 1973, 36). This is emblematic of what Ahern (2002) has identified as the shifting project of northward expansion taking place in the mid-sixteenth century, when a more pragmatic project of establishing mining settlements and converting indigenous populations was replacing the days of dreams of miracles and mythic golden cities. "Hacia 1564, 'la Nueva España de los primeros tiempos, la de los conquistadores y misoneros intrépidos, la de las conversiones masivas y casi milagrosas, ya no era más que un recuerdo' [Toward 1564 'The New Spain of the early days, the con-quistadors and intrepid missionaries, of the mass and almost miraculous conversions were now nothing more than a memory']" (Solange Alberro, quoted in Solodkow 2009, 113).

If world view is necessarily constructed out of the social and physical setting, as Tuan (1974, 79) argues, in addition to culture, Obregón's textu-alscape is informed in equal measure by his sociohistoric circumstances and the mining milieu of an expanding New Spain. In this context, the competing interests of evangelization and securing a large pool of forced labor are informed by two intimately related and human-based practices: (1) the de facto conversion of people to Christianity and (2) the distribution of land and people under the economic systems of slavery, encomienda and *repartimiento*.

The Christian Frontier

Although the roles of religious *reducciones* and missions in northern Mex-ico were paramount beginning in the 1590s when Jesuit missionaries began to establish themselves in the region, in 1584 Obregón would have been writing about a region precariously held with crosses and but a few rustic structures.[1] To that point, the evangelization of indigenous peoples in the region had been under the purview of the Franciscans, who, beginning in the 1550s, enjoyed exclusive jurisdiction over the conversion of the Tepe-huanes (Jones 1988, 28). The first missionary to evangelize in the region, Fray Juan de Tapia, reached the Guadiana Valley in 1556, establishing a temporary mission among the Tepehuanes. During his one-month stay he reports having administered 2,500 baptisms, however, the area would not be revisited again until 1561 when Francisco de Ibarra escorted a group of four Franciscans from San Martín (20–21). Although one missionary, Gerónimo de Mendoza, had died, the three that remained, Pedro de Espinareda, Diego de la Carrera, and Jacinto de San Francisco established the first permanent mission at Nombre de Dios, a "crude structure of adobe walls topped by a straw roof" (21). The next friars to evangelize in the north were those that accompanied Ibarra on his expedition two years later, Fray Pablo Azevedo, Brother Juan de Herrera, and a third whose name is unknown. Obregón's support of these friars is clear throughout his text, and he insists that "la cosa más útil y conveniente en la guerra es llevar frailes [The most useful and advisable thing in war is to bring along friars]" (199).

By the time of Obregón's writing, the Franciscans, desirous to locate new populations and convert them to Christianity, wanted to take advantage of this period of northward expansion. A mendicant order that vowed poverty, chastity, and obedience, the Franciscan project in the New World "inherited a rich eschatological tradition expressed in a spirit of apocalyptic conversion" (West 1989, 293). Many Franciscans believed themselves to be the evangelical order of the Third Age on the basis of the twelfth-century writings of Joachim of Fiore, who predicted an evangelical order would convert the world and lead it into an age of peace. "Spain is interpreted as the spiritual Jerusalem to whom God has shown a new world to save" (311). Combined with the steps taken by the Crown in 1572 to replace Franciscans with secular clergy so as to rein in their power, and the dwindling numbers of neophytes in Central Mexico because of Western diseases, this conversion mission took on an "urgency to action" for friars who set their sights on the populations to the north (West 1989; Phelan 1970). "By the time the century ended, the friars were left with but two alternatives—to retire peacefully to their monasteries or to transfer their missionary enthusiasm to the colonial frontiers among the less civilized natives" (Phelan 1970, 54).

Throughout the *Historia*, Obregón cites Ibarra's insistence on the primacy of building a church or placing a cross in a central location of the pueblo visited.[2] Directly after founding the villas of Nombre de Dios and Durango, Ibarra "Puso y edificó por su mano el cimiento y primer edificio de las iglesias para el ejemplo de los de su campo [Placed and built by his own hand the cement and first building of the churches for the example of all of his men]" (75). This process of erecting crosses to mark Christian territory had already begun with Álvar Núñez Cabeza de Vaca: "When conversion of the Indians was sealed . . . they were entreated to mark their villages with the Christian emblem and to meet the Spanish with crosses, not bows" (Ahern 1993, 224). This also informed indigenous perception of

Europeans. Obregón relates how "querechos," recalling Cabeza de Vaca, expect Ibarra's group to perform a ritual similar to the one that Cabeza de Vaca had performed: "Eran muy continos [*sic*] e importunos a que los tocásemos y santiguásemos, que es ceremonia que uso Álvar Núñez Cabeza de Vaca" (179).

Fray Marcos de Niza and other Franciscan friars likewise utilized the cross as a sign to demarcate territory: "Fray Marcos and Esteban agreed upon a code of crosses that would transmit geographical information about the territory" (Ahern 1993, 226). Just as the act of naming referred to in chapter 2 serves as a means of Christianizing the landscape, the act of demarcating space with a cross establishes a Christian frontier, an act repeated throughout the duration of the Ibarra Expedition. In Topia, for example, not only is a huge cross erected, but any and every indigenous idol hidden high and away in the mountains and caves that can be found is buried underneath it, a common practice among Franciscan missionaries.[3] The space is appropriated as "Christian" by the symbolic placing of the cross, but the cross also writes over the indigenous religious symbols as if they were a palimpsest. Obregón relates that in Cinaro (Río Fuerte region) the cross also appropriates space, and the intention to repeat this act demonstrates its function in the larger agenda of *pacificación*.

[El maestre de campo] Tomó por defensor y abogado de ella al santo apóstol y evangelista San Juan y para su principio hizo, amasó y empezó el primer barro, cimiento y tapia, de manera que con su solicitud trabajo y cuidado fue fundada la iglesia en la provincia de Cinaro. . . . Puso el maese de campo en el patio de la iglesia un altar y hermosa cruz y por consiguiente la mandó poner en medio de todos los pueblos comarcanos a la villa.

· [(The first lieutenant) took as defender and advocate of it the holy apostle and evangelist Saint John and to start he made, mixed and set the first mortar, cement, and wall, in such a way that with soliciting work and care, the church was founded in the province of Cinaro. . . . The first lieutenant put an altar and a beautiful cross in the patio of the church and next ordered that one (a cross) be put in the middle of all of the pueblos surrounding the villa.] (108)

The cross acts as a semiotic tool in the ceremonial act of taking possession in the Roman tradition, marking presence on the land and declaring intent to remain, but it should be noted that the cross is not limited to the land (Seed 1993, 112). Antonio de Espejo reports that the querechos he encounters in the Valle de Señora are wearing crosses on their foreheads because Francisco Sánchez Chamuscado, who had been there before Espejo, had ordered them to wear them so that future Spanish explorers could read this as a sign not to harm them.[4] The cross functions as synecdoche, signifying intent to remain, but also signifying the Church and Christianity, "expand[ing] a spatial element in order to make it play the role of a 'more' (a totality) and take its place" (dc Certeau 1984, 101). In this way, the vestige of the cross alters the physical landscape as well as the "spiritual landscape," to borrow a term from Harley (1989, 294). This is evinced by Obregón in the case of Chiametla, where the cross serves the semiotic function of taking possession in the interim of church construction:

> En la provincia de Chiametla y frontera de tierra de cristianos, tomó posesión el gobernador de la provincia de Chiametla, que es frontera de tierra de cristianos, en nombre de vuestra S.C.C.R.M., lo cual fue por mano y testimonio de su secretario Sebastián de Quirós y firma. Mandó hacer una iglesia y él por su mano enarboló y puso una alta cruz en medio del pueblo.

> [In the province of Chiametla and frontier of land of Christians, the governor took possession of the province of Chiametla, which is frontier of Christian lands, in the name of your Sacred Cesarean Catholic Royal Majesty, which was done by the hand and testimony of his secretary, Sebastián de Quirós, and signed. He ordered a church be built and by his own had he hoisted and placed a tall cross in the middle of the town.] (118)

In addition to communicating the establishment of a "frontera de tierra de cristianos," erecting a cross would also demonstrate the expedition's adherence to the orders and instructions given to the Ibarra Expedition by the viceroy, and Obregón is emphatic about how those orders are carried out in the Christian way. From the inauguration of the expedition at San Martín, Ibarra orders the reading of the instructions given to him by the viceroy, Luis de Velazco, insisting to his men that they be carried out with "mucha cristiandad, equidad y concierto de acertada guerra y modo de proceder en ella; las cuales siempre hizo guardar, cumplir y ejecutar con gran prudencia, cristiandad y cuidado, en cuyos efectos y su cumplimiento siempre hubo conformidad y cristiano efecto [with much Christianity, equity and accordance of proper war and war procedure; he always observed, fulfilled and executed the orders with great prudence, Christianity and care in their results and their compliance there was always conformity and Christian effect]" (73). Although the Ibarra expedition had taken place before the newer set of edicts had come into being in 1573, Obregón composed *Historia* during their mandate, and the importance that expeditions follow a Christian code of behavior in expanding the mining enterprise would certainly have filtered down from the vice regal bureaucracy. Demonstrating compliance to the Christian mission would have been imperative to establishing the legitimacy of the exploration, but Obregón also insists that in future endeavors, explorers "guarden las ordenanzas de guerra y minas . . . con cristiana equidad [observe the orders of war and mining . . . with Christian equity]" (204). While Obregón certainly proclaims this to demonstrate compliance, his arguments reveal two other motivations for carrying out these explorations with care and consideration: his messianic mentality and the more secular consideration of successfully establishing mining operations.

Obregón expounds at length throughout the text on the spiritual nature of the Ibarra Expedition and his own personal religious conviction, often employing Biblical exegesis and elaborating theological arguments that reflect the debates of his day. He is emphatic that the conversion project is paramount to all worldly endeavors and writes at length on the spiritual responsibilities of the encomienda system. His extensive theological musings and repeated insistence on a just conversion process are demonstrative of a sincere zeal for the Christian mission. While material gain motivated explorers (Obregón himself refers frequently to the greed and shortsightedness of his fellow soldiers), others, including he, were fueled in equal part by a messianic mission. Their zeal stemmed from the common belief of their day that the world was awaiting a new age of peace, one that depended on the salvation of the natives. Just as the conquest was not exclusively carried out by soldiers but rather miners, sailors, merchants, friars, townspeople, secretaries, and members of the lower nobility, the messianic mission was not the exclusive terrain of the missionaries. Apocalyptic thinking extended outside the religious realm, and Obregón views the landscape in terms of divine Providence, Godly intervention in the secular world, and above all else, the conversion mandate.

While it is not clear from the text that Obregón shares any of the apocalyptic notions held by many missionaries and explorers of the time, he definitively places the conversion of the indigenous peoples in a "universal" historical framework rooted in what he calls, "Católica memoria." He shares with the Franciscan missionaries a firmly held belief in divine

Providence in which the Spanish are a chosen people and part of God's larger plan. The (erroneous) coincidence that Obregón draws between the birth of Martin Luther and that of Hernán Cortés referred to in chapter 1 intimates that he shared the commonly held conviction of his day that the project of Spanish expansion in the New World was absolutely a matter of divine Providence in which "the Spanish race under the leadership of her 'blessed kings' had been chosen to undertake the final conversion of the Jews, the Moslems, and the Gentiles" (Phelan 1970, 11).

> Tiénese por experiencia verdadera que los descubrimientos de gentes, naciones y tierras nuevas han estado y están ocultas hasta que Dios nuestro Señor es servido llegue el tiempo de su limitación y orden acordada por su divino concierto, cuyo secreto de estar mucha suma de años sin descubrirse es reservado al altísimo secreto de Dios nuestro Señor, porque vemos que en nuestros tiempos se han descubierto y sujetado gran suma de naciones de gentes.

> [It is taken as truth that the discoveries of peoples, nations and new lands have been and are hidden until God our Lord is served and it is determined according to His divine will that the time has arrived, whose secret of existence for so many years without being discovered is reserved to the most high secret of God our Lord, because we see that in our time a great number of nations and peoples have been discovered and subjugated.] (Obregón 1584, 227)

His use of *nosotros* indicates more than his mere participation in the expedition; rather, it signifies his inclusion in the providential plan. In "nuestros tiempos" ("our time"), argues Obregón, these nations are being discovered and subjugated by the Spanish Empire, an empire of which he is a part and in whose expansion project he has been an active participant. Of all the known nations, none is equal to Spain, reasons Obregón, and it is by the holy Catholic faith, the Sacred Scriptures, doctrine, and theology, that Spain has vanquished enemies and subjected strange, remote nations, protecting them with "el tesoro de nuestra inestimable Fe católica [the treasure of our inestimable Catholic Faith]" (178). It is only by His mercy and permission that the miracles that have occurred in the Indies have occurred, so as to save the "bárbaros infieles" (178).[5]

His belief in miracles and strongly held conviction that the discovery of a new world is providential bespeak Obregón's adherence to the medieval view of the active intervention of God and the Devil in its fulfillment. The result is a textualscape replete with both divine and diabolic acts in the secular world. Particularly, the expedition's successes are credited to the acts of a merciful God aiding, protecting, and defending the Spanish soldiers in the terrifying landscape of the borderlands.[6] Yet, while God is doubtless on the side of the Crown and by extension the expedition, the evangelizing mission is threatened by the Devil who conspires to undermine Spanish efforts to convert the natives to Christianity. This occurs principally in moments when either indigenous inhabitants or Spanish soldiers are inspired by the Devil to perform violent or evil acts, bringing the violence occurring on the borderlands to the forefront and the contentious issue of forceful conversion.

The issue of forceful conversion continued to be debated at length in Spain and the New World, culminating, but not ending in the Junta de Valladolid (1550–51).[7] This debate had caused philosophical and moral tension not only between soldiers and missionaries but also internally between and within different religious orders. A subtle example of this tension occurs when a Franciscan friar in Jalisco refuses Obregón's confession because of the former's contention that soldiers kill indigenous inhabitants: "Quise confesarme por la obligación y peligro en que iba, así de la enfermedad como por pasar tierra de guerra, y no me quiso confesar un fraile franciscano por la mala opinión que tenía de soldados, diciendo que matan indios [I tried to confess as is my obligation, and (also because of) the danger into which I was heading and my illness and because I was passing through lands of war, and a Franciscan friar did not want to give me confession due to the bad opinion that he had of soldiers, saying that they kill Indians]" (126). This detail brings to light the larger issue of the internal conflict within and between religious orders involved in the expansion project in New Spain. While some Franciscans, such as Gerónimo de Mendieta ([1596] 1997), defended the "moderate" use of coercion as a practical necessity for extirpation of idolatry and the conversion of indigenous people to Christianity, Dominican theologians on the other hand "usually minimized and often repudiated the principle of force" (Phelan 1970, 10). Furthermore, as evidenced in the case of the Franciscan who denied Obregón confession, the use of violent coercion would have been debated even between members of the same religious order.

Violence is acceptable to Obregón, but only as a means to the end of conversion in circumstances of just war. Obregón insists that it is imperative there be severe punishment at the very first sign of insolence so that the Indians never see cowardice or weakness in the soldiers (133). As a soldier, Obregón invokes the cry to battle "¡Santiago a ellos!," an exercise that has its roots in the medieval battle tradition (Obregón 79, 170).[8] Evoking the name of the patron saint of Spain blesses necessary and just battle. Yet it would be erroneous to conclude that Obregón advocates violence—in fact, he emphatically warns his Christian readers that excessive mistreatment of the recently converted indigenous vassals is only counterproductive because "aunque bárbaros, quieren que les trate en verdad en se les haga buen tratamiento [although barbarians, they want to be treated truthfully and given fair treatment]" (133). To wit, God's intervention will punish the Spaniards who abuse their power. When Diego de Alcaraz (see chapter 2) and his men exact excessive tribute, steal, and otherwise abuse the Indians, God punishes them for their misconduct and the bad example they set for those who should have been converted to Christianity (155). According to Obregón, violence, while essentially unavoidable, must be exercised judiciously, and peaceful means of pacification must be employed wherever possible:

> Echar y repartir los servicios personales en los naturales nuevamente poblados con moderación y espacio de tiempo, porque por ocasión de oprimirlos y apremiarles a que tributen suelen alzarse como lo hicieron los de las provincias de Cinaro, Chiametla, Jalisco y valles de Señora, en las cuales mataron y asolaron a sus encomenderos y en las dos partes quedaron victoriosos y sin haberlos podido tornar a sujetarlos.

> [Distributing and doling out the personal services of the natives in the newly settled areas should be done with moderation and over a space of time, because if they are oppressed and forced to give tribute they will rebel, as they did in the provinces of Cinaro, Chiametla, Jalisco and the Valley of Sonora, where they killed and destroyed their encomenderos and in both places have remained victorious and have not been subjugated again.] (204)

Excessive force will only be counterproductive. How can the indigenous subjects be evangelized if they are so oppressed that they rebel? By forcing excessive tribute too quickly the Spanish run the risk of losing an opportunity that, in Obregón's view, inures to the collective benefit of the indigenous populous.

What Bravo (1997, 19) calls "la concepción mesiánica del conquistador" informs to a significant degree the narrator's worldview and his sense of purpose. Obregón is insistent that his readers know that the battles on the northern frontier are just and waged in the name of God. This is not to say that Obregón harbors no worldly motivations or ambitions (he does); rather, his insistence that the enterprise on the frontier of New Spain is a spiritual endeavor indicates an equally influential (and in my reading, sincere) messianic conception of historical events and his role in them. This conception of the world at once informs the version of past events he provides, the present landscape that he (re)presents, and the ideal future of extensive mining operations he projects onto the northern frontier. "Empires move outward in space as a way of moving forward in time; the 'prospect' that opens up is not just a spatial scene but a projected future of 'development' and exploitation" (Mitchell 2002, 170). As Obregón advocates for the expansion of New Spain's mining enterprise, the inexorable interdependency between evangelization and the encomienda takes shape, the implication being that those peoples perceived as not conducive to conversion, or conversely as living in lands not conducive to mining, are quickly dismissed.

The Mining Mission

In *Power and Penury* (1988), David Charles Goodman examines mining operations in Spain and the Americas under the reign of Phillip II (1556–98) and concludes, "Nowhere was mining attempted on the scale of the Spanish monarch's operations" (151). Along with the important site in Spain of Guadalcanal (about twelve leagues, or roughly sixty miles, north of Seville in the foothills of the remote Sierra Morena), the Americas, including San Luis Potosí and Zacatecas, made up a crucial portion of the Crown's mining operations. Between 1555 and 1600, more than 23,827 million *maravedías* (about one quarter of the king's income) derived from the Americas. After 1560, silver production exceeded gold, and the silver boom in Zacatecas of 1546 (which had enriched Ibarra) coupled with the production at the great hill of Potosí (1545) centralized the production of mercury and silver as "the twin foci of the crown's mining policy in the Indies" (183).[9]

Another factor contributing to the focus on the potential wealth of mines to the north of New Spain was the dwindling production of the mine at Guadalcanal in Spain. Once described by García Martín de la Bastida, a shareholder in the mine, as "the richest [mine] that has ever been discovered in Christendom," Guadalcanal had begun to show signs of decline by 1560 (200). This decline in production coincided with a sharp dip in silver coming from the Indies. Compounding these financial strains were the Crown's rising military expenditures as Phillip II added to the tremendous debt he had inherited fighting the Ottoman Turks and putting down the Morisco Revolt (1568–71) and the Revolt of the Netherlands (1568).[10] The discovery of new mines in northern New Spain, and securing existing ones, was a top priority and a major factor of imperial expansion at precisely the time that Obregón was composing his *Historia* to send to the Crown.

Indications of the criollo's awareness of the importance of mining to the larger imperial enterprise abound in *Historia*, and the more topophilic passages reveal a palpable bias for lands that are viewed as conducive to permanent mining settlements. Furthermore, Obregón's depictions reflect the acute dependency of Spanish mining settlements on the ability to exploit an easily "pacified" labor force for distribution among soldiers and explorers. He refers repeatedly to two systems that the Crown had officially sanctioned at different points in time to that end: the encomienda and the repartimiento. The encomienda, a system under which native people were effectively distributed between soldiers along with land, had come under intense scrutiny under Carlos V because of reports of the cruel abuses of indigenous peoples at the hands of Spanish encomenderos. With the passage of Las Leyes Nuevas in 1542, Carlos V had aimed to curtail this abuse and replaced the encomienda with the more bureaucratic repartimiento system, limiting forced labor or tribute to specific projects for limited periods of time. However, encomenderos resisted and regulation of Las Leyes Nuevas was never effectively implemented (even less so in Nueva Vizcaya), and by 1545 the encomienda was once again a legitimized institution under the Crown. In either case, encomienda or repartimiento, "the major institutions of the first century of Spanish rule thus exerted authority over people" and "relied centrally upon articulating a relationship between Europeans and a living, breathing Other" (Seed 1993, 127, 130).

From Obregón's text, one can glean that these two systems of land and labor distribution—the bread and butter of the mining enterprise—greatly inform his conception of the region. Obregón mentions the repartimiento and encomienda frequently as he describes Ibarra's distribution of land and people to members of the expedition in terms of the number of men that are "encomendados." Near Culiacán, he relates, Ibarra left the indigenous people who had rebelled encomendados again in two encomiendas for Pedro Tovar: "Que eran dos encomiendas: la una de mil hombres y la otra de cuatrocientos, los cuales prometieron reconocer, tributar y obedecer de nuevo a su encomendero don Pedro de Tovar [There were two encomiendas: one of one thousand men and the other of four hundred, (all of whom) promised to recognize, (pay) tribute (to) and obey again their encomendero, don Pedro de Tovar]" (93).

Obregón's language reflects not only his familiarity with these systems of land and labor distribution but also their coexistence in the region. What is more, his descriptions testify to the role of the repartimiento and encomienda in the sociopolitical mentality of the day, which implies that distribution naturally has as much to do with people as it does with land. In fact, when employing each term, Obregón speaks of the number of people, not the size of the parcel. While Las Leyes Nuevas had attempted to address the inherent tension that existed between the Crown's moral preoccupations with the treatment of the indigenous labor force and its increasing dependence on the income generated from it, Obregón's text reflects the on-the-ground reality of its persistence and the entrenched assumption in the criollo's mind that such a labor force was a given. Far from lessening after the passage of Las Leyes Nuevas, the dependence on forced labor in New Spain was only increasing as mining expanded northward. In fact, in 1562 Ibarra was given express permission to dole out encomiendas as he saw fit, inaugurating the legality of the encomienda in the north (Cuello 1988, 688).

Despite Las Nuevas Leyes, encomenderos in the north treated indigenous people harshly, and the system, while on paper not technically slavery, operated much like it. Moreover, although the encomienda was not unique to the northern frontier, its duration absolutely was, lasting in Nueva Vizcaya into the late seventeenth and early eighteenth centuries. Cuello cites the Mixtón War and the discovery of silver in Zacatecas as justifications for maintaining the status quo of the encomienda, but adds that the mere fact that northern conquest began later than central Mexico meant that the encomienda, the principle reward for exploration, was fated to continue: How else would soldiers be compensated, especially when impresarios like Ibarra bore the expense of these exploratory undertakings in return for future power and profit? Worse still, in large part because of the remoteness of the region, the encomienda often resembled slavery more than repartimiento—encomenderos often treated indigenous residents as personal property, even branding them. The result was the three labor systems— slavery (reported as late as 1738 in Nuevo León), the encomienda, and the repartimiento—while differentiated in theory, coexisted and overlapped in practice (684–88).

The persistence of forced labor in all its variants may have also been in part because of the more labor-intensive processes involved in silver mining. In earlier days under Carlos V, "mining often meant no more than panning for gold in the river-beds of the Antilles, [and] Indian mining labor could be restricted to 'sifting, washing or other light work.'" (Goodman 1988,

185). However, the conditions of silver mining were far more demanding and posed new problems for Phillip II. "Faced with the inherited debts of Castile and soaring military expenditures, and presented with the prospects of Potosí and Huancavélica, Phillip showed less open opposition to Indian labour in mines" (186). Thus the increased acceptance of using indigenous labor under Phillip II, coupled with the persistence of the repartimiento and encomienda systems, only perpetuated and grew an economy dependent on the exploitation of indigenous labor, an exploitation that was justified by the laborers' conversion to Christianity. As Seed (1993, 115) succinctly states, "Legitimacy (the right to rule or even be present in the New World) was contingent on evangelization of the natives." In terms of landscape perception, this raises the following question: is the spiritual (i.e., an easily pacified indigenous populace) a prerequisite for the material, or is the material (i.e., the presence of precious metals) a prerequisite for the spiritual?

It is telling that Tuan utilizes the Spanish-versus-indigenous model to exemplify his point that while one culture may view a landscape as "uninhabitable," the peoples indigenous to that landscape are quite at home in it. Tuan (1974, 14) also recognizes how *purpose* constitutes an important factor in *perception*. Ibarra's principle function as governor of Nueva Vizcaya was "granting the Indians in *encomienda* for the purpose of exploiting their labor and giving them religions instruction" (Mecham 1927, 108). Doubtless with these seemingly contradictory missions in mind, Obregón dismisses landscapes wholesale with the phrase "no se puede poblar" wherever people are not perceived as predisposed to conversion or potential riches are not encountered. Recall that Obregón had argued that the inhabitants of Topia showed little potential for conversion, "por estar como están en tierras tan remotas, ásperas e imposibilitadas de poblarlas cristianos, ¿dónde se harán cristianos si no es poblando algunas minas buenas o poniendo Dios nuestro Señor el remedio necesario? [being as they are in lands so remote, rough and impossible for Christians to inhabit; How can they be made Christians if no good mines are settled there or with God our Lord's necessary assistance?]" (90). Lands are "uninhabitable" for Spaniards wherever the interdependent institutions of encomienda and evangelization may not flourish, hence the emerging places of potential referenced in the last chapter would have needed to facilitate both projects. On examination, Obregón's places of potential exemplify the ways topophilia and topophobia may be informed by specific sociohistorical circumstances.

When Obregón relates Chamuscado's encounters with indigenous inhabitants along the Río Conchas, he begins by dismissing the "indios silvestres" that will be "malos de sujetar" ["wild Indians" that will be "difficult to subjugate"]. However, there may be potential nearby as these inhabitants tell the explorers about a large settlement to the north: "toda la cual será poblada y sujeta de cristianos *si se descubren buenos metales para convertirlos a nuestra santa Fe católica* aunque con trabajo y dificultad por no ser gente de asiento y posible que los obligue a sujeción porque imitan a los gitanos que llevan consigo todo posible [all of which will be settled and made Christian *if good metals are discovered there to convert them to our Holy Catholic Faith* although with work and difficulty because they are not sedentary people and it is possible (they will have to be) obligated to settle because they imitate the gypsies that carry everything with them]" (229, my emphasis). They could be pacified, albeit with some trouble, but even this is contingent on the presence of precious metals. The metals make it worth the trouble, and living on lands suited for mining increases their chances for conversion. Similarly, Obregón reads Chiametla (the place Ibarra would reside until his death in 1575) as a place of potential:

En esta provincia [Chiametla] hay muchos bastimentos de maíz frijol, calabaza, gallinas de la tierra, frutos de la tierra y vacas. . . . Hay mucho pescado, hostia [*sic*], camarón, sal y algodón, de todas las cuales cosas hay entre los vecinos granjerías, especialmente en el pescado, sal y labores de maíz *para las minas*, de las cuales han sacado y sacan mucha plata.

[In this province (Chiametla) there are many supplies of maize, bean(s), squash, hens of the earth, fruits of the earth, and cows. . . . There are many fish, oysters, shrimp, salt and cotton, of all which there are among the farming residents, especially fish, salt and cultivated maize *for the mines*, from which they have extracted and (continue to) extract much silver.] (131, my emphasis)[11]

The word "para" is indicative of the value-laden lens through which the narrator reads the landscape—the land *and* its peoples. Chiametla is but a litany of resources that are already in existence and seemingly there for the taking. That is, Chiametla's landscape is cultivated to a degree and now simply needs to be put to "proper" use to supply a mining enterprise.

Of course, Chiametla had been settled before, but that settlement had failed. Obregón relates the story of the abandonment of the encomienda that Nuño de Guzmán had founded there because of the "gente indómita y encenegada en el bestial y abominable vicio de sus malas costumbres y vidas y no consentir sujeción y servidumbre a los cristianos [the indomitable people blinded in the bestial and abominable vice of their evil customs and lives and would not consent to settlement and service to the Christians]" (115). Unlike Diego de Alcaraz, who had abused the indigenous people under his charge, Obregón depicts de Guzmán in this instance as a victim of the "bestial Indian," not the other way around. The encomienda, a legitimate, legal institution by his standards, is undermined by a hostile indigenous people who refuse to accept civilization and Christianity.[12] At the same time, Obregón insists that Chiametla presents possibility, and his narration reveals a strong sense of place. "An already produced space can be decoded, can be read" (Lefebvre [1974] 1991, 17). The allure of Chiametla may lie in part in the fact that it is recognizable enough to be read. Famed for its riches of gold, silver, and metals, in addition to an abundance of food and clothed people, the soldiers had been excited about Chiametla despite the fact that de Guzmán's encomienda had been abandoned. This may be because the place of abandonment, forced or otherwise, can at least be read and decoded by the members of the Ibarra Expedition as a place of potential because of the very idea that people of their own ilk have lived there before. "The presences of diverse absences" at Chiametla is at once collectively read by the Ibarra group in terms of what is there, what was there, and what could be there in the future (de Certeau 1984, 108). Obregón's use of the past perfect and the present tenses, "han sacado y sacan mucha plata [have extracted and are extracting much silver]" presuppose a gaze of possession while simultaneously emphasizing proof of value and reassuring the reader that this resource has not been exhausted. "The colonizing imagination takes for granted that the land and its resources belong to those who are best able to exploit them" (Spurr 1993, 31). This is a landscape that is seemingly ready-made. "Everything is in order; it is simply a question of substitution and supplement rather than true transformation . . . the valley calls for the colonizer to bring it in to being" (30).

In his "pitch" for Cinaro as a focal place for the development of an enterprise of expansion, Obregón reveals a keen eye for all of the elements conducive to permanent settlement. Obregón is insistent that Cinaro will offer a strategic location from which to operate in the banda del norte, providing a landscape conducive to establishing Spanish missionary and mining settlements and serving as a base of operations from which to expand Spanish holdings. "In America, it was from the cities that the European subject organized the conquest of the land," and the establishment of a permanent city on the "Christian frontier" would have been imperative to future expansion (Verdesio 2002, 138). To borrow a term from Powell, Cinaro could serve as an "outpost of empire" on a distant, unstable frontier (Powell 1944, 179). There must be thirty thousand people from Petatlán to

Mayombo, reckons Obregón, in addition to access to water, food supplies, and a great quantity of metals.[13] "Sácanse de las de San Andrés mucha plata y se hubiera sacado de los demás descubrimientos *si estuvieran poblados* [Lots of silver is extracted from San Andrés, and even more would from the other discoveries, *if they were settled*]" (112, my emphasis).[14] Obregón reasons that it can be settled and held with as few as one hundred men, so long as they have a strong fort and "moderation" is exercised in exacting personal service and tributes from the aborigines (ibid.). While Obregón had referred to the soldiers' disappointment in Cinaro not being "Otro México," he also noted that the people had been viewed positively by himself as well as the soldiers. What is more, Obregón depicts Cinaro as strategically located to offer access to other focal places: Cibola, Corazones, Paquimé, and San Felipe de Nuevo México. Furthermore, all of the resources for establishing settlement are found there: people, supplies, and metals (141).

Y así lo vi y experimenté por las partes que la otra vez y lo afirma Álvar Núñez Cabeza de Vaca en su historia. . . . Y estando estas provincias pobladas, V.M. hará notable servicio a Dios nuestro Señor y aumentará en su real Corona *vasallos, tributos y quintos en cantidad.*

[And thus I saw and experienced it throughout the region as confirmed by Álvar Núñez Cabeza de Vaca in his history. . . . And once these provinces are settled, Your Majesty will make notable service to God our Lord and your royal Crown will increase its *vassals, tributes and fifths in (great) quantity.*] (141–42, my emphasis)

Obregón's argument seems tailor-made to address the principal problems faced by the Crown and its viceroys in the northern borderlands, mainly the rough terrain and continuous raids from indigenous resistors who seriously outnumbered the Spanish. As Powell (1944, 174) explains, principal mining sites were in arid climates, hundreds of miles from the coast and surrounded by mountains and under constant attack. "The mining camps of the far frontier, many but newly opened by the activities of Francisco de Ibarra, were suffering particularly from the disastrous effects of constant Indian raids" (188). If it were "poblado," Obregón reasons, Cinaro would provide a future strategic location from which soldiers could "ir poblando y reduciendo." As Seed (1993, 123) indicates, "'poblar' defines the arrival of people, rather than the construction of buildings or dwellings, as the critical step in occupying a region." Cinaro is already considered part of the larger empire in Obregón's textualscape, it now only needs to be molded in the image of that empire by Spanish or criollo vassals to better and more effectively serve the Crown.

In all matters material, Obregón demonstrates what Spurr calls a "doctrine of natural inheritance" in which the indigenous people are depicted as foolishly sitting on wealth, ignorant to the potential of the landscape in which they live, and thereby not deserving of its governance (29): "Y aunque es verdad que no han sacado plata ni oro en aquellas provincias los naturales, por no saber sus beneficios ni haberlo usado, es certísimo estar en aquella gran serranía y sus ramos de ellas la mayor gruesa de metales de todas las Indias [And even though it is true that the natives have not extracted silver nor gold from these provinces, for not knowing their benefits nor having used them, the largest lode of metals in all of the Indies is certain to be in those great mountains and their branches]" (60). If only they were under the charge of the civilized European, lands wasted—or "desusada," a term Obregón employs repeatedly—could be put to proper use.[15]

(Re)producing Social Space and Textualscapes

In "Frontera, ciudad y plaza pública americana del siglo XVI," (2005) Álvarez Félix Bolaños demonstrates how the foundation of the city in New Spain (and in particular the construction of the central plaza) was formulated by the imposition of apartheid: the reproduction of European intellectual and physical structures (legislatures, buildings, and religious iconography), public displays of punishment for dissidence, and "el obsesivo y masivo registro textual de estos procesos en una forma discursiva llamada 'relación' [the obsessive and massive textual registry of those processes in a discursive form called 'relación']" (27). A strikingly similar project is born out of Obregón's *Historia*, in which both the landscaping processes he relates and the very act of textualizing those processes are a means for reproducing a Europeanized landscape. Borrowing from Lefebvre, the Spanish "social space" need only be produced and reproduced throughout the banda del norte for it to be brought under control. The message is one of endless, yet realistic, possibility. The lands are inhabitable, peopled, bountiful, and rich in mineral wealth. The Spanish can cultivate many of the same crops as they do in Castile and, with care, Christianize the population and institute their economic systems (214). The Spanish self-image, encapsulated in Castile, would have allowed his readers to visualize a Hispanicized America, one that could sustain the transference of Christianity in the form of the evangelization project, as well as the economic institutions that the Spanish brought with them, the encomienda and repartimiento. The Spanish—or more precisely in the case of Obregón, criollo—textualization of the landscape of the northern frontier belies an occidental desire to at once reaffirm and sustain Spain's social space in the Old World while reproducing it in the New World.

Recalling Cosgrove's emphasis on the cogent influence that Roman imperial expansion wielded in the dissemination of conceptions of spatiality in Europe may lend insight into a similar diffusion of such a view in New Spain. This is a "spatiality of distant control radiating from a powerful center" and involves mapping and plotting appropriated lands on surveyors' grids (Cosgrove 1998, 66). As far back as Pliny the Elder (23–79 CE) landscape figures into assertions of dominion (Murphy 2004, 15). However, Obregón's text reveals that this top-down view of spatiality does not occur to the exclusion of the on-the-ground, bottom-up textualscapes that inform the centers of power. Obregón recognizes the power of writing in imperial expansion:

La suma potestad y sabiduría de Dios Todopoderoso que con incomparable equidad y concierto crió sustenta y conserva a todas sus criaturas, puso en mayor merecimiento y grado al hombre sacado del dechado y grandeza de su retrato divino, al cual dio y ordenó el loable y virtuoso ejercicio de *letras* para que con él sepan y alcancen los secretos y casos convenientes y dificultosos para que se rijan y gobiernen en justicia, paz, equidad y concierto con que justamente puso, ordenó y permite *la milicia para el castigo* de los sucesos y casos desordenados de que tenemos verdadera experiencia.

[The supreme power and wisdom of God Almighty, who, with incomparable equity and concert, created and conserves all of His creatures, placed in man the greatest worthiness and rank, and (created) him from the greatness and perfect model of His own divine image; and He gave and ordered unto him the laudable and virtuous exercise of *letters* so that with it, he would learn and come to understand secrets and advisable and difficult cases so that they may regulate and govern in justice, peace, equity and concert, along with which He (also) justly placed, ordered and permitted *discipline for the punishment* of disorderly events and cases, of which we have true experience.] (233, my emphasis)

That Obregón segues from recognizing the power of writing to the power of physical punishment, both powers and privileges given by God, attests to the ways discourse and violence converge in the project of colonial dominance (see Rabasa 2000). The discourse produced in the New World, the relación, crónica, and historia, assured colonial readers of three important things, Bolaños (2005, 12) tells us: the veracity of events and accounts, the legitimacy of the civilizing mission, and above all else, the possibility of the reproduction of the processes in future times and places by other explorers. The production of a meticulous discursive record, as far as it at least attempted to serve as a means of reproduction of Europeanized space, goes hand in hand with relations of power at work and the physical violence inflicted during this tumultuous period in the borderlands. This is not to say that the influence of the center is not present (it clearly is). However, as we see in Obregón, who wrote a highly descriptive, itinerary-driven history of northward expansion to send to Spanish officials, a criollo was just as capable of the appropriating gaze and attempts to reproduce European social space as the panoptic eye of the Empire.

Conclusions

The recognition that the larger project of imperial expansion is inextricably linked to its purported spiritual purposes is not new, and clearly Obregón's perception of the landscape would have been informed in no small part by the importance of evangelization and the mining mission, institutions that in turn would have driven the creation of his textualscape. What Obregón's textualscape offers is a reading of how the moral anxiety over what Ahern described as the "coyuntura contradictoria de evangelizar y explotar [contradictory conjunction of evangelization and exploitation]" (2001, 44) of the Spanish expansion project informs landscape perception and the immeasurable consequences of that process. Just as Obregón projects a past (history) and a present (itinerary) onto the landscape, he likewise projects a future onto it, a future that he transcribes onto the textualscape. The textualscape provides more than a surface or a theatre: it provides a space in and on which the potential of the northern frontier forms a tangible part of the Spanish empire that officials on the other side of the Atlantic can hold and possess, an affirmation that, from a far-off place called Cinaro, the Spanish empire can extend its holdings and increase its vassals and tributes. While Obregón recognizes the "tailed" landscapes, the violence and injustices of the "empty" despoblado, he at once mourns their loss while infusing them with life. The living landscape is decoded through the occidental cultural lens and translated into a textualscape that reveals at once the projection and reflection of a Spanish past, present, and future.

Moreover, the production of this textualscape, and so many others like it, would have also served to (re)produce spatial knowledge. Bookending his account with the notion that "Nuevo" Mexico holds the potential for the repetition of the successful imposition of Spanish culture over an indigenous civilization, coupled with chapter after chapter between highlighting the pragmatic processes of stabilizing the borderlands, *Historia* presents its readers with a dynamic, contentious, confusing moment in time in the long life of this landscape. And, if we consider *Historia* as part of a larger imperial discourse, the landscape is negotiated and created not in the top-down fashion of the survey or the map but rather in the bottom-up fashion of the itinerary. This bespeaks a more organic conception of landscape in which, while the panoptic eye of the distant empire certainly plays a major role, the faceless soldier, *escribano*, Nahua, African, Pima, Yaqui, friar, Xixime, Opata, prospector, tradesman, Suma, translator, Concho, *relator*, Acaxee, mestizo, and criollo are the active participants creating their social space and determining how the representation of that landscape is exported back to the "center" of the empire.

Conclusion

*If space is a product, our knowledge of it must be expected to
reproduce and expound the process of production.*
—HENRI LEFEBVRE, 1974

*Geographical discoveries are pushing back the ancient frontiers
around the world, places where monsters have been located; and
the monsters fade from the horizon. On the other hand, blacks and
Indians are discovered; the Others are no longer monstrous beings,
just different men. As for the monsters, they are internalized: their
place is no longer "out there" but in the depths of the very soul.*
—PAUL ZUMTHOR, 1986

*Written texts contain an often hidden geography and an examination
of that geography may clarify the unreflected ideologies of the text.*
—JAMES DUNCAN AND DAVID LEY, 1993

Historia de los descubrimientos de Nueva España presents its reader with
much more than the title would indicate. It is a text that does not merely
tell and describe but rather one that appropriates and molds the dynamic
site perceived in the occidental image. In fact, as Sauer's complaint (1932)
about the text as "confused" would indicate, *Historia* presents a complicated case in which the functions of the relación and the historia converge
and overlap, resulting in a dual projection of a Spanish past, present, and
future onto the landscape in a textualscape that infuses the northern borderlands with a sense of place and history. Obregón views himself as an
active participant in the Spanish project of imperial expansion in both
economic and spiritual terms despite what any reader may have perceived
as a precarious social standing. As Obregón projects his vision of mining
and evangelization onto the borderlands of New Spain, they emerge as a
landscape to be worked by indigenous hands, but ruled by European ones.
Of course, whatever the textualscape attempts or claims to (re)present,

121

it is composed over an a priori indigenous social space that existed long before becoming existential by "discovery." This study has aimed to pick apart Obregón's filter to gain insight into authorial worldview while also recognizing the myriad moments of negotiation that can be glimpsed in which the indigenous inhabitants are active participants in the production and reproduction of social space.

The extensive landscape depictions reveal Obregón's topophilia and topophobia as they are informed culturally and individually, and how his particular sociohistorical circumstances inform them. As part and parcel of this, humanscapes, reduced to the most fundamental elements of shelter, clothing, and crop production, are largely limited to their presence or absence, their perceived material value rather than cultural value. However, the fissures found in Obregón's textualscape attest that the notions of the indigenous person as passive receptacle or bellicose savage emerge from the ideals of the mining and evangelization projects rather than from the reality on the ground, one in which the mythical conceptions from the earlier days of exploration were at once being reimagined. For that very reason it is precisely what is omitted in the textualscape of the *Historia* that is most telling. Although the projection of an imagined European landscape often eclipses more than it reveals, by comparing the textualscape against cultural studies it becomes clear that it has been constructed over a palimpsest of indigenous landscapes that had been negotiated and renegotiated for thousands of years. Moreover, given the social, cultural, and environmental upheaval of this period and the myriad ways that Spanish encroachment would have affected indigenous identity, we must concede that even as it is put to paper, the banda del norte is a landscape being constructed and reconstructed by multiple cultures and societies with competing visions. So while the textualscape serves as a tool in the reproduction of knowledge of socially produced space, it represents a landscape that can never be attained, a simulacrum, or in the words of Cosgrove (1998, 81), "the realized image of a reality that never existed."

If, as Mitchell (2002, 19) argues, the Whig narrative of science, reason, and naturalistic representation overcame contradictions for the British colonial project in the Pacific in the eighteenth and nineteenth centuries, for Spain in the sixteenth it was evangelization, the encomienda, and the textualscape, in which "the real subject" is not the borderlands of New Spain but rather the narrator's vision of what should be there. The encomienda "naturalized" Spanish imperial expansion in New Spain by subsuming the humans that lived in that landscape as part of a "civilized" march toward progress and "salvation" in both space and time, a naturalization played out by the everyday participants in imperial expansion and the way they committed their participation to paper.

> Any text is taken to represent [in much scholarship of Spanish American literature] a reality that is "pre-given," whose existence has the status of an objective fact, an object unmediated by any symbolic system. . . . It is in a literature seemingly most concerned with representing a "real" that we are presented with a radical defamiliarization [*sic*] of established notions of the "real" in terms of both the experience of the settler socie-ties seeking to "naturalize" their relationship to their surroundings and of that of native populations which see their "real" reshaped by the actions and representations of the colonizing people. In reading this literature of the "real" we, as readers, are made all the more conscious of the real's artificial, re-constructed quality. (Higgins 2002, 159–60)

Of course, the principle function of this representation that I would like to stress is its role in human identity creation and imposition. In this endeavor we gain insight from the field of Human Geography, which considers the effects of mapping on the human experience through time. Many scholars in this field, (Gregory, Thrift, and Pred, among others) have sought to "locate geographical concerns at the heart of social theory by showing how the engagements between the individual and the social are always played out in particular arenas—places, domains, locales" (Agnew, Livingstone, and Rogers 1996, 136). In this view, Obregón's "landscap-ing project" cannot be disengaged from his situación enunciativa, nor its human participants (European, indigenous, and African) and how that project is informed by oppositions that are culturally defined and reliant on one another (Derrida 1978). "One way to investigate the duality of the representations of places is by situating the sites within an analysis of dis-courses about the Other. Such an analysis highlights the duality by showing how difference in the site of the Other is 'recuperated' by appropriating it into a categorical framework that is familiar and useful within the site from which the representation emanates" (Duncan 1993b, 39).

Obregón was writing from a very particular locus of annunciation at a time when new means of defining and categorizing became imperative to the Spanish imperial project, and "the need to draw administrative bound-aries and to make inventories of assets became important" (Agnew, Living-stone, and Rogers 1996, 367). Such "assets" included human beings who were likewise defined and categorized, indicating a human hierarchy in the parlance of those on the ground as much as those residing on the Iberian

Peninsula. The land and the people are interwoven in the representations created of the landscape of the borderlands of New Spain. Just as Duncan proposes that discourses about people reveal much about representations of place, discourses of landscape likewise reveal much about the representations of people.

> The bodies, not only of so-called primitive peoples but of all the colonized, have been a focal point of colonialist interest which, as in the case of landscape description, proceeds from the visual to various kinds of valorization: the material value of the body as labor supply, its aesthetic value as object of artistic representation, its ethical value as a mark of innocence or degradation, its scientific value as evidence of racial difference or inferiority, its humanitarian value as the sign of suffering, its erotic value as the object of desire. (Spurr 1993, 22)

Landscape studies, then, can serve as a useful critical platform from which to approach discourses that attempt to textualize, all at once, humans and the lands in which they live.

As we continue to grapple with the spatial turn in literary and cultural studies, landscape theories offer a useful critical platform. Westphal (2013, 43) contends that the "distinction between space and place has been examined from all angles, all latitudes, and all seams, without coming to satisfying conclusions," yet landscape has been arguably underexamined. Quoniam (1988) asserts that landscape provokes debate and discussion, and that is a "good thing." Yet despite popping up everywhere in the discourse, landscape has been largely relegated to the position of backdrop or setting. Theories involving landscape would be particularly insightful in the field of Latin American colonial literature, in which studies point to the "imagined" and "invented" America (O'Gorman 1958; Rabasa 1993). Indeed, Obregón's textualscape demonstrates just one humble contribution in a massive discursive undertaking of producing meaning in the form of social space.

By the end of the fifteenth century in Europe, Leon Battista Alberti's *On Painting* (1435–36) had become "the handbook of the new orthodoxy in the arts, elevat[ing] *storia* to the highest point of artistic endeavor" (Cosgrove and Daniels 1993, 65). The export of humanist texts to New Spain, where a "monomania for scribal matters," as Weckmann ([1984] 1992, 469) calls it, had taken hold, coupled with the continuation of the Roman way of thinking about law as permanent written text (predominantly in the form of the relación, crónica, or historia) imbued the textual production of space with a certain degree of unquestioned authority. In New Spain, this "almost sacred aura" of writing, to borrow at term from Rama (1996, 24), only increased exponentially, as writing legitimized and fomented the Spanish project of imperial expansion. The extensive discursive production in New Spain not only created a tremendous administrative bureaucracy of *letrados* consisting of myriad "administrators, educators, professionals, notaries, religious personnel, and other wielders of pen and paper," but also served as a way to provide some semblance of control over the landscape for vice regal and peninsular officials (18). As Derrida (1978) argued that language is not a medium for conveying meaning, but for the production of meaning, the symbolic representations of landscape in Obregón's textualscape hoped to produce knowledge of a faraway region both for future explorers and for a readership that may never see it but sought to count it among its possessions. This unquestioned authority in the textual production of landscape must be taken into account as we consider the representation of the-land-and-its-people as it is constructed discursively, and its role in imperial expansion. If we recall the deceptively innocuous discursive tool of "description" cited by Padrón (2004), on decoding that description we see that writing is arguably the most violent landscaping weapon and, once in the hands of its readers, a violent "mindscaping" weapon, to borrow a term from Olwig (2002).

In heeding Mitchell's call to consider "landscape" as a verb, I would add that we also recognize it as verbal. The textualscape stands out as a critical means of spatial reproduction in the borderlands of sixteenth-century New Spain. Obregón's text exhibits how the textualscape, which at first may appear to consist of nothing more than benign description, reveals much more when decoded and alternative lived experiences are teased out. This work of decoding is particularly urgent as the pernicious and erroneous presupposition persists that before the arrival of the European to the Americas no socially produced space had existed. I emphasize this point to call attention to the need to avoid the pitfalls of what Verdesio (2002, 156) refers to as the "image of the blank page." This takes on a greater sense of urgency when we recognize that that image has contemporary implications. "That impoverished vision of the past will, eventually, have an effect on the way in which projects for the future—for which that past is the foundation—are conceived" (ibid.). When considered within the framework of Westphal's (2013) geocentric approach in which one singular place is considered over time (as opposed to an author, genre or historical period) to explore how it has been represented in various media, we can examine how the same region has been presented and re-presented from Obregón to today via myriad modes: literature, oral tradition, guide books, movies, maps, art, architecture, webpages, newspapers, radio, etc. What do these textualscapes tell us over time about multicultural perspective, identity, and the creation and re-creation of social space? As Sheridan-Prieto (2002) argues, and West-phal (2013) acknowledges, what sources does one include and exclude in such a study? How do we account for the "conflicting forces and views that condition the way in which various spaces come to be recognizable places" (Westphal xiii)? How can this process help us to "produce a less Eurocentric representation of the present as well as more solid projects for the future" (Verdesio 2002, 156)?

The textualscape, recalling Appadurai's (1993) use of the suffix -scape as connoting "fluid" and "perspectival," is a creative narrative act that represents the landscape as perceived by the narrator. It attempts to embody (textually or even visually) the dynamic site perceived, the land, and its people, and it bespeaks the cultural function of landscape. It is a means for the (re)production of social space and, most important to this investigation, has real human consequences. This does not necessarily imply a sinister plot on the part of the narrator. Space, Lefebvre ([1974] 1991, 37) cautions, cannot be produced "with a perfectly clear understanding of cause and effect, motive and implication," and neither can landscape or its textualization. It is because of that lack of understanding that the landscape and the textualscape remain cultural phenomena that must be addressed, if only to attend to the following question: to what degree have we been "mindscaped"?

Notes

Introduction

1. Both Parsons and West were protégés of renowned American geographer Carl Sauer.

2. *Cultural landscape* is a term that was coined by Carl Sauer in 1925 to describe man's shaping force on the landscape, a point upon which I elaborate later.

3. Francisco de Ibarra (c. 1539–1575) was born to a noble family in the Basque province of Guipúzcoa in northeast Spain. He began preliminary explorations of the lands north of Zacatecas during 1554–62, but he is best known for the major exploration described in Baltasar Obregón's chronicle *Historia de los descubrimientos de Nueva España* and the period of organizational consolidation of Nueva Vizcaya, an ever-shifting territory throughout the sixteenth century comprising the modern-day Mexican states of Durango, Chihuahua, Sinaloa, and Sonora. For a detailed account of Francisco de Ibarra's life, see Mecham 1927.

4. Leib and Walker (2002) also note the limitations of photographs to tell the whole story: "Yet, just as Parson's photographs did not tell the entire story of the Topia Road 1940–1941, we recognize that our photographic replication provides but a small window into the changes that have occurred since then. The repeat photographs, therefore, are a catalyst for our discussion of change along the Topia Road rather than the story of change in its entirety" (578).

5. "Chichimeca" is a Nahuatl word that the Spanish picked up from the Nahua auxiliary soldiers. While some Nahua used the term with pride to refer to their ancestors who had migrated from the north, others used it to refer to a variety of ethnic groups that they viewed as nomadic savages (Rojos 2014, 1362). The Spanish used it pejoratively, hence the name for these uprisings, which lasted until the turn of the century (see Powell 1977). Sheridan-Prieto (2002) points out that chichimeca is not a cultural group at all, but rather a way to designate a limit that draws a clear distance between a "we" and an "other" (18). The term is generic and completely ignores cultural difference, a topic I explore in chapter 3.

6. Obregón's crónica of northward expansion was not published in the author's lifetime, but was sent to the Consejo de Indias. The original, only discovered in the

first quarter of the twentieth century, is held in the Archivo General de Indias in Seville, Spain (AGI. Patronato. 22. R7. fol. 603–850). The first known published edition was produced by Father Mariano Cuevas in 1924 and then reedited in 1989. Cuevas transcribed the entire work in only ten days, and consequently there are many errors in interpretation as well as omissions. The Cuevas version was later translated into English by Hammond and Rey and published in 1928. Finally, in 1990, the University of Seville published a paleographic edition in microfiche along with a philological study of the work, edited by Eva María Bravo. I have referred to this paleographic edition in microfiche, however, the edition to which I will refer as a primary source, and from which I will cite, will be the published edition with modernized language, also edited by Bravo (1997).

7. Born in New Spain to a wealthy family in the silver mining town of Zacatecas, Juan de Oñate was appointed by Phillip II in part because the former "was an experienced leader from a prestigious family that possessed a substantial fortune, and he had the ear of the viceroy, Luis de Velasco" (Weber 1992, 60).

However, Oñate would later become renowned for the abuses of the indigenous pueblo peoples during his tenure, abuses that included the extortion of crops and violence.

8. While the word *historia* may refer to "stories," the point that I wish to emphasize is the compilation of stories from various sources and his role as editor, both functions of compiling a *History* with a capital *H*.

9. Notable studies that deal with Obregón's discourse include Rosa Camelo's "La idea de la historia en Baltasar de Obregón" (1971), which examines what the text reveals about Obregón's own conceptions of History; Elide Pittarello's "Scienza/ Esperienza nella *Historia de los descubrimientos antiguos y modernos de la Nueva España* di Baltasar de Obregón" (1984) in which Pittarello explores the emphasis that Obregón places on eyewitness experience; and Eva María Bravo's extensive and indispensable introduction to her 1997 transcription.

.10. Scholarly attention has been paid to a much greater extent to the Coronado corpus, including *La relación del descubrimiento de las siete ciudades* by Fray Marcos de Niza (1539), Fernando de Alarcón's relación (1556), and *Relación de la Jornada de Cíbola* by Pedro de Castañeda y Nájera (1563). See Ahern 1989, 1993, 1994a, 1994b, 2003; Aiton 1925, 1940; Arias 1993, 1996, 2002; Bancroft 1834–74; Herbert E. Bolton 1949; Day 1940; Flint and Flint 1992, 2002, 2003, 2005; Gordon 2006; Hammond 1966; Hammond and Rey 1940; Hodge 1865; Reff 1987, 1991a, 1996; Riley 1974; Sánchez 1997, 2007; and Weber 1992. Translations: Craddock 1996; Flint and Flint 2002, 2003, 2005; Montané Martí 1995, 2002, [1556] 2004.

11. Arjun Appadurai employs the suffix "scape" to what he cites as the five "dimensions of global cultural flow" and the very building blocks of imagined worlds, contending that cultural flow in the globalized world occurs in and through the growing disjunctures between ethnoscapes, mediascapes, technoscapes, finanscapes, and ideoscapes.

What is of interest to this study is his use of the suffix "scape." The significance of this regarding "textualscape" will be treated in greater detail, but here it should be noted that Appadurai (1993) employs the suffix to speak to fluid and perspectival constructs (275–76).

12. Cynthia Radding's environmental and cultural history, *Landscapes of Power and Identity* (2005) is a noteworthy exception.

13. Theorists such as Foucault (1986), de Certeau (1984), and Lefebvre ([1974] 1991) have wielded great influence in scholarship across disciplines, and Mitchell (2002), Arias and Meléndez (2002), Basso (1996) and Hirsch and O'Hanlon (1995) all reference the influence of one or more of these scholars in their respective fields. This "spatial turn" has greatly informed studies of colonial Spanish America over the past several decades. In their introduction to *Mapping Colonial Spanish America: Places and Commonplaces of Identity, Culture, and Experience* (2002), Santa Arias and Mariselle Meléndez cite some of the most important works in the study of colonial Spanish America (Gruzinski 1991; Mignolo 1995; Pratt 1992; Zamora 1993; among others) and demonstrate the degree to which space has played a fundamental role in them. "Space influenced the way colonial Spanish America was created discursively, historically, culturally, politically, and legally" (21). These theories of space and place have provided a particularly productive stance from which to examine colonial discourse in terms of mapping (Ahern 1999, 2002, 2003; Hill-Boone 1994, 1998; Mignolo 1992, 1994, 1995; Mundy 1996; Padrón 2004).

14. Denis Cosgrove (1998, 68) dates this usage of a "new and more pictorial meaning of landscape" even earlier, stating that it had been established by the turn of the sixteenth century. Olwig would probably caution that such a pictorial meaning did, however, include depictions of culture and people.

15. These depictions that showed man in his relationship to the country may reflect, at least in part, the shift in the view of nature taking place in the sixteenth and seventeenth centuries. Antithetical to the Greek view of nature as saturated or permeated by mind, this conception of nature was based on the "denial that the world of nature is an organism, and the assertion that it is devoid both of intelligence and life" (Collingwood 1945, 5). In this view the natural world is a like a machine—an arrangement of parts designed and constructed for a definite purpose by an intellectual mind outside itself. Just as a clockmaker is to a clock, so is God to nature (3–9). This also reflects the Biblical notion that man has dominion over nature.

16. A different version of this chapter has been published separately as an article: Rebecca Carte, "Mapping an Occidental History in Baltasar Obregón's *Historia de los descubrimientos de Nueva España*," *Journal of the Southwest* 53 (2011): 279–304.

Chapter One

1. In Spain, "banda" was almost exclusively a nautical term: "mientras que en América desde Oviedo se extiende hasta significar 'zona' y 'orilla; margen' [while in the Americas from (the time of) Oviedo it comes to mean 'zone' and 'border; margin']" (Corominas 1954, 1:485).

2. The expedition led by Francisco Vázquez de Coronado y Lúxan (more commonly referred to as simply "Coronado") set out from New Spain in 1540 and penetrated as far north as Kansas and as far west as the Grand Canyon. However, the Coronado expedition was viewed as a failure on its return to New Spain in 1542 having found no golden cities. It was relegated to memory until twenty years later when a participant in the two-year trek, Pedro de Castañeda y Nájera, wrote an

account of events that described the regions traversed. See Flint and Flint 1992, 2002, 2003, 2005.

3. "Ninguna persona de qualquier estado y condiçion que sea haga por su propia autoridad nueuo descubrimiento por mar ni por tierra ni entrada nueua poblaçion ni rancheria en lo que estuuiere descubierto o se descubriere sin licencia y prouission o de quien tuuiere nuestro poder para la dar so pena de muerte y de perdimiento de todos sus bienes para nuestra camara y mandamos a los nuestros visorreyes audiencias y gouernadores y otras justiçias de las Indias que no den licencia para hazer nueuos descubrimientos sin enbiaroslo primero a consultar y tener para ello primero licencia nuestra" (*Transcripciónón de las Ordenanzas* 1573). Of course, Ibarra would have followed the instructions of the 1525 Ordenanzas, however, I refer to those of 1573 throughout this study, as those were in use at the time of Obregón's writing. *Las Ordenanzas de descubrimiento nueva población y pacificación de las Indias* are held in the AGI in Seville. I reference a transcription of the original document. See *Transcripción de las Ordenanzas* 1573.

4. In the case of Francisco Ibarra, the governor would not receive compensation from the Crown until 1574 in the form of an annual salary of 2,000 ducats. In addition, he and his followers were excused from the *alcabala* (a sort of sales tax) for twenty years. Finally, instead of the customary *quinto*, or one-fifth of all the precious metals extracted, the settlers of Nueva Vizcaya were only made to pay the Crown one-twentieth (Mecham 1927, 109). However, it is important to bear in mind that this compensation would come much later, and during the actual expedition Ibarra's principal means for compensating his soldiers was the granting of encomiendas.

5. "Poblar" is derived from "pueblo," defined in Corominas (1987, 480) as a "conjunto de los ciudadanos," and it communicates the action of founding and making inhabitable. I have translated it as "to settle" because this word connotes both "peopling" and inhabiting.

6. Álvar Núñez Cabeza de Vaca was the royal treasurer of the expedition led by Pánfilo de Narváez, which landed on the coast of Florida in 1528 with four hundred men. While three hundred men set out by land in search of riches, the ships were to follow the coast. However, the sea and land crews were separated, and after a year of searching, the sailors gave up hope and headed back to Cuba. The abandoned land expedition suffered storms, hunger, thirst, and native attacks, ultimately creating makeshift rafts to try to reach Mexico, but to no avail. Cabeza de Vaca was one of the four survivors of the expedition who made his way to present-day Sinaloa, Mexico, on foot, practicing cures as a medicine man for food and lodging with three other survivors (see Weber 1992; Adorno 1993, 1994, 1999).

7. It is interesting to note that this association of Antilla with Seven Cities represented the amalgamation of two legends: "Of all the legendary islands the most famous and most persistent was Antilla (Antilia, Antiglia, Annthilia, Antillia, Atilae, Atalae), sometimes also called Hidden Island or *Insula Perdita*, and often confused with the island of the Seven Cities (though more often located opposite it: its *ante ilha*). . . . The island of Antilla was the prototype of the supernatural paradise and a kind of theocracy, which according to the chronicler Herrera [1601] eluded navigators by becoming invisible" (Weckmann [1984] 1992, 17).

8. Rojo (2014) describes the commonalities between different versions of this foundation narrative, which are built around a theme of foreign ancestry and primordial migration, indicating a common birthplace of the various groups in the region. Different versions include an underworld with seven caves and an urban settlement surrounded by water, the people of whom are sent on a pilgrimage by a deity to a "promised land."

9. Rojo argues that by Obregón's time the "Medieval hypothesis" of seven bishops would have been debunked, and in fact cites Obregón's text as the "final blow" to that narrative. Rojo's study exposes our own blind spots in failing to recognize the tremendous influence of indigenous local knowledge and cosmology in this period of exploration. As she points out, Ibarra's group included Nahuatl-speaking interpreters as well as soldiers from the Coronado Expedition who had been to Cíbola. Also, Obregón frequently refers to the soldiers' hopes of finding "Otro México." Additionally, Rojo adds that they would have been following pre-Columbian routes of migration, commerce, and ritual exchange. "Indigenous views were neither completely neglected nor entirely suppressed. On the contrary, they became part of the conquistadors' cognitive repertoire, molding their expectations and informing their interpretations of the landscape and people they subsequently came across" (3356). She effectively shows that "Nuevo México" would have been a "transcultural object of desire" (3408). However, I don't agree that this necessarily means the abandonment of Medieval tropes nor that the two could not have coexisted. It is plausible that one only served to strengthen the other. Much like indigenous lore and knowledge spread by word of mouth, European lore and knowledge would have done so as well. At the time of de Niza's reporting the European legend may have persisted, and by Obregón's if only in stories told by conquistador fathers to their sons, the first generation criollos. Clissold confirms that "Antillia—'Ante-ilha' the island out opposite, the island in front" was still believed to exist in the sixteenth century, and a number of attempts were made to reach it (1961, 25). Also, Guzmán refers to it as he does to the legend of Las Islas Amazonas as late as the 1530s. Finally, "Antonio Galvano or Galvão, writing at the end of the second half of the sixteenth century, believes that the Seven Cities, Antilla, and New Spain are a single and identical entity" (Weckmann [1984] 1992, 17). Of course, in the previous century the Medieval legend may have held considerably more water. Antilia is included in many fifteenth-century maps, and the Western Antilles are named so because Europeans at first believed that Columbus had landed on Antilia (Weber 1992).

10. In 1548 the Spanish created the Audiencia de Nueva Galicia, which was charged with overseeing the region north and west of Mexico City, and many explorations left from Nueva Galicia (Jones 1988, 17).

11. The oidores of Nueva Galicia were incensed that Ibarra settled Chiametla, claiming that Morones's grant should have been passed on to them. They tried, but failed, to have Ibarra ousted (see Mecham 1927).

12. Obregón's mission in joining the Ibarra Expedition in Chiametla was to warn Ibarra that an enemy of his, Juan de Avellaneda, had acquired a mandate charging Ibarra and his men (falsely, according to Obregón) with having stolen horses before departing from San Martín. At the time, Ibarra was planning to explore farther north

and had asked Hernando de Trejo to come to Chiametla to serve as *maese de campo* (first lieutenant) in his absence. Obregón joined Trejo in Compostela to make the journey to Chiametla together, but only after Obregón had travelled forty leagues alone during the rainy season in "lands of war," which he relates in chapter 18 of the first book.

13. Additionally, *Historia* exemplifies other discursive characteristics that Mignolo (1982, 103–10) cites as salient features that emerge during particular periods in New Spain. It is interesting to note that in Obregón, we see an overlap of these periods. For example, Mignolo argues that the *historia indiana* during the period between 1480 and 1543 included the following characteristics, all of which are reflected in *Historia*: "la expansión territorial de España"; "el impulso humanístico en la historiografía"; "el abandono de tipo de crónica medieval"; "el auge de las historias nacionales y nuevo capítulo en la historiografía castellana"; and "la historia de las Indias" (104). While Obregón's text does not reflect the "preocupación por la historia indígena" cited as a hallmark of the period between 1543 and 1592, or "el auge de los cronistas oficiales y consolidación de la historiografía oficial," it is a text indicative of "la profusión de géneros" (105). Finally, Obregón's *Historia* demonstrates "la predicación del cristianismo se aneja a la historia eclesiástica," a salient feature of the period 1592–1623.

14. Although the Ordenanzas of 1573 had condemned the use of the word *conquistar* in favor of the euphemism *pacificar*, Obregón regardless uses *conquistar* alongside *pacificar* and *poblar* throughout the text. Likewise he employs "encomienda" despite the Crown's efforts to abolish that institution with Las Leyes Nuevas (1542), which intended to avoid the maltreatment of indigenous people in the New World by regulating and eventually abolishing the encomienda system. However, these edicts fomented discontent among the colonists, including a revolt in Perú, and the Crown repealed the New Laws in 1545. I treat the topic of the persistence of the encomienda and other forms of forced labor in chapter 4. (See *Las leyes nuevas, 1542–1543; ordenanzas para la gobernación de las Indias y buen tratamiento y conservación de los indios. Edición, estudio y notas por Antonio Muro Orejón*. Ed. Antonio Muro Orejón. Sevilla: 1961.)

15. Rosa Camelo's article "La idea de la historia en Baltasar de Obregón" (1971) examines what the text reveals about Obregón's own conceptions of History, citing three major functions of History in Obregón: to serve as an example for other men, to preserve memory and fame of the conquistadors that they may be recognized for their efforts, and to tell the truth.

16. María Bravo also notes that in addition to Obregón himself, various *escribanos* had added to and otherwise "intervened" in the text. The escribano served as "a combination secretary, scribe, and notary [and] could be either a government or private position" (Flint and Flint 2005, 706). Bravo's linguistic analysis of *Historia* indicates that in terms of phonetic-phonological aspects, "surgen las características del español meridional y los vulgarismos extendidos por toda la Península, que aparecen arraigados en el habla de los escribanos que intervienen en la redacción del texto" (1997, 28). See Adorno (1995) for more on the complexity of the "yo" in juridical documents and the role of the escribano and relator.

17. "Aunque hurtando el oficio y natural ejercicio de la abeja, que recogiendo la sustancia de muchas y diversas flores la junta y convierte en dulce miel y a [semejanza

de] este ejemplo no debo ser culpado de lo que pareciere haber tomado de otras historias, siendo traídas a la memoria con razones, ejemplos y necesario cuadrante a la utilidad de lo que tratare" (42).

18. "Por su lengua, sus fuentes literarias e históricas y su conocimiento de tópicos y modelos de la tradición, hay que adscribir este autor a un estrato social no muy culto, pero con una formación que abarca el conocimiento de las armas y de algunas letras" (Bravo 1997, 13).

19. Vitulli and Solodkow examine "lo criollo" as a cultural concept under constant construction, recognizing not only the discontinuities and transformations of the term, but also the particularities of the term's connotations depending on its situación enunciativa (9, 17). They demarcate three historical stages of the term's transformation: (1) stereotype, or fixity and ambiguity (1560–1600); (2) agency, or linguistic reappropriation (1600–1700); and (3) formation of a criollo consciousness (1700–1810) (17). The term, as I use it here, would not have conjured the same provincial connotations as it would in the eighteenth century when "Creole pioneers" (as Benedict Anderson refers to them) emerged as visible social groups increasingly possessing their own cultural and political identities. See Benedict Anderson's Imagined Communities for more on the role of the Creole and the newspaper in nineteenth-century independence movements.

20. Le Riverend and Venegas demonstrate how the image of the criollo as inferior emerged in order to justify power relations and maintain the status quo in New Spain, counteracting the growing influence and number of criollos. This was accomplished in three principal ways, the first of which was to put obstacles in place that prevented the extension of the encomienda. From the second half the sixteenth century until the beginnings of the eighteenth, a bitter debate raged over the rule of "por dos vidas," under which the encomienda extended from father to son, but not to descendants thereafter (27). A second tactic involved control of the land. "Plena propiedad" for the criollo meant that he had to take on prohibitively expensive and hard to prove legal battles, "dilatados y costosos procesos legales." Finally, *prelación*—the priority or right that the criollos had to seek vacant administrative or religious posts, while initially favorable to criollos, changed dramatically when arguments of their defects abounded, depicting the criollo as incapable of governing (27–28).

21. Benítez elequently captures the milieu of the time thusly: "Los criollos habían perdido una gran batalla histórica y el paraíso de las Indias se convirtió en un lugar incómodo y miserable. Las encomiendas—la razón de su vida—se liquidaban y el fragmento de idílica caballería . . . se venía abajo sin remedio triunfando la Inquisición, los advenedizos, los burócratas y los agiotistas" (Fernando Benítez 237).

22. Obregón contextualizes the indigenous revolt as resulting from the excesses and abuses that the Spanish perpetrated against the indigenous inhabitants:

[Los indígenas] Asolaron, derrocaron y robaron la villa que estuvo poblada en este valle y mataron al capitán Diego de Alcaraz y a cien hombres que dejó avecindados Francisco Vázquez Coronado por ocasiones desordenadas y ofensas que hicieron a los naturales, así de aprovecharse de sus mujeres e hijas como en cargarles con demasiados tributos y servicios personales y asimismo por el desorden que tenían en el tomarles bastimentos y gritarlos con desorden, tomándoselos sin pagárselos y sin consentimiento de su voluntades. . . . Y el mayor daño de todo fue emponzoñarlos y acancerarles los corazones con la ponzoña y carcoma del celo porque les tomaban, quitaban y aprovechaban de sus mujeres e hijas, con tanta disolución y poco secreto que me han certificado los que se hallaron presentes que cuando entraron asolando la villa los enemigos, estaba el capitán acostado con dos indias. . . . Dios nuestro Señor lo permitió por castigar como castigó sus desconciertos y mal ejemplo a gente que iban a poner en orden y concierto de nuestra santa Fe católica. (Obregón 1584, 155–56)

23. Obregón refers to the indigenous people as potential vassals throughout the text. Weckmann examines what the word meant in the sixteenth century in juridical and social terms. He finds that the Crown identified vassalage with "the payment of a tribute of considerable worth," made by the encomenderos, the true vassals. However the explorers often used "vassal" to refer to indigenous people, reflecting the word's classical feudal meaning, in which a vassal could refer to a free fief holder or to an unfree famer, or *solariegos* (Weckmann [1984] 1992, 75). "Éstos de Chiametla han sido de paz de muchos años a esta parte y de ordinario han tratado y contratado con los pasajeros y caminantes que han pasado por su pueblo y vendídoles bastimentos por mercaderías de menudencias. Prometieron al gobernador serían obedientes *vasallos* de vuestra S.C.C.R.M. . . . Ofreciéronse a la ayuda y pacificación y conquista de los caribes serranos" (119).

24. Maureen Ahern (1995b, 155) has argued that many texts from this period would have served as guides for future expeditions. I treat the issue of the historia as itinerary description in chapter 3.

25. Sauer also notes in the same essay that he preferred to refer to the Mariano Cuevas edition as he found Hammond and Rey's English translation to be unreliable.

26. While scholars such as Walter Mignolo have warned against such literary interpretations, emphasizing that relaciones were written out of an obligation to inform the Crown and not with the goal of being read as literature, it would be hard to overlook the literary elements in Obregón. In "Discurso jurídico, discurso literario: el reto de leer en el siglo XX los escritores del XVI" (1995), Rolena Adorno argues that the relación represents a type of discourse unto itself, apart from, yet related to, the traditional concept of literature. While the model for the relación was primarily the judicial format rather than any literary one at the same time, the modern reader recognizes elements of both in the relación. Adorno suggests that attempts to differentiate between these texts as juridical or literary are arbitrary, as both genres are interpretive constructions and neither is purely transparent nor purely self-reflective (17). In this sense, to categorize the relación as one or the other is as limiting as it is irrelevant. For the purposes of this analysis, the greater import lies in understanding how and why the narrating subject employs literary elements to relate what is seen and how this plays a role in landscape appropriation.

27. "Cuando Dios nuestro Señor permitió la infernal y abominable secta contagiosa, daño en las almas por las culpas y pecados de los hombres de la secta del abominable y ponzoñoso basilisco Martín Lutero, fue servido permitir y ordenar que el día que nació este pérfido dañador y enemigo de nuestra santa Fe católica, nació el católico y cristianísimo marqués don Hernando Cortés para el remedio, conversión y salvación del gran número de indios idólatras" (Obregón 1584, 46–47).

John Leddy Phelan demonstrates that this parallel between Luther and Cortés was not an uncommon one, citing the Franciscan missionary Gerónimo de Mendieta and his contemporaries as disseminators of such a narrative. It would seem that Obregón further disseminates a critical error: "Mendieta had again confused his dates. Luther was born in 1483, and Cortés in 1485" (Phelan 1970, 32).

28. A Turco-Mongol conqueror, Timur Lang invaded Anatolia and defeated Bayezid and the Ottoman Empire in 1402. Timur saw the Seljuks as the rightful rulers of Anatolia.

29. While *Historia* is divided into two books, the first book is much larger in scope, consisting of thirty-eight chapters, while the second book, which primarily deals with the later expeditions of Chamuscado-Rodríguez and Antonio Espejo, comprises only ten. The first five chapters of book 1 summarize the period between Hernán Cortés's arrival at Tenochtitlán through the departure of the Ibarra expedition from San Martín.

30. "Ordinario" indicated "daily" (Corominas 1954, 4:291). "Descaecer" intimates a gradual decrease in health, authority, credit, or wealth (*Diccionario de Autoridades* 1726–39).

31. In the Bravo edition from which I cite, "Topía" is spelled with the í. However, I employ the more common spelling of "Topia" when not quoting directly from Bravo's edition.

32. Mecham points out that Castañeda only wrote his account once Ibarra, in his initial entradas north of Nueva Galicia, had begun claiming territories that Coronado had already traversed.

Chapter Two

1. Murphy (2004, 131) argues that Pliny the Elder's *Naturalis historia* set a precedent for the organization of knowledge under imperial authority, assimilating the unfamiliar into the realm of Roman culture. "This kind of survey occurs often in the rhetoric of ancient history and poetry; these parallels in turn force us to think further about the political implications of such geographical description."

2. Portuondo addresses the distinctive functions of cosmographers in the Casa de la Contratación, the Consejo de Indias, and those appointed for ad hoc committees or to work for the Court. Because Obregón addresses his text specifically to the Consejo de Indias, I have limited my analysis of the particular aspects cited as germane to that institution (see Portuondo 2009, chapter 2, "Cosmographical Styles at the Casa, Consejo, and Corte" in *Secret Science*).

3. Specifically, Obregón relates how much it had greatly pained the participants of the Coronado Expedition to turn back from Quivira "porque desearon saber y descubrir los secretos de aquella gran tierra y su remate en la mar, mayormente porque hubo insignias y sospecha [de que] llegaron cerca del gran río Salado y de la Mar del Norte, adonde se tiene por cierta ser del Estrecho de los Bacalaos hacia Irlanda; este estrecho y costa ha sido deseado su descubrimiento para continuar desde él viaje a España y descubrir las naciones de gentes que habitan en sus rededores y comarcas" (61). Obregón reasons that the Straight of Bacalaos should be in that area, since Quivira lies in the general direction and region of Ireland, the cattle found there are similar to those of Ireland, and it is cold like Ireland.

4. Padrón considers conceptions of space in the process of the invention of America, arguing that throughout the sixteenth century a medieval perception of space persisted, one grounded in a linear sense of space based on embodied experience. To be clear, Westphal (2013, 38) reminds us that "space" was not always a spatial concept, but rather more akin to movement. The more abstract meaning of the word "space" as we use it today would not come into usage until Descartes's *Principes de la Philsophic* (1644).

5. "Luego que los descubridores lleguen a las provincias y tierras que descubrieren juntamente con los offiçiales pongan nombre a toda la tierra a cada prouincia por si a los montes y rios mas principales que en ellas ouiere y a los pueblos y ciudades que allaren en la tierra y ellos fundaren" (*Transcripción de las Ordenanzas* 1973, 16).

6. Rojos demonstrates that "Nuevo México" is the only toponym formed by Europeans during the early colonial period that reproduced the name of an Amerindian place (227). Rojos also points out that the Nahuatl term for "nuevo," "yancuic," connoted the idea of "new," but also "original" or "primeval," and contends that many Spanish would have understood this usage.

7. Bravo defines "poblazón" as "el efecto de poblar" (286). The *Diccionario crítico etimológico castellano e hispánico Corominas* (1954) includes "poblazón" as deriving from "pueblo": "Es corriente desde la Edad Media el uso de 'pueblo' con el valor de congregación numerosa de gente afectada por una común condición política" (4:673).

8. It is possible that the Chamuscado routes were actually, at least in part, new ones that visited more than sixty indigenous settlements, many of which represent first contact with many pueblos that Coronado did not visit.

9. Bernardino de Luna was a participant in the Espejo Expedition who Obregón explains "murió en servicio de V.M." Luna's descendants provided the testimony for the *Historia*.

10. When Mendoza did not grant Hernán Cortés the commission he desired to explore the north, Cortés tried to go over the viceroy's head. However his plea to the Real Consejo in Spain fell on deaf ears. Later, the second viceroy of New Spain, Luis de Velasco, gave a commission to Cortés's son. The latter's expedition was cut short, and Obregón contends that had Luis Cortés been permitted to continue his journey he would have discovered "las naciones que habitan en casas de gran altura que llaman Nuevo México" later discovered by Francisco Sánchez Chamuscado in 1581 (71).

11. Diego de Ibarra was born in the village of Ybar in Guipúzcoa and arrived in New Spain in 1540, whereupon he joined Viceroy Mendoza in Nueva Galicia in fighting the Mixtón War, during which he lost his leg. He remained in the frontier region and had become extremely wealthy when Juan de Tolosa, a Basque explorer (and incidentally, Hernán Cortés's son-in-law) shared his silver discovery in Zacatecas with him, along with Cristobal de Oñate and Batlasar Temiño de Bolaños. The four men formed an agreement to found a town near the mines and Zacatecas and in a very short time were the wealthiest men not just in New Spain, but in the Americas (see Mecham 1927, 43–47).

12. Mecham notes that the *alcalde mayor* of San Martín, Diego de Colio, viewed Ibarra's men as marauders more than explorers and accused them of stealing from

and harassing the inhabitants of his village. Colio also apparently claimed that he had preceded Ibarra to Nombre de Dios by two months and seventeen days (1927, 114). Later, Obregón will reference the unseemly behavior of his fellow soldiers despite not having witnessed any of the events in San Martín.

13. Ibarra first sent a small scouting party consisting of Salvador Ponce and four soldiers to confirm the existence of Topia. On their return, Ibarra sent twenty soldiers and several more guides along with the maestre de campo, Martín Gamón (see chapter 1). Ibarra himself led the expedition to Topia after Easter and spent several months in the Sierras around Topia after fighting a battle with the Acaxee warriors (Obregón 81–90).

14. Rivera-Ayala (2002) says that the horse served an imperative social function during the colonial period: "Its use was an exclusive privilege of the European population. . . . Within the chivalric environment of the sixteenth century the horse was not just a means of transportation or for moving goods but rather represented a social status" (261).

15. I have translated "politica" and "policia" to "civilized" throughout the text. Corominas indicates the term "politica"'s association as early as the year 1399 with the idea of "buena crianza" (467, 1987).

16. Lawson-Peebles applies the idea of perceptual geography in his textual analysis of writings of the American Revolutionary era, using the term *landscape* to mean "the land as percept [*sic*]" (1988, 4). Drawing partially from the polemical Sapir-Whorf hypothesis, in which thinking depends on language, Lawson-Peebles aims to establish the nature of the relationship between language and landscape, contending that perception and language exist together. While Lawson-Peebles does not embrace Whorf's notion that language is the key to cognition, he recognizes that "perception and language exist together," thereby eliminating a direct connection, as he puts it, between "Word" and the "World" (5).

17. "Cinaro" refers to the modern-day region around the Río Fuerte and the Valle Carapoa, about 30 kilometers north of the modern-day city of Los Mochis in the state of Sinaloa. Obregón uses the names "Cinaro" and "Tigueco y Cinaro" when referring to these lands to the north of Culiacán. The rivers of Petatlán (Río Sinaloa) and Ocoroni (a tributary to Río Sinaloa) are included in his depictions of this region, as well as the villages of Petlatlán, Ocoroni, Ciguini, and Tigueco y Cinaro.

18. While the repartimiento was not introduced in New Spain until 1575, several years after Obregón's participation in the Ibarra expedition, the notion of it clearly formed a part of Obregón's conception of the region when he was composing his text. Furthermore, Obregón employs the term *encomienda* just as frequently to describe Ibarra's distribution of land and people to members of the expedition. I elaborate on the persistence and coexistence of these forced labor systems in the northern reaches of New Spain in chapter 4.

19. The speech in its entirety reads as follows:

> Escogidos y esforzados cristianos y amigos míos: Yo quisiera haber descubierto y conquistado otra nueva y riquísima Constantinopla y otra próspera y fortísima Venecia o, a lo menos, otro insigne y rico México u otro atesorado Perú, para apoderaros y haceros señores de sus señoríos y riquezas con mayor título y grandeza

que lo poseen, señorean y gozan [*sic*] los que los tienen. Mas es justa y moderada consideración, como de católicos y esforzados soldados, que los tesoros, riquezas y señoríos los de Dios nuestro sumo bien, a quién y cómo y cuándo Él es servido. Y considerando la recta obligación que a su santo servicio tenemos los que somos cristianos y hemos prometido y profesado la santa obediencia y dirección de las cosas pertenecientes al uso y ejercicio de nuestra santa Fe católica, es justo ocurrir a su santo servicio aumentando en ella a esta nación bárbara, rústica y desconocida de su Dios criador y salvador, para que conozcan, gocen y alcancen luz de sus inestimable y resplandeciente sol de justicia y seamos principio, parte y medio para rescatarlos de las eternas penas del infierno. . . . Buscaremos otros medios que consigan y aumenten la grandeza y colmo de mi deseo para que empareje a la gratificación de vuestros méritos obras y leales servicios, y os certifico es el fundamento de mis hechos, promesas e intención después del que enderezo y consigo al servicio de la potestad de Dios nuestro Señor y el de la imperial majestad de nuestro católico y poderoso Emperador y señor natural. (103–4)

20. The reader must take pause here and wonder if relating this speech supposedly delivered by Ibarra is also somehow a way for Obregón to demonstrate compliance with the Ordenanzas.

21. Here Obregón indicates that this occurs in June of 1567, although this is clearly an error.

22. "Puso en condición y término de despoblarse la villa por no dejar repartida la tierra" (140). Ibarra's troubles with desertion continued later in the expedition when he determined to settle the area along the river Yaquimi (Yaqui in present-day Sonora). He sent word to the maestre de campo in Cinaro to send soldiers to help, but he was informed of their discontent for not having yet received land grants: "Y asimismo le dio aviso del descontento que tenían los soldados que le había dejado en no dejarles señalados sus repartimientos, ocasión de haberse huido los que estaban ausentes, y que importaba su ida a Cinaro para muchos efectos, mayormente para el amparo de la villa de Cinaro, las demás de su gobernación y que la de Cinaro estaba en términos de despoblarse" (217).

Chapter Three

1. Quoniam's explanation of this inversion of text and image elucidates the impossible nature of attempting to definitively (re)present landscape:

This desire to see does not imply truth in the vision developed by the artist considering landscape and space. Thus, the betrayal of images is enriched by false writing which becomes the symbolic commentary on spatial structure. This text is illegible. However, a word, a part of a sentence written in French (I am French) or in English (the space is in Arizona) can be read. This emphasizes the impossibility of really defining the space and landscape which surround us. Words and their use betray both the discourse of the geographer and the space which originates this discourse. Painting becomes the text of my ideas and the text becomes the descriptive picture of the landscape. The spatial structuring of the text goes back and forth between legible phenomenon (intelligibility) and illegible phenomenon (unintelligibility) in the continuity/discontinuity of our experience, of our perceptions, and their commentary. One cannot forget that the discovery of writing allowed people to open up new spaces. In my work, the text represents another space. (1988, 9)

2. The traditional categorization of "sedentary" or "nomadic" has been recently called into question in studies about the region. Likewise, the complexities of indigenous identity are continuously coming to light (Areti Hers and Mirafuente 2000; Rojo 2014; Deeds 2003). Rojo points out that scholars are increasingly grappling with the limitations of traditional models of categorization based on "cultural areas" such as that advanced by Paul Kirchhoff in which three geocultural groups are identified (Mesoamerica, Aridamerica, and Oasisamerica). This model, as well as the "Greater Southwest" and "American Southwest" model (which represent the equivalent of Kirchhoff's Oasisamerica and Aridamerica) are driven by settlement patterns, subsistance methods, and sociopolitcal concerns. The term "Gran Chichimeca," coined by Charles di Peso and Beatriz Braniff is likewise problematic. "Nowadays it is clear that the equation 'Mesoamerican/sedentism/agricultural versus Aridamerican/nomadism/ hunting-gathering' ingrained in Kirchhoff's model is a gross simplification" (Rojo 2014, 1089).

3. One aspect of the landscape, the desert fauna, even "followed" the Yaqui into exile to the United States. The Yaqui, many of whom now reside in Arizona as the descendants of exiled refugees who fled Mexico in the late nineteenth century, still make a yearly pilgrimage to Magdalena in the state of Sonora to honor a Catholic saint, but do so in their own way: "They bring musical instruments and dance regalia and perform the deer and pascola dances for their saint—dances that blend Yaqui and European heritages and reflect a strong traditional relationship between people and the creatures of the desert" (Griffith 1993, xv).

4. Lawson-Peebles (1988) makes the case for a similarly strong connection between language and landscape, however not in the direct manner of Spirn.

5. Sheridan-Prieto points to recent historiography that "tierra de Guerra Chichimecas" cultural contrast and diversity. "Muchos estudios parten ahora de las identidades multiples que afloran, casi acidentalmente, en la documentación [occidental]" (2002, 15).

6. Documents from this period are demonstrative of the Spanish inability to recognize ethnic, cultural, and political differences between groups. Deeds (2003) explores the persistence of ethnic identity in some cases and its demise in others under conditions of conquest, employing a comparative and chronological approach to studying semisedentary and nonsedentary groups. She points out that the Spanish did not differentiate between *naciones*, *villas*, etc., thereby eliminating difference. In fact, Ahern has demonstrated how the Spanish were purposefully deceived and manipulated by the Chichimecas who used this ignorance to their advantage in fighting the Spanish: "Los chichimecas rápidamente desviaron esta ceguera étnica en una arma táctica importante: la traición" (1998, 70). This also demonstrates the crucial role that auxiliary soldiers and interpreters, who did recognize difference, played in the negotiation of identity.

7. Hopkins Durazo cites these sons as the first "mestizos sonorenses" (1988, 37). The question of miscegenation also arises in Sauer's study of the region. He argues that the institution of the encomienda would have increased contact and miscegenation between different groups from Jalisco, Michoacán, Mexico, or African slaves "who promptly bred a mulatto progeny." Sauer concludes that the "encomienda meant quickly the end of tribal individuality" (Sauer 1932, 2).

While Sauer's assessment may be debated, the Spanish expansion project and the institutions inherent in its mission, such as the encomienda and the establishment of mining camps would have served to increase forced migration. Furthermore, due to the inability of the Spanish to recognize individual differences, more than likely different cultural identities were not perceived or encouraged to thrive by the Spanish.

8. Mesoamerica was more diverse than is commonly believed. Recently, scholars have begun abandoning the conception of this region as a cultural unit and stressing differences more than commonalites, marked by "extreme population mobility" and "complex multi-ethnic aggregation and disaggregation within fairly centralized political units" (Rojo 2014, 1130).

9. Coronado left New Spain in 1540 with several hundred auxiliary indigenous allies, including women; however, he did not return with as many. Riley explains: "The exact number of [Indian allies] will probably never be known, but there were at least several hundred Indians. Castañeda gives the figure 'more than 1,000 persons.'... It seems likely that a number of women went on the expedition, though there is very little mention of them. Only three women (one Indian and two Spaniards) are specifically noted as wives of soldiers.... Women and children actually do not seem to have been considered exceptional. In the Jaramillo narrative, for example, there is passing mention of a black slave of Melchior Pérez who has his wife and children at Tiguex and remained there" (1974, 28). Despite their great numbers, little is known about auxiliary soldiers. Ahern argues that documents written in Nahuatl from the settlement of Nombre de Dios attest to and claim acknowledgement of the Nahua auxiliaries' important role in the war, a dimension that is otherwise suppressed in Obregón and Ibarra's official reports (Ahern 1998).

10. Hopkins Durazo (1988) views the familiarity of groups in the Sonora Valley with objects from the sea as indicative of exchange prior to European contact: "Es notable también el aprecio en que tienen los indígenas de la sierra los objetos provenientes del mar, como conchas y caracoles, así como los plumajes elegantes de aves de otras latitudes, lo que demuestra que entre las diversas tribus existía un comercio o intercambio de productos de su región" (23). Also, Riley (1974) rejects the notion that Mesoamerican influences to pueblo ceremonialism such as masked religious dances and mythology occurred in the sixteenth century, arguing that this influence had occurred in pre-Columbian times. Recent studies have lent credence to the notion that complex trade routes existed. Kokrda (2005) cites the "frequent appearance of a plumed or horned serpent found in central and southern Mexico is imagery also depicted on Casas Grandes ceramics" as an indication of such connections that existed long before the arrival of the Spanish (113). Griffith (1993) also makes an argument for longstanding exchange between the peoples of Mesoamerica (dating to 1060–1340 CE) that reached as far north as Paquimé in the present-day state of Chihuahua. He cites the late archeologist Charles Di Peso: "Di Peso's contention,

supported by a good deal of impressive evidence, is that ruin he calls Paquimé was a sort of staging area for a deliberate attempt at trade and proselytization that were carried on by immigrants from Central Mexico's high cultures" (10).

11. The Coronado Expedition had instilled such terror in the indigenous with whom they came in contact, argues Ahern, that Hernán Gallegos would later marvel at "la reacción de gran temor y huida que provocó la mera aparición de su compañía compuesta por nueve soldados y tres frailes" (1994, 196). Adorno and Rabasa's work illuminates the tremendous effect of fear both in terms of the Spaniards' attempts to control theirs and the ways they learned to inspire fear in the aboriginal peoples: "Fear of the other was a weapon by both sides, the Native American and the European" (1991, 167). For example, Deeds (2003) suggests that the indigenous may have feigned or exaggerated cannibalism to scare the Spanish.

12. The effects of warfare, migration, subsistence changes, and disease have caused scholars to call into question the ranchería pattern advanced by Edward H. Spicer.

13. It follows that culture must be viewed as agent, the natural landscape (the area prior to the man's introduction to it) as medium, and the cultural landscape as result. This represents an important empirical turn in the field of human geography. Agnew (1996) notes the coincidence in the early part of the twentieth century of Sauer's notion of cultural geography and the overwhelming abandonment of the notion of environmental determinism in the field of human geography, an abandonment that would be replaced by historical particularism (135). While one may take issue with a subject-object conceptual framework that presupposes a "natural landscape," Sauer's study does provide several critical tools. In the first place, he brings landscape to the table in the field of geography. Second, although he adds "cultural" to "landscape," which, viewed in light of the term's etymology, may be criticized as redundant, he recognizes the human element in landscape as well as the idea that landscape is dynamic in space and time. Finally, he calls attention to cultural manifestations in landscape, manifestations that reveal themselves frequently in textual production.

14. In Obregón's words: "Vacas que hallaron multiplicadas de las que dejó perdidas Francisco Vázquez de Coronado cuando iba al viaje de Cíbola, y de las que iban dejando vecinos de Culiacán cuando metían ganado en su villa" (131). In the Valle de Señora they find melons "de la semilla que les quedó de cuando mataron a ls de Alcaraz" (153). For more on this topic, see Riley 1974.

15. Powell describes the development of a system of presidios and defensive towns placed at strategic points in the tierra de guerra of the silver frontier, a system that began during the administration of the second viceroy of New Spain, Luis de Velasco (1551–64), and reached its greatest development under the fourth viceroy, Martín Enríquez de Almanza (1568–80) (Powell 1977, 181).

16. Pratt uses the phrase "contact zone" to refer to "social spaces where cultures meet, clash, and grapple with each other, often in contexts of highly asymmetrical relations of power, such as colonialism, slavery, or the aftermaths" (2002, 34). This concept offers a useful point of analytical departure in colonial studies because the idea of the contact zone illuminates encounters between two cultures (or more as the case may be here) as a dialogue and an exchange. That said, at this very specific moment that Obregón is attempting to capture, power was not asymmetrical, and the colonial machine was not yet as entrenched as it would be even in ten more years.

By the following century the concept of the "contact zone" may offer a useful tool in studying the region.

17. It is here in the Valle de San Juan that the soldiers hear of Topia for the first time, and when Ibarra sends Martín Gamón on the scouting expedition during which he hangs the guides (see chapter 1). Obregón also contends that during this time, Martín Gamón is jealous that Ibarra has left Martín de Arana as Gamón's substitute in the San Juan Valley. Gamón recruits a few soldiers to his side and causes discontent among the soldiers and is later condemned to death.

18. Many scholars (Arens, 1998; Hulme 1986, 1998; Jáuregui 2005) point out that "cannibalism" was not a new phenomenon to the Spanish but rather a classic trope of the European imagination dating from Herodotus. "The locations moved but the descriptions of Amazons, Anthropophagi and Cynocephali remained constant throughout Ctesias, Pliny, Solinus, and many others" (Hulme 1998, 21). Hulme cites a passage from Diego Alvarez Chanca, who sailed with Columbus on his second voyage, in which Chanca reports that Columbus and some of his men entered an indigenous person's house and retrieved several material items, including "four or five bones of the arms and legs of men." Chanca has only reported second-hand information and infers cannibalism a priori. This original passage is then rewritten in several texts (including, Hulme points out, Peter Martyr who "never got nearer to the Caribbean than Andalucía"), and with each new depiction, increasingly horrifying elements are added, such as pieces of human flesh on a spit ready for roasting and the head of a young boy dripping blood hanging from a beam (1998, 16–18). Hulme sustains that Arens's argument (1979), which questions the adequacy of documentation regarding cannibalism, has been misrepresented. Whether people eat each other and what their motivations are less important to discuss than "the fact that the idea that they do so is commonly accepted without adequate documentation" (Hulme 1998, 7).

19. Ashcroft (2000) postulates that the superseding of "anthropophagi" by "cannibalism" was not a simple change in the description of the practice of eating human flesh but rather the replacement of the descriptive term with an ontological category.

20. As a final note on cannibalism, "El tropo caníbal funciona como estereotipo colonial; fija o significa al *Otro*; produce la *diferencia* y también el terror de reconocimiento en ella" (28). Catholic transubstantiation, under attack from the Reformation: "Los sacrificios mexicas producirían un reconocimiento siniestro e intolerable a perversión del sacramento Eucharistic" (29).

21. "Todos estos daños, carnicerías, robos y matanzas y ofensas a Dios nuestro Señor, daños de los vecinos y moradores de la villa y minas, caminos de San Miguel de Culiacán, cesaron con el remedio y pacificación del gobernador Francisco de Ibarra y sus soldados [All of this harm, carnage, robbing and killing, and offenses to God our Lord, harm of the residents and inhabitants of the town and mines, paths from San Miguel de Culiacán, they stopped with the remedy and pacification of the governor Francisco de Ibarra and his soldiers]"(93). Thanks to Ibarra, the indigenous inhabitants had been pacified and re-encomendados, "los cuales prometieron reconocer, tributar y obedecer a su encomendero don Pedro de Tovar [they promised to recognize, pay tribute to, and obey their encomendero, don Pedro de Tovar]" (93).

22. "Gandul 'moro o indio joven y belicoso' 2.a mitad S.XV." (Corominas 1987, 291).

23. Hopkins Durazo (1988, 22) hypothesizes that Oera "pudo estar localizado en algún lugar sobre el alto río Yaqui . . . cerca del actual San Pedro de la Cueva." Obregón contends that the Oera were enemies of the peoples of Cinaro, Corazones, Guaraspi, and Asenmuça, and comments on the Oera's "bellicose nature" (174).

24. For more on the archaeological site of Paquimé, see Di Peso 1974.

25. Obregón does relate a story about "un indio valiente y osado." When he and six other soldiers enter a village he calls Temosa along the Río Mayombo, they begin to take corn from a man's house. "Nos salió a flechar y hacer daño en las personas y caballos de cargar sin temer del daño que les [*sic*] podíamos hacer. . . . Fue caso digno de loa y memoria atreverse un solo indio a cinco soldados" (146). However, this is quickly dismissed as the exception to the norm when Obregón immediately adds that the hundred other Indians in the village did not dare to come down to aid the *indio valiente*, or even come near the Spaniards. In case of Luisa, while Obregón does acknowledge Luisa's intelligence and ability, "these traits are largely negated by his repeated and confusing emphasis on Luisa as the wife of various male caciques, some of whom purportedly kept her captive, which implied that Luisa's husbands rather than Luisa exercised ultimate authority" (Reff and Kelley 2008, 17).

26. Westphal's section entitled "Cabeza de Vaca or the Possibility of Space" in *Plausible World* (2013, 103–8) provides an insightful and refreshing reading of the famous *Naufragios* and Nicolás Echeverría's 1991 film interpretation.

Chapter Four

1. A valuable source for the project of Jesuit reducciones is Pérez de Ribas 1999, 1645.

2. Ibarra is often recognized as preferring to use gifts and persuasion as opposed to war to expand Spanish territory, and Obregón is insistent regarding his Christian leadership. See Jones 1988 and Mecham 1927.

3. "[Ibarra] Mandó poner en el pueblo una gran cruz, que fue necesaria mucha gente para la traída del madero y levantarla en alto. Enteró en la peña de ella todos los ídolos que pudo descubrir, tenían y halló, y los demás que tenían en la gran altura, sierras y cuevas de aquella serranía" (88).

4. The signs were also used in reverse, with the indigenous people reading them. Obregón relates that, recalling Cabeza de Vaca, the querechos expect Ibarra's group to perform a ritual similar to the one that the former had performed: "Eran muy continos [*sic*] e importunos a que los tocásemos y santiguásemos, que es ceremonia que uso Álvar Núñez Cabeza de Vaca" (179). Not only does this prior contact with the Cabeza de Vaca contingency affect indigenous perception of Spaniards, presumably leading them to believe the Spaniards to be "hijos del sol," it equally affects Spanish perception of the indigenous, who here are depicted as docile subjects, serving and adoring the Spanish visitors. A similar encounter takes place in Fernando de Alarcón's 1556 account when he uses the identity of a "hijo del sol" to garner friendly treatment ([1556] 1967, [1556] 2004; see also King 1996). Finally, Ahern has also noted this phenomenon in Gallegos when the Spanish erect crosses and the Conchos recognize the men as "hijos del sol." The Spanish then take advantage of reports such as Cabeza de Vaca's

in dealing with the indigenous people: "Ciertas relaciones anteriores aportaron la formación del paradigma de primer contacto" (Ahern 2001, 385).

5. Following is another passage that speaks to Obregón's sense of Providence:

> Entre todas las naciones que hasta hoy están descubiertas, vistas y experimentadas y conocidas, ninguna iguala y empareja con la española. . . . Asimismo han sido vencedores y destructores de estos pérfidos competidores y enemigos de nuestra santa Fe católica, ayudándola y defendiéndola con el tesoro y limpieza de las Sagradas Escrituras, doctrina y teología han conquistado y sujetado muchas extrañas, diversas y remotas naciones, llegándolas y amparándolas al gremio y tesoro de nuestra inestimable Fe católica y nacen con esta virtuosa indignación, esfuerzo y firmeza y gran espíritu de aumentar y añadir este rebaño, el cual es fe de ser uno junto sin división de reino, mando, ley y costumbres y preceptos; de la cual nación ha acontecido pasar por tierras de bárbaros infieles desconocidos de nuestro Dios creador y salvador, adonde por su suma y piadosa y misericordia y permisión ha hecho milagros, porque esta gente desconocida y ciega del conocimiento de Dios y de su ley evangélica se aficione a ser cristiana. (178)

This sentiment of Providence applies not only to the greater Spanish empire but also operates on the more regional level of New Spain, in which who discovers what and when is likewise attributed to God's divine plan. Why else, reasons Obregón, would the Ibarra Expedition have come so close to the famous coveted pueblos of Nuevo México but never reach them? Obregón misjudges or exaggerates the expedition's proximity to the pueblos of New Mexico that would later be reached by "los descubridores nuevos," namely Chamuscado and later Espejo (187):

> Por cuyos inconvenientes y sucesos y la voluntad de Dios nuestro Señor ante todas cosas, que no permitió ni fue servido que se descubriesen las poblazones del Nuevo México y porque permitió poblase y diese lumbre de fe a los de Cinaro, Chiametla y las demás villas como gente más poca y pobre que la de los llanos . . . pues es notorio llegamos dos jornadas de lo primero poblado de ellas si fuera servido con facilidad permitiera fuéramos los descubridores de estas provincias tan deseadas, trabajadas y buscadas. (184)

6. Obregón is insistent that it is the intervention of a merciful God that protects and aids the Ibarra expedition in times of peril:

> Ninguna cosa ni suceso hay de tanta utilidad y provecho como en la ocasión de los peligros, trabajos y naufragios pedir remedio, amparo y socorro a la poderosa mano y misericordia de Dios nuestro Señor, el cual en la mayor necesidad le ampara y remedia con su infinita y gran providencia con la medicina celestial de su bendita e incomparable misericordia. . . . Con este santo y clementísimo remedio estoy cierto guardó, amparó y sacó el altísimo poder de Dios nuestro Señor de tantos y tan espantosos trabajos y peligros al general Francisco de Ibarra y los de su campo, amparándolos y defendiéndolos de la temerosa boca del hambriento enemigo y de su fiera cólera y de ser señoreados y cautivos de gente tan bárbara, rústica y desconocida del resplandeciente sol de justicia y misericordia. (174–75)

7. The Junta de Valladolid had been held over one year (1550–51) during which Bartolomé de Las Casas and Juan Inés de Sepúlveda debated the sovereignty, rights, and very nature of indigenous populations so that the junta could decide "si es lícito a Su Majestad hacer guerra a aquellos indios antes que se les predique la fe, para subjectallos a su Imperio, y que después de subjectados puedan más fácil y cómodamente ser enseñados y alumbrados por la doctrina evangélica del conoscimiento de sus errores y de la verdad cristiana" (Domingo de Soto 1552).

8. "The appeal to the patron saint of Spain, Santiago the Great (St. James), dates from the battle of Clavijo in 844 when according to the legend and in response to the Christians' call, the apostle fought on horseback on the Christian side against the emir of Córdoba" (Weckmann [1984] 1992, 111).

9. The process used for extracting silver from its ore in New Spain and Peru was at first smelting, as at Guadalcanal; later, smelting with bellows was established in New Spain. However, a much more important technological change transforming silver production came with the successful introduction of the cold process of amalgamation, first in New Spain in 1555 and much later in Potosí in 1572. This process used mercury. See Goodman 1988, 175.

10. The Ottoman Empire was a rising power in the Mediterranean while Phillip II was on the throne and posed a significant threat as late as 1585. In 1560, Phillip formed the Holy League with various republics on the Mediterranean to fight the Turks, financing hundreds of ships and soldiers for more than twenty years. During the same period, Moorish residents of Granada who had been forced to convert to Christianity were fighting against the strict suppression of their customs. Expenses were also high in Phillip's fight to quell Protestant heresy and secession in the Netherlands.

11. I have read "hostia" as "ostión."

12. While Obregón's depiction of the indigenous people at Chiametla is one of bellicose war mongers, quite to the contrary, they had treated Guzmán's party well, providing 150 porters, helping the expedition transport its supplies from Aztatlán to the Río Baluarte, and then even supplying Guzmán and his men with supplies for two months: "At the end of this period, in January 1531 once his army was replenished, Guzmán repaid his hosts by provoking them to acts of hostility that resulted in the destruction of many native settlements and the enslavement of their inhabitants" (Reff 1991, 24). In fact, recall that the nefarious de Guzmán had terrorized the indigenous peoples to such an extent that he was eventually arrested and jailed in 1536. As Reff points out citing the case of Petatlán, the northernmost settlement visited by one of de Guzmán's scouting parties, de Guzmán's effect on the population was not isolated to Chiametla: "Petatlán reportedly had eighty houses, but recently had been abandoned. Although Guzmán attributed the absence of people to the fact that the river had overflowed its banks, inundating the village, the inhabitants of Petatlán probably fled to avoid capture and enslavement. This proved to be the case almost everywhere Guzmán traveled" (Reff 1991, 32).

13. In another section, Obregón estimates 25,000 inhabitants (141).

14. Obregón even frames this pitch in terms of return on royal investment, pointing out that a mere one hundred men will suffice:

Es averiguado que vuestra S.C.C.R.M. acrecentará en sus reales y riesgos de pocos pobladores, porque cien hombres son bastantes sustentarla, poblarla y defenderla con buen fuerte, rescate y moderación en los servicios personales y tributos en los naturales, a los cuales ante todas cosas se les ha de hacer buen tratamiento, porque de lo contrario sucedió alzarse y matar a los que allí estuvieron poblados cinco años como declararé en su capítulo y lugar conveniente. Y poblada esta villa, desde ella irán conquistando y poblando las de más adelante. (Obregón 1584, 112)

15. This echoes a Eurocentric notion that persists to this day in what could be considered the new genre of the textualscape, the Hollywood film:

In the manner of Western historiography, Eurocentric cinema narrates penetration into the Third World through the figure of the "discoverer." In most Western films about the colonies . . . the status of hero falls to the voyager (often a scientist) who masters a new land and its treasures, the value of which the "primitive" residents had been unaware. It is this construction of the consciousness of "value" as a pretext for (capitalist) ownership that legitimizes the colonizer's act of appropriation. In *Lawrence of Arabia* and the *Indiana Jones* series of the 1980s, the camera relays the hero's dynamic movement across a passive, static space, gradually stripping the land of its "enigma" as the spectator wins visual access to oriental treasures through the eyes of the explorer-protagonist. (Shohat and Stam 1994, 146)

Bibliography

Abrahamsson, Kurt Viking. 1999. "Landscapes Lost and Gained: On Changes in Semiotic Resources." *Human Ecology Review* 6, no. 2: 51–61.

Adorno, Rolena, and Patrick Charles Pautz, eds. and trans. 1999. *Álvar Núñez Cabeza de Vaca: His Account, His Life, and the Expedition of Pánfilo de Narváez.* 3 vols. Lincoln: University of Nebraska Press.

———. 1995. "Discurso jurídico, discurso literario: el reto de leer en el siglo XX los escritos del XVI." *Memorias: Jornadas andinas de literatura latino americana* 3 (1995): 15–25.

———. 1994. "Peaceful Conquest and Law in the Relación of Alvar Nuñez Cabeza de Vaca." In *Coded Encounters*, 75–86. Amherst: University of Massachusetts Press.

———. 1993. "The Negotiation of Fear in Cabeza de Vaca's Naufragios." In *New World Encounters.* Edited by Stephen Greenblatt, 163–99. Oakland: University of California Press.

Agnew, John, David N. Livingstone, and Alisdair Rogers, eds. 1996. *Human Geography: An Essential Anthology.* Cambridge: Blackwell.

Ahern, Maureen. 2003. "Mapping, Measuring, and Naming Cultural Spaces in Casteñada's *Relación de la jornada de Cíbola.*" In *The Coronado Expedition: From the Distance of 460 Years.* Edited by Richard and Shirley Flint, 265–89. Albuquerque: University of New Mexico Press.

———. 2002. "Llebando el norte sobre el ojo izquierdo." In *Mapping Colonial Spanish America*, 24–47. Lewisburg, PA: Bucknell University Press and Associated University Press.

———. 2001. "*La relación y conçudio* de Hernán Gallegos: glosa, guía y memoria de Nuevo México 1581–1582." *Lexis* XXV: 381–406.

———. 1999. "La narración cartográfica de *La Relación de la de Cibola* de Pedro de Castañeda y Náxera, 1563." In *Literatura de viajes: El viejo mundo y el nuevo.* Edited by Salvador García, 51–60. Madrid: Castalia/Ohio State University.

———. 1998. "Fronteras mudables: un informe náhuatl de la Guerra Chichimeca, 1563." In *Indigenismo hacia el fin del milenio.* Edited by Mabel Moraña, 61–76.

Pittsburg: Instituto Internacional de Literatura Iberoamericana/Pittsburg University.

———. 1995. "Testimonio oral, memoria y violencia en el diario de Diego Pérez de Lúxan: Nuevo México 1583." *Revista de Crítica Literaria Latinoamericana* 41: 153–63.

———. 1994. "The Articulation of Alterity on the Northern Frontier: The *Relatione della navigatione & scoperta* by Fernando de Alarcón, 1540." In *Coded Encounters*. Edited by Francisco Javier Cevallos Candau, 46–61. Amherst: University of Massachusetts Press.

———. 1994. "*La relación de la Jornada de Cibola*: Los espacios orales y culturales." In *Conquista y contraconquista: La escritura del Nuevo Mundo: Actas del XXVIII Congreso del Instituto de Literatura Iberoamericana*. Edited by Julio Ortega and José Amor y Vázquez, 187–99. México, DF: Colegio de México; Providence, RI: Brown University.

———. 1993. "The Cross and the Gourd: The Appropriation of Ritual Signs in the *Relaciones* of Alvar Núñez Cabeza de Vaca and Fray Marcos de Niza." In *Early Images of the Americas*. Edited by Jerry M. Williams and Robert E. Lewis, 9–16. Tucson: University of Arizona Press.

———. 1990. "Alarcón on the Colorado River: Communication Strategies in his *Relatione delle navigatione* (1540)." *Ideas '92* 6: 25–34.

———. 1989. "The Certification of Cibola: Discursive Strategies in *La relación del descubrimiento de las siete ciudades* by Fray Marcos de Niza (1539)." *Dispositio* 14: 303–13.

Aiton, Arthur S. 1940. "Coronado's Commission as Captain General." *Hispanic Latin American Review* 20: 83–84.

———. 1925. "The Later Career of Coronado." *Hispanic Latin American Review* 30: 298–304.

Alarcón, Fernando. [1556] 2004. *Los indios de todo se maravillaban: La relación de Hernando de Alarcón*. Translated by Julio César Montané Martí. Zapopan, Jalisco, México: El Colegio de Jalisco.

———. [1556] 1967. [Report of the 3rd ed. 1606] *Relatione della navigatione & scoperta. Che fece il Capitano Fernando Alarchone per ordine dello Illustrissimo Signor Don Antonio di Mendoza Vice Re della nuoua Spagna, data in Colima, porto della nuoua Spagna*. In Gian Battista Ramusio. *Navigationi et viaggi*, vol. 3, 303d–309d. Venice: Theatrvm Orbis Terrarvm Ltd.

Anderson, Benedict. 1983. *Imagined Communities*. London and New York: Verso.

Appadurai, Arjun. 1993. "Disjuncture and Difference in the Global Cultural Economy." In *The Phantom Public Sphere*. Edited by Bruce Robbins, 269–95. Minneapolis: University of Minnesota Press.

Arens, William. 1998. "Rethinking Anthropophagy." In *Cannibalism and the Colonial World*, 39–62. Cambridge: Cambridge University Press.

Areti Hers, Marie, and José Luis Mirafuente, comp. 2000. *Nómadas sedentarios en el Norte de México*. México, DF: Universidad Nacional Autónoma de México.

Arias, Santa, and Mariselle Meléndez, eds. 2002. *Mapping Colonial Spanish America: Places and Commonplaces of Identity, Culture, and Experience*. Lewisburg, PA: Bucknell University Press and Associated University Press.

———. 1996. "Entre instrucciones, experiencia y mundos posibles en la *Relación* del descubrimiento de las siete ciudades de Fray Marcos de Niza (1539)." *Cuadernos Americanos* 55: 204–16.

———. 1993. "Empowerment through the Writing of History." In *Early Images of the Americas*, 163–79. Tucson: University of Arizona Press.

Ashcroft, Bill, Gareth Griffiths, and Helen Tiffin, comps. 2000. *Post-Colonial Studies: Key Concepts*. New York: Routledge.

Bancroft, George. 1834–75. *A History of the United States from the Discovery of the American Continent*. Boston: Little, Brown and Co.

Barrera López, Trinidad. 2001. Introduction to *Alvar Núñez Cabeza de Vaca: Naufragios*, 7–57. Madrid: Alianza Editorial.

Basso, Keith. 1996. Introduction to *Senses of Place*, 3–10. Santa Fe, NM: School of American Research Press.

Battista, Agnese. World Map. 1544. In *Portolan Atlas of Nine Charts and a World Map*. Library of Congress Geography and Map Division, Washington, DC.

Benítez, Fernando. 1962. *Los primeros mexicanos*. In *De la conquista a la independencia*, 2012. México, DF: Ediciones Era.

Bolaños, Álvaro Félix. 2005. "Frontera, ciudad y plaza pública americana del siglo XVI: escritura, violencia y *status quo* deseado en cronistas españoles de la conquista." *Boletín Cultural y Bibliográfico* 41, no. 65: 3–31.

———. 2002. "A Place to Live, a Place to Think, and a Place to Die: Sixteenth-Century Frontier Cities, Plazas, and *Relaciones* in Spanish America." *Mapping Colonial Spanish America: Places and Commonplaces of Identity, Culture and Experience*. Edited by Mariselle Meléndez and Santa Arias, 275–93. Lewisburg, PA: Bucknell University Press and Associated University Press.

Bolton, Herbert E. 1949. *Coronado and the Turquoise Trail: Knight of Pueblos and Plains*. Albuquerque: University of New Mexico Press.

Boucher, Phillip. 1992. *Cannibal Encounters: Europeans and Island Caribs, 1492–1763*. Baltimore: Johns Hopkins University Press.

Bravo, Eva María. 1997. Introduction to *Historia de los descubrimientos de Nueva España by Baltasar Obregón*, 12–34. Sevilla, España: Ediciones Alfar.

———. 1989. *Transcripción y estudio lingüístico de la "Historia de los descubrimientos de Nueva España" de Baltasar Obregón*. PhD diss., Universidad de Sevilla.

Camelo, Rosa. 1971. "La idea de la historia en Baltasar de Obregón." In *Estudios de historia novohispana*, 51–57. México, DF: Instituto de Investigaciones Históricas, Universidad Nacional Autónoma de México.

Carter, Paul. 1987. *The Road to Botany Bay: An Essay in Spatial History*. London: Faber & Faber.

Castañeda de Nájera, Pedro de. [1563] 2005. *Relación de la jornada de Cíbola compuesta por Pedro de Castañeda de Nájera donde se trata de todos aquellos poblados y ritos, y costumbres la qual fue el año de 1540*. Transcription in *Documents of the Coronado Expedition 1539–1542*. Edited by Richard Flint and Shirley Cushing Flint, 378–493. Dallas: Southern Methodist University Press.

———. 2002. *Relación de la jornada de Cíbola compuesta por Pedro de Castañeda de Nájera donde se trata de todos aquellos poblados y ritos, y costumbres la qual fue el año de 1540*. In *Francisco Vázquez Coronado: sueño y decepción*. Edited by Julio César Montané Martí. Zapopan, Jalisco, México: El Colegio de Jalisco.

Certeau, Michel de. 1984. *The Practice of Everyday Life*. Translated by Steven Rendall. Berkeley: University of California Press.

Clissold, Stephen. 1961. *The Seven Cities of Cíbola*. London: Shenval Press.

Collingwood, R. G. 1945. *The Idea of Nature*. Oxford: Clarendon.

Corominas, Joan. 1987. *Diccionario etimológico de la lengua castellana*, 3rd ed. 2 vols. Madrid: Gredos.

———. 1954. *Diccionario crítico etimológico de la lengua castellana*. 8 vols. Madrid: Gredos.

Cosgrove, Denis. 1998. "Cultural Landscapes." In *A European Geography*. Edited by Tim Unwin, 65–81. Harlow, Essex, UK; New York: Longman.

Cosgrove, Denis, and Stephen Daniels. 1993. "Spectacle and Text." In *Place/Culture/Representation*. Edited by James Duncan and David Ley, 57–75. New York: Routledge.

Cosgrove, Denis, and Mona Domosh. 1993. "Author and Authority." In *Place/Culture/Representation*. Edited by James Duncan and David Ley, 25–38. New York: Routledge.

Craddock, Jerry. 1996. "Philological Notes on the Hammond and Rey Translation of *de la entrada que hizo . . .*" *Romance Philology* 49: 69–118.

Cuello, José. 1988. "The Persistence of Indian Slavery and Encomienda in the Northeast of Colonial Mexico (1577–1723)." *Journal of Social History* 21, no. 4: 683–700.

Day, Grove A. 1940. *Coronado's Quest*. Berkeley: University of California Press.

Deeds, Susan M. 2003. *Defiance and Deference in Mexico's Colonial North: Indians under Spanish Rule in Nueva Vizcaya*. Austin: University of Texas Press.

Derrida, Jaques. 1978. "Structure, Sign, and Play in the Discourse of the Human Sciences." In *Writing and Difference*. Translated by Alan Bass, 278–94. New York: Routledge.

Diccionario de Autoridades (1726–1739). Real Academia Española. http://web.frl .es/DA.html.

Di Peso, Charles C. 1974. *Casas Grandes: A Fallen Trading Center of the Gran Chichimeca*, vols. 1–3. Flagstaff, AZ: Northland.

Di Peso, Charles C., John B. Rinaldo, and Gloria J. Fenner. 1974. *Casas Grandes: A Fallen Trading Center of the Gran Chichimeca*, vols. 4–8. Flagstaff, AZ: Northland.

Domingo de Soto, Fray. 1552. "Prólogo del maestro Soto." *Ibero-American Electronic Text Series*, accessed July 10, 2013, http://digicoll.library.wisc.edu/cgi-bin/ IbrAmerTxt/IbrAmerTxt-idx?type=HTML&rgn=div1&byte=1401467.

Duncan, James. 1993. Introduction to *Place/Culture/Representation*. Edited by James Duncan and David Ley, 1–24. New York: Routledge.

———. 1993. "Sites of Representation: Place, Time and the Discourse of the Other." In *Place/Culture/Representation*, 39–56. New York: Routledge.

Epstein, Jeremiah. 1991. "Cabeza de Vaca and the Sixteenth-Century Copper Trade in Northern Mexico." *American Antiquity* 56: 472–82.

Espejo, Antonio de. [1586] 1975. "Relación." In Juan González de Mendoza, *Historia de las cosas mas notables, ritos y costumbres del gran reyno de la China sabidas assi por los libros de los mismos Chinas, como por relacion de los religiosos, y otras personas que han estado en el dicho reyno.* Madrid: Querino Gerardo Flamenco, a costa de Blas de Robles.

———. 1966. "Report of Antonio de Espejo." In *The Rediscovery of New Mexico, 1580–1594.* Edited by George P. Hammond, 213–31. Albuquerque: University of New Mexico Press.

Flint, Richard, and Shirley Flint, eds. 2005. *Documents of the Coronado Expedition, 1539–1542.* Dallas: Southern Methodist University Press.

———. 2003. *The Coronado Expedition: From the Distance of 460 Years.* Albuquerque: University of New Mexico Press.

———. 2002. *Great Cruelties Have Been Reported: The 1544 Investigation of the Coronado Expedition.* Dallas: Southern Methodist University Press.

———. 1992. "The Coronado Expedition: Cicuye to the Rio de Cicuye Bridge." *New Mexico Historical Review* 67: 123–38.

Foucault, Michel. 1986. "Of Other Spaces." *Diacritics* 16: 22–27.

Gallegos, Hernán. [1582] 1966. "Gallegos' Relation of the Chamuscado-Rodríguez Expedition." In *The Rediscovery of New Mexico, 1580–1594.* Edited by George P. Hammond, 67–114. Albuquerque: University of New Mexico Press.

Gerbi, Antonello. 1985. *Nature in the New World.* Translated by Jeremy Moyle. Pittsburgh: University of Pittsburgh Press.

———. 1973. *The Dispute of the New World: The History of a Polemic, 1750–1900.* Pittsburgh: University of Pittsburgh Press.

Glantz, Margo. 2005. *La desnudez como naufragio.* Madrid: Iberoamericana.

Goodman David Charles. 1988. *Power and Penury.* Cambridge: Cambridge University Press.

Gordon, Richard. 2006. "Following Estevanico: The Influential Presence of an African Slave in Sixteenth-Century New World Historiography." *Colonial Latin American Review* 15: 183–206.

Greider, T., and L. Garkovich. 1994. "Landscapes: The Social Construction of Nature and the Environment." *Rural Sociology* 59: 1–24.

Griffith, James S. 1993. *Beliefs and Holy Places: A Spiritual Geography of the Pimería Alta.* Tucson: University of Arizona Press.

Gruzinski, Serge. 1991. *La colonialización de lo imaginario.* México, DF: Fondo de Cultura Económica.

Guy, Donna, and Thomas Sheridan, eds. 1998. *Contested Ground Comparative Frontiers on the Northern and Southern Edges of the Spanish Empire.* Southwest Center Series. Tucson: University of Arizona Press.

Hammond, George. 1966. Introduction to *The Rediscovery of the Southwest, 1580–1594.* Edited by George P. Hammond. Albuquerque: University of New Mexico Press.

Hammond, George, and Agapito Rey, eds. 1940. *Narratives of the Coronado Expedition, 1540–1542.* Albuquerque: University of New Mexico Press.

———. 1928. *Obregón's History of 16th Century Explorations in Western America, entitled Chronicle Commentary, or Relation of the Ancient and Modern Discoveries in New Spain and New Mexico, Mexico, 1584*. Los Angeles: Wetzel Publishing Company.

Harley, John Brian. 1989. "Maps, Knowledge, and Power." In *The Iconography of Landscape*. Edited by Dennis Cosgrove and Stephen Daniels, 277–305. Cambridge: Cambridge University Press.

Herrera y Tordesillas, Antonio de. 1601. *Descripción de las Indias Occidentales*. Madrid: Imprento Real.

Higgins, Anthony. 2002. "'Enlightened' Reconfigurations of Colonial Space in the *Rusticatio Mexicana*." In *Mapping Colonial Spanish America: Places and Commonplaces of Identity, Culture, and Experience*, 159–80. Lewisburg, PA: Bucknell University Press and Associated University Press.

Hill-Boone, Elizabeth. 1998. "Pictorial Documents and Visual Thinking in Postconquest Mexico." In *Native Traditions in the Postconquest World*. Edited by Elizabeth Hill-Boone and Tom Cummins, 149–99. Washington, DC: Dumbarton Oaks Research Library and Collection.

———. 1994. "Aztec Pictorial Histories: Records without Words." In *Writing Without Words: Alternative Literacies in Mesoamerica and the Andes*. Edited by Elizabeth Hill-Boone and Walter Mignolo, 50–76. Durham, NC: Duke University Press.

Hirsch, Eric. 1995. Introduction to *The Anthropology of Landscape: Perception of Space and Place*. Edited by Eric Hirsch and M. O'Hanlon, 1–30. Oxford: Clarendon.

Hodge, F. W., ed. 1865. *Descubrimiento de las siete ciudades*. Madrid: M.B. de Quiros.

Hopkins Durazo, Armando. 1988. *Imágenes prehispánicas de Sonora: la expedición de don Francisco de Ibarra a Sonora en 1565, según el relato de don Baltazar de Obregón*. Hermosillo, Sonora, México: Armando Hopkins Durazo.

Hulme, Peter. 1998. Introduction to *Cannibalism and the Colonial World*, edited by Francis Barker, Peter Hulme, and Margaret Iversen, 1–38. Cambridge: Cambridge University Press.

———. 1986. *Colonial Encounters: Europe and the Native Caribbean 1492–1797*. London: Methuan.

Jáuregui, Carlos. 2005. *Canibalia: canibalismo, calibanismo, antropofagia cultural y consume en América Latina*. Córdoba, España: Casas de las Américas.

Jones, Oakah L. 1988. *Nueva Vizcaya: Heartland of the Spanish Frontier*. Albuquerque: University of New Mexico Press.

King, Willard F. 1996. "El México de Alarcón (1580–1613)." *Lectura crítica de la literatura americana: Inventarios, invenciones y revisores. Tomo I*. Edited by Saúl Sosnowski, 576–99. Caracas, Venesuela: Ayacucho.

Kirchhoff, Paul. 1954. "Gatherers and Farmers in the Greater Southwest: A Problem in Classification." *American Anthropology* 4: 529–60.

Kokrda, Ken. 2005. "Approaching Casas Grandes." *Casas Grandes and the Ceramic Art of the Ancient Southwest*. Chicago and New Haven, CT: The Art Institute of Chicago and Yale University Press.

Las leyes nuevas, 1542–1543; ordenanzas para la gobernación de las Indias y buen tratamiento y conservación de los indios. Edición, estudio y notas por Antonio Muro Orejón. 1961. Edited by Antonio Muro Orejón. Sevilla, España: Publicaciones de la Escuela de Estudios Hispano-Americanos de Sevilla.

Lawson-Peebles, Robert. 1988. *Landscape and Written Expression In Revolutionary America: The World Turned Upside Down.* Cambridge: Cambridge University Press.

Le Riverend, Julio, and Hernán Venegas Delgado. 2005. *Estudios sobre el criollo.* La Habana, Cuba: Editora Política.

Lefebvre, Henri. [1974] 1991. *The Production of Space.* Translated by Donald Nicholson-Smith. Oxford: Blackwell.

López de Velasco, Juan. [1571] 1971. *Geografía y descripción universal de las Indias recopiladas por el cosmógrafo-cronista Juan López de Velasco desde el año 1571 al de 1574.* Madrid: Ediciones Atlas.

Lowenthal, David. 1975. "Past Time, Present Place: Landscape and Memory." *Geographical Review* 65, no. 1: 1–36.

Mecham, John Lloyd. 1927. *Francsico de Ibarra and Nueva Vizcaya.* Durham, NC: Duke University Press.

Méndez García, Benjamín. 2005. "Ecología y senderismo: La lectura y el respeto a cada paisaje en su contexto." *Páxina Cultural de Lena/Tsena.* Accessed February 26, 2015. http://www.xuliocs.com/ecologiasend.htm.

Mendieta, Gerónimo de. [1596] 1997. *Historia eclesiástica indiana.* México, DF: Consejo Nacional para la Cultura y las Artes, 1997.

Mignolo, Walter. 1995. *The Darker Side of the Renaissance.* Ann Arbor: University of Michigan Press.

———. 1994. "The Moveable Center." In *Coded Encounters: Writing, Gender, and Ethnicity in Colonial Latin America.* Edited by Francisco Javier Cevallos, 15–45. Amherst: University of Massachusetts Press.

———. 1992. "Putting the Americas on the Map. Colonialism and Post Colonialism in Latin American Mirages." *Colonial Latin American Review* 1: 25–63.

———. 1982. "Cartas, crónicas y relaciones del descubrimiento y la conquista." In *Historia de la literatura hispanoamericana: Tomo I.* Edited by Luis Iñigo-Madrigal, 57–116. Madrid: Ediciones Cátedra.

Mitchell, W. J. T., ed. 2002. *Landscape and Power,* 2nd ed., vii–xii. Chicago: University of Chicago Press.

———. 2002. Introduction to *Landscape and Power,* 2nd ed., 1–4. Chicago: University of Chicago Press.

———. 2002. "Imperial Landscape." In *Landscape and Power,* 2nd ed., 5–34. Chicago: University of Chicago Press.

Montané Martí, Julio César, trans. [1556] 2004. *Los indios de todo se maravillaban: La relación de Hernando de Alarcón.* Fernando Alarcón. Zapopan, Jalisco, México: El Colegio de Jalisco.

———, ed. 2002. *Relación de la jornada de Cíbola compuesta por Pedro de Castañeda de Nájera donde se trata de todos aquellos poblados y ritos, y costumbres la qual fue el año de 1540.* In *Francisco Vázquez Coronado: sueño y decepción,* 163–234. Zapopan, Jalisco, México: El Colegio de Jalisco.

———, ed. 1995. "Relación (1539)." In *Por los senderos de la quimera: El viaje de Fray Marcos de Niza,* 79–97. Hermosillo, Sonoro, México: Instituto Sonorense de la Cultura.

Mundy, Barbara E. 1996. *The Mapping of New Spain: Indigenous Cartography and the Maps of the Relaciones Geográficas.* Chicago: University of Chicago Press.

Murphy, Trevor. 2004. *Pliny the Elder's* Natural History: *The Empire in the Encyclopedia.* Oxford: Oxford University Press.

Niza, Fray Marcos de. 1987. "La relación del descubrimiento de las siete ciudades (1539)." In *The Journey of Fray Marcos de Niza.* Edited by Cleve Hallenbeck, li–lxxi. Dallas: Southern Methodist University Press.

———. 1999. "Fray Marcos de Niza, Relación (1539)." Edited by Jerry R. Craddock. *Romance Philology* 53: 69–118.

———. 1995. "Relación (1539)." In *Por los senderos de la quimera: El viaje de Fray Marcos de Niza.* Edited by Julio César Montané Martí, 79–97. Hermosillo, Sonoro, México: Instituto Sonorense de la Cultura.

Núñez Cabeza de Vaca, Álvarez. [1542, 1555] 1999. "Relación." In *Álvar Núñez Cabeza de Vaca: His Account, His Life, and the Expedition of Pánfilo de Narváez.* 3 vols. Edited and translated by Rolena Adorno and Patrick Charles Pautz, 13–279. Lincoln: University of Nebraska Press.

Obregón, Baltasar de. 1997. *Historia de los descubrimientos de Nueva España.* Edited by Eva María Bravo. Sevilla, España: Ediciones Alfar.

———. 1989. *Historia de los descubrimientos antiguos y modernos de la Nueva España.* Prologue by Mariano Cuevas. México, DF: Editorial Porrúa.

———. 1928. *Obregón's History of 16th Century Explorations in Western America, entitled* Chronicle Commentary, or Relation of the Ancient and Modern Discoveries in New Spain and New Mexico, Mexico, 1584. Translated by George P. Hammond and Agapito Rey. Los Angeles: Wetzel Publishing Company.

———. 1584. *Historia de los descubrimientos antiguos y modernos de Nueva España.* AGI. Patronato. 22. R7. fol. 603–850.

O'Gorman, Edmundo. 1958. *La invención de América.* México, DF: Fondo de Cultura Económica.

Olwig, Kenneth. 2002. *Landscape, Nature and the Body Politic: From Britain's Renaissance to America's New World.* Madison: University of Wisconsin Press.

Padrón, Ricardo. 2004. *The Spacious Word: Cartography, Literature, and Empire in Early Modern Spain.* Chicago: University of Chicago Press.

Pérez de Luxán, Diego. 1966. "Diego Pérez de Luxán´s Account of the Espejo Expedition into New Mexico, 1582." In *The Rediscovery of New Mexico, 1580–1594.* Edited by George P. Hammond, 153–212. Albuquerque: University of New Mexico Press.

Pérez de Ribas, Andrés. 1999. *History of the Triumphs of Our Holy Faith amongst the Most Barbarous and Fierce Peoples of the New World.* Translated by Daniel T. Reff, Maureen Ahern, and Richard K. Danford. Tucson: University of Arizona Press.

———. 1645. *Historia de los trivmphos de nvestra santa fee entre gentes las mas barbaras, y fieras del Nueuo orbe, conseguidos por los soldados de la milicia de la Compañia de Iesvs en las missiones de la prouincia de Nueua-España Refierense assimismo las costvmbres, ritos, y supersticiones que vsauan estas gentes, sus puestos, y temples, las vitorias que de algunas dellas alcancaron con las armas los catolicos españoles, quando les obligaron à tomarlas, y las dichosas muertes de veinte religiosos de la Compañia, que en varios puestos, y a manos de varias naciones, dieron sus vidas por la predicacion del santo euangelio.* Madrid: A. de Paredes.

Phelan, John Leddy. 1970. *The Millennial Kingdom of the Franciscans in the New World.* Berkeley: University of California Press.

Phillips, Jerry. 1998. "Cannibalism qua Capitalism." In *Cannibalism and the Colonial World*, 183–203. Cambridge: Cambridge University Press.

Pittarello, Elide. 1984. "Scienza/Esperienza nella *Historia de los descubrimientos antiguos y modernos de la Nueva España* di Baltasar de Obregón." *Studi di Letteratura Ispano-Americana* 17: 45–67.

Portuondo, María M. 2009. *Secret Science: Spanish Cosmography and the New World*. Chicago: University of Chicago Press.

Powell, Philip Wayne. 1977. *La Guerra Chichimeca*. México, DF: Fondo de Cultura Económica.

———. 1944. "Presidios and Towns on the Silver Frontier of New Spain, 1550–1580." *Hispanic American Historical Review* 24: 179–200.

Pratt, Mary Louise. 2002. "Arts of the Contact Zone." *Professing in the Contact Zone: Bringing Theory and Practice Together*. Edited by Janice M. Wolff, 33–40. Urbana, IL: National Council of Teachers of English.

———. 1992. *Imperial Eyes*. New York: Routledge.

Pred, Allen. 1977. "The Choreography of Existence: Comments on Hägerstrand's Time-Geography and its Usefulness." *Economic Geography* 53: 207–21. Reprinted in Agnew, Livingstone, and Rogers 1996, 636–49.

Quoniam, S. 1988. "A Painter, Geographer of Arizona." *Environment and Planning D: Society and Space* 6, no. 1: 3–14.

Rabasa, José. 2000. *Writing Violence on the Northern Frontier: The Historiography of Sixteenth-Century New Mexico and Florida and the Legacy of Conquest*. Durham, NC: Duke University Press.

———. 1993. *Inventing America: Spanish Historiography and the Formation of Eurocentrism*. Norman: University of Oklahoma Press.

Radding, Cynthia. 2005. *Landscapes of Power and Identity*. Durham, NC: Duke University Press.

Rama, Angel. 1996. *The Lettered City*. Translated by John Charles Chasteen. Durham, NC: Duke University Press.

Reff, Daniel T. 1996. "Text and Context: Cures, Miracles and Fear in the Relación of Alvar Núñez Cabeza de Vaca." *Journal of the Southwest* 38: 115–18.

———. 1991. *Disease, Depopulation, and Culture Change in Northwestern New Spain: 1518–1764*. Salt Lake City: University of Utah Press.

———. 1991. "Anthropological Analysis of Exploration Texts: Cultural Discourse and the Ethnological Import of Fray Marcos de Niza's Journey to Cibola." *American Anthropologist* 93, no. 3: 636–55.

———. 1987. "The Introduction of Smallpox in the Greater Southwest." *American Anthropologist* 89: 704–8.

Reff, Daniel T., and Courtney Kelley. 2008. "Good Witch, Bad Witch, and a Little in Between: Gender and Writing of History in Colonial Mexico." Unpublished paper, Ohio State University.

Riley, Carroll L. 1987. *The Frontier People: The Greater Southwest in the Protohistoric Period*. Albuquerque: University of New Mexico Press.

———. 1974. "Mesoamerican Indians in the Early Southwest." *Ethnohistory* 21: 25–36.

———. 1971. "Early Spanish-Indian Communication in the Greater Southwest." *New Mexico Historical Review* 46: 284–314.

Rivera-Ayala, Sergio. 2002. "Riding High, the Horseman's View: Urban Space and Body in México in 1554." In *Mapping Colonial Spanish America: Places and Commonplaces of Identity, Culture, and Experience*, 251–74. Lewisburg, PA: Bucknell University Press and Associated University Press.

Rojo, Danna A. Levin. 2014. *Return to Aztlan: Indians, Spaniards, and the Invention of Nuevo México*. Norman: Univeristy of Oklahoma Press.

Roskill, Mark. 1997. *The Languages of Landscape*. University Park: Pennsylvania State University Press.

Ross, Kathleen. 2000. "Chisme, exceso y agencia criolla: *Tratado del descubrimiento de las Indias y su conquista (1589)* de Juan Suárez de Peralta." In *Agencias criollas: la ambigüedad "colonial" en las letras hispanoamericanas*. Edited by José Antonio Mazzotti, 131–41. Pittsburg, PA: Iberoamericana.

Sánchez, Joseph P., Bruce A. Erickson, and Jerry Gurulé. 2007. *Between Two Countries: A History of Coronado National Memorial, 1939–1990*. Albuquerque, NM: Rio Grande Books.

———. 1997. *Explorers, Traders, Slavers*. Salt Lake City: University of Utah Press.

Sauer, Carl. 1925. "The Morphology of Landscape." *Geography* 2, no. 2: 19–54.

———. 1932. *The Road to Cíbola*. Berkeley: University of California Press.

Seed, Patricia. 1993. "Taking Possession and Reading Texts: Establishing the Authority of Overseas Empires." In *Early Images of the Americas*, 112–33. Tucson: University of Arizona Press.

Sheridan-Prieto, Cecilia. 2002. "Diversidad nativa, territorios y fronteras en el noroeste novohispano." *Desacatos* 10: 13–29.

Shohat, Ella, and Robert Stam. 1994. *Unthinking Eurocentrism*. New York: Routledge.

Solodkow, David. 2009. "La aristocracia de los desposeídos: Baltasar Dorantes de Carranza y la primera generación de criollos novohispanos." In *Poéticas de lo criollo*. Edited by Juan M. Vitullio and David Solodkow, 105–43. Buenos Aires: Corregidor.

Spirn, Anne Whiston. 1998. *The Language of Landscape*. New Haven, CT: Yale University Press.

Spurr, David. 1993. *The Rhetoric of Empire*. Durham, NC: Duke University Press.

Thrift, Nigel. 1981. "Owner's Time and Own Time: The Making of a Capitalist Time-Consciousness 1300–1800." In *Space and Time in Geography: Essays Dedicated to Torsten Hägerstrand*, 56–84. Lund, Sweden: CWK Gleerup. Reprinted in Agnew, Livingstone, and Rogers 1996, 552–70.

Transcripción de las Ordenanzas de descubrimiento, nueva población y pacificación de Las Indias dadas por Felipe II, el 13 de julio de 1573, en el Bosque de Segovia, según el original que se conserva en el Archivo General de Indias de Sevilla. 1973. Madrid: Ministerio de la Vivienda.

Trigo, Abril. 1997. "Fronteras de la epistemología: Epistemologías de la frontera." *Papeles de Montevideo. Literatura y Cultura. La crítica literaria como problema* 1: 71–87.

Tuan, Yi-fu. 1979. *Landscapes of Fear*. New York: Pantheon.

———. 1974. *Topophilia: A Study of Environmental Perception, Attitudes and Values*. Englewood Cliffs, NJ: Prentice-Hall, 1974.

Turchi, Peter. 2004. *Maps of the Imagination: The Writer as Cartographer*. San Antonio, TX: Trinity University Press.

———. 2001. "The Writer as Cartographer." In *Bringing the Devil to His Knees: The Craft of Fiction and the Writing Life*. Edited by Charles Baxter and Peter Turchi, 162–79. Ann Arbor: University of Michigan Press.

Vas Mingo, Marta Milagros del. 1985–93. "Las Ordenanzas de 1573, sus antecedentes y consecuencias." In *Quinto Centenario del descubrimiento de América, encuentro de dos mundos*, no. 8, 83–101. Washington, DC: Secretaría General, Organización de los Estados Americanos.

Verdesio, Gustavo. 2002. "The Original Sin behind the Creation of a New Europe: Economic and Ecological Imperialism in the River Plate." In *Mapping Colonial Spanish America: Places and Commonplaces of Identity, Culture, and Experience*, 137–58. Lewisburg, PA: Bucknell University Press and Associated University Press.

Vitulli, Juan M., and David Solodkow, eds. 2009. Introduciton to *Poéticas de lo criollo*. Buenos Aires: Corregidor.

Walker, Johnathan, and Jonathan Leib. 2002. "Walking in the Footsteps of West and Parsons." *Geographical Review* 92: 555–81.

Watson, J. Wreford. 1970. "Image Geography: The Myth of America in the American Scene." *Advancement of Science* 27: 71–79.

———. 1967. "Spanish Fur Trade from New Mexico, 1540–1821." *Americas* 24: 122–36.

Weckmann, Luis. [1984] 1992. *The Medieval Heritage of Mexico*. Translated by Frances M. López-Morillas. New York: Fordham University Press.

West, Delno C. 1989. "Medieval Ideas of Apocalyptic Mission and the Early Franciscans in Mexico." *Americas* 45: 293–313.

West, Robert C., and James J. Parsons. 1941. "Revisiting the Topia Road: Walking in the Footsteps of West and Parsons." *Geographical Review* 31: 406–13.

Westphal, Bertrand. 2013. *The Plausible World: A Geocritical Approach to Space, Place, and Maps*. Translated by Amy D. Wells. New York: Palgrave Macmillan.

Woll, Dieter. 1997. "Español criollo y portugues criollo; volviendo a la cuestión del origen y la historia de las dos palabras." *Latinitas et Romanitas*: 517–35.

Zamora, Margarita. 1993. *Reading Columbus*. Berkeley: University of California Press.

Zumthor, Paul. 1986. *Speaking of the Middle Ages*. Translated by Sarah White. Lincoln: University of Nebraska Press.

Zumthor, Paul, and Catherine Peebles. 1994. "The Medieval Travel Narrative." *New Literary History* 25: 809–24.

Index

cannibals and cannibalism. *See*
  anthropophagy
Cárdenas, Juan de, 28
caribe, 87–94, 134
Carrera, Diego de la, 103
Carter, Paul, 40
Casas Grandes. *See* Paquimé
Castañeda y Nájera, Pedro de, 22, 40–41,
  85, 128n10, 129n2, 135n32, 140n9
Castile (Castilla), 16, 29, 35, 47, 113, 117
Centicpas, 65
Certeau, Michel de, 16, 35, 38, 41, 43,
  51, 85, 101, 105, 115, 129n13
Chalchihuites, 7
Chamuscado-Rodríguez expedition, xiv,
  8, 23, 49, 51, 55–56, 83, 105, 113,
  135n29, 136n8, 144n5
Chanca, Diego Alvarez, 142n18
Chiametla, 22–23, 30, 51, 65, 72, 89,
  92–94, 105, 109, 114–15, 131n11,
  131–32n12, 134n23, 144n5, 145n12
Chichimeca, 7, 40, 81, 86, 96, 127n5,
  139n2, 139nn5–6
Chihuahua, 15, 94, 127n3, 140n10
chivalry. See *caballería*
Cíbola, 20, 36, 40, 54–56, 82, 116,
  128n10, 131n9, 141n14
Cinaro, 64–67, 104, 109, 115–16, 119,
  137n17, 138n22, 143n23, 144n5
Clissold, Stephen, 131n9
Colio, Diego de, 136–37n12
Collingwood, R. G., 129n15
Columbus, Cristobal de, 23, 32, 40, 51,
  88, 131n9, 142n18
Compostela, 14, 132n12
Conchas River. *See* Río Conchas
Concho, 9, 83, 120, 143n4
Consejo de Indias, xiv, 8, 11, 23, 31, 42,
  43–45, 49, 127n6, 135n2
Constantinople, 66–67
Copala, 58
Corazones, 116, 143n23
Corominas, Joan, 13, 28, 65, 129n1,
  130n5, 135n30, 136n7, 137n15,
  142n22
Coronado, Francisco Vázquez de, xiii, 8,
  11, 12, 14, 17, 20–21, 22, 30, 36, 37,

39, 40–41, 44, 49, 52, 54–57, 58, 73,
  81–82, 85, 128n10, 129n2, 131n9,
  133n22, 135n32, 135n3 (chap. 2),
  136n8, 140n9, 141n11, 141n14
Cortés, Hernán (Hernando), 11, 22, 27,
  33–35, 58, 107, 134–35n27, 135n29,
  136nn10–11
Cortés, Luis, 136n10
Cosgrove, Denis, 10, 73, 74, 118, 122,
  124, 129n14
Counter-Reformation, 34–35
Craddock, Jerry, 128n10
criollo, 8, 11, 16–17, 23, 27–30, 33, 36,
  39, 41, 93, 98, 100, 111, 112, 117,
  118, 119, 120, 131n9, 133nn19–21
Cuello, José, 112
Cuevas, Mariano, 13, 128n6, 134n25
Culiacán, xiii, 3, 4, 14, 18, 22, 36, 63,
  65, 71, 82, 85, 91, 92, 111, 137n17,
  141n14, 142n21
cultural landscape, 5, 84, 127n2, 141n13
Cumupa, 90
Cunca'ac, 78
Cuzco, xiii, 12

Daniels, Stephen, 124
Deeds, Susan M., 75, 79, 80, 82–84,
  139n2, 139n6, 141n11
Derrida, Jaques, 123, 125
despoblado, 92, 119
Diccionario de Autoridades,13, 88,
  135n30
Di Peso, Charles C., 139n2, 140n10,
  143n24
Domingo de Soto, Fray, 145n7
Dominican (Order), 108
Domosh, Mona, 73, 74
Duncan, James, 121, 123–24
Durango, xiii, 4, 15, 22, 59, 87, 103,
  127n3

El Estrecho de los Bacalaos, 47, 135n3
El Turco (The Turk), 56–57
encomendados. See encomiendas
encomenderos. See encomiendas
encomiendas, xiii, 7, 17, 27–30, 35–36,
  49, 67, 82–83, 86, 89, 92, 102, 106,

About the Author

Dr. Rebecca A. Carte's research focuses on indigenous representation in colonial and modern discourses from Mesoamerica and the Andes and has been published in *Journal of the Southwest, Latin American Literary Review,* and *Studies in Latin American Popular Culture.* She earned her PhD from Ohio State University in Columbus, Ohio, in 2008. A native of the Cleveland, Ohio, area, she is currently an assistant professor of Spanish at Cuyahoga Community College.

The Southwest Center Series

Joseph C. Wilder, Editor

Ignaz Pfefferkorn, *Sonora: A Description of the Province*

Carl Lumholtz, *New Trails in Mexico*

Buford Pickens, *The Missions of Northern Sonora: A 1935 Field Documentation*

Gary Paul Nabhan, editor, *Counting Sheep: Twenty Ways of Seeing Desert Bighorn*

Eileen Oktavec, *Answered Prayers: Miracles and Milagros along the Border*

Curtis M. Hinsley and David R. Wilcox, editors, *Frank Hamilton Cushing and the Hemenway Southwestern Archaeological Expedition, 1886–1889*, volume 1: *The Southwest in the American Imagination: The Writings of Sylvester Baxter, 1881–1899*

Lawrence J. Taylor and Maeve Hickey, *The Road to Mexico*

Donna J. Guy and Thomas E. Sheridan, editors, *Contested Ground: Comparative Frontiers on the Northern and Southern Edges of the Spanish Empire*

Julian D. Hayden, *The Sierra Pinacate*

Paul S. Martin, David Yetman, Mark Fishbein, Phil Jenkins, Thomas R. Van Devender, and Rebecca K. Wilson, editors, *Gentry's Rio Mayo Plants: The Tropical Deciduous Forest and Environs of Northwest Mexico*

W. J. McGee, *Trails to Tiburón: The 1894 and 1895 Field Diaries of W J McGee*, transcribed by Hazel McFeely Fontana, annotated and with an introduction by Bernard L. Fontana

Richard Stephen Felger, *Flora of the Gran Desierto and Río Colorado of Northwestern Mexico*

Donald Bahr, editor, *O'odham Creation and Related Events: As Told to Ruth Benedict in 1927 in Prose, Oratory, and Song by the Pimas William Blackwater, Thomas Vanyiko, Clara Ahiel, William Stevens, Oliver Wellington, and Kisto*

Dan L. Fischer, *Early Southwest Ornithologists, 1528–1900*

Thomas Bowen, editor, *Backcountry Pilot: Flying Adventures with Ike Russell*

Federico José María Ronstadt, *Borderman: Memoirs of Federico José María Ronstadt*, edited by Edward F. Ronstadt

The Southwest Center Series (continued)

Curtis M. Hinsley and David R. Wilcox, editors, *Frank Hamilton Cushing and the Hemenway Southwestern Archaeological Expedition, 1886–1889*, volume 2: *The Lost Itinerary of Frank Hamilton Cushing*

Neil Goodwin, *Like a Brother: Grenville Goodwin's Apache Years, 1928–1939*

Katherine G. Morrissey and Kirsten Jensen, editors, *Picturing Arizona: The Photographic Record of the 1930s*

Bill Broyles and Michael Berman, *Sunshot: Peril and Wonder in the Gran Desierto*

David W. Lazaroff, Philip C. Rosen, and Charles H. Lowe, Jr., *Amphibians, Reptiles, and Their Habitats at Sabino Canyon*

David Yetman, *The Organ Pipe Cactus*

Gloria Fraser Giffords, *Sanctuaries of Earth, Stone, and Light: The Churches of Northern New Spain, 1530–1821*

David Yetman, *The Great Cacti: Ethnobotany and Biogeography*

John Messina, *Álamos, Sonora: Architecture and Urbanism in the Dry Tropics*

Laura L. Cummings, *Pachucas and Pachucos in Tucson: Situated Border Lives*

Bernard L. Fontana and Edward McCain, *A Gift of Angels: The Art of Mission San Xavier del Bac*

David A. Yetman, *The Ópatas: In Search of a Sonoran People*

Julian D. Hayden, *Field Man: The Life of a Desert Archaeologist*, edited by Bill Broyles and Diane Boyer

Bill Broyles, Gayle Harrison Hartmann, Thomas E. Sheridan, Gary Paul Nabhan, and Mary Charlotte Thurtle, *Last Water on the Devil's Highway: A Cultural and Natural History of Tinajas Altas*

Thomas E. Sheridan, *Arizona: A History, Revised Edition*

Richard S. Felger and Benjamin Theodore Wilder, *Plant Life of a Desert Archipelago: Flora of the Sonoran Islands in the Gulf of California*

David Burckhalter, *Baja California Missions: In the Footsteps of the Padres*

Guillermo Núñez Noriega, *Just Between Us: An Ethnography of Male Identity and Intimacy in Rural Communities of Northern Mexico*

Cathy Moser Marlett, *Shells on a Desert Shore: Mollusks in the Seri World*

Rebecca A. Carte, *Capturing the Landscape of New Spain: Baltasar Obregón and the 1564 Ibarra Expedition*